The Invisibility Bargain

The Invisibility Bargain

Governance Networks and Migrant Human Security

JEFFREY D. PUGH

OXFORD
UNIVERSITY PRESS

OXFORD
UNIVERSITY PRESS

Oxford University Press is a department of the University of Oxford. It furthers
the University's objective of excellence in research, scholarship, and education
by publishing worldwide. Oxford is a registered trade mark of Oxford University
Press in the UK and certain other countries.

Published in the United States of America by Oxford University Press
198 Madison Avenue, New York, NY 10016, United States of America.

Library of Congress Cataloging-in-Publication Data
Names: Pugh, Jeffrey D., author.
Title: The invisibility bargain : governance networks and migrant human security /
Jeffrey D. Pugh.
Description: New York, NY : Oxford University Press, 2021. |
Includes bibliographical references and index.
Identifiers: LCCN 2020038367 (print) | LCCN 2020038368 (ebook) |
ISBN 9780197538692 (hardback) | ISBN 9780197553916 (paperback) |
ISBN 9780197538715 (epub)
Subjects: LCSH: Refugees—Colombia—Social conditions. |
Refugees—Ecuador—Social conditions. | Colombians—Ecuador—Social conditions. |
Refugees—Social networks—Case studies. | Human security—Ecuador. |
Social sciences—Network analysis. | Ecuador—Emigration and immigration—Social aspects. |
Ecuador—Emigration and immigration—Government policy.
Classification: LCC HV640.5.C7 P77 2021 (print) |
LCC HV640.5.C7 (ebook) | DDC 362.870986—dc23
LC record available at https://lccn.loc.gov/2020038367
LC ebook record available at https://lccn.loc.gov/2020038368

DOI: 10.1093/oso/9780197538692.001.0001

3 5 7 9 8 6 4 2

Paperback printed by Marquis, Inc., Canada
Hardback printed by Bridgeport National Bindery, Inc., United States of America

For Sophie

Contents

List of Illustrations

Figures

Tables

Acknowledgments

During a June week in 2005, I helped to facilitate a series of dialogues between Ecuadorian and Colombian women in the municipal building of Ibarra, Ecuador, together with the staff of the nongovernmental organization (NGO) I founded, the Center for Mediation, Peace, and Resolution of Conflict; guest trainers from several countries; and officials from United Nations High Commissioner for Refugees (UNHCR) and the United Nations Development Fund for Women. That experience, and the questions arising from it about how nonstate actors and networks can facilitate protection and peacebuilding in migrant-receiving communities, marked my entry point into my current research agenda, and was one of the motivations to carry out the research presented in this book. After fifteen years working on this set of research questions, and watching the migration context in Ecuador change significantly, it is a pleasure and a relief to be able to share the results here. Most books are the product of an enormous amount of collaborative effort. This one is no exception. I am grateful to many people who have helped me along the way, and the final product is much better because of helpful critiques, discussions, suggestions, encouragement, and intellectual engagement from numerous colleagues around the world. Many shortcomings undoubtedly still exist, for which I am solely responsible.

I wish to express my most sincere gratitude to all of the interviewees, migrants, NGO personnel, international organization and state officials whose experiences, insights, and stories are reflected in these pages and whose generosity in sharing them have made this book possible. Many organizations in Ecuador have partnered with me to facilitate data collection, and I am especially grateful to Asylum Access, the Hebrew Immigrant Aid Society, and UNHCR for facilitating contacts in nearly all of the provinces I studied. At Oxford University Press, I am very appreciative to Angela Chnapko for believing in this project and shepherding it through the editorial process with patience and insight. The two anonymous reviewers contributed enormously to improving and tightening this book, making it more accessible, and broadening its audience. I thank them for their time and service. I also appreciate Alexcee Bechthold's logistical assistance with the editorial process.

Over the years, I have benefited from the advice of many mentors, especially Margaret Keck, Renee Marlin-Bennett, Fausto Sarmiento, Julia Jordan-Zachery, and Sammy Barkin, and I appreciate their guidance and support, which has influenced my career and this book in many ways. Johns Hopkins University, Providence College, and the University of Massachusetts, Boston have been supportive home institutions for me as I worked on this project, providing rich intellectual communities. Likewise, the opportunity to be a visiting researcher at FLACSO Ecuador, the University of the Witwatersrand in South Africa, and the Johns Hopkins School of Advanced International Studies (SAIS) has enriched my work and led to fruitful exchanges with new colleagues. The research in this book has benefited from the financial support of the Fulbright Commission in Ecuador (special thanks to Karen Aguilar and Susana Cabeza de Vaca in Ecuador and Kris Monahan in the United States), two Providence College Committee on Aid for Faculty Research (CAFR) grants, and support from Johns Hopkins University, the University of Georgia, and the UMass Boston McCormack Dean's Office Faculty Fund for Enhancing Research (DOFFFER) grant.

For thoughtful discussions and feedback over the years on portions of the research contained in this book, I thank Rameez Abbas, Michelle Arevelo-Carpenter, Renny Barbiarz, Fabian Bauwens, Patricio Benalcazar, Carlos Beristain, Bianca Bersani, Duncan Breen, Joe Brown, Kara Cebulko, Emma Cervone, Erin Chung, Sarah Clarke, Jennifer Culbert, Steven David, Daniel Deudney, Bill Dixon, Susan Engel, Volker Frank, Gabriela García, Carmen Gomez, Michael Hanchard, Leila Hudson, Karen Jacobsen, Yves-Renee Jennings, Luis Jimenez, Lili Knorr, Paul Kowert, Hitomi Koyama, Loren Landau, Paulina Larreategui, Peter Lewis, Noora Lori, Sherry Lowrance, Cheryl Martens, Michael McCarthy, Noelia Montagud, Paola Moreno, Cecile Mouly, Rebecca Furst Nichols, Sarah O'Byrne, Nobotaka Otobe, Sarah Parkinson, Luicy Pedroza, Tara Polzer, Debbie Poole, Andres Quintero, Joel Quirk, Fredy Rivera, Adriana Salcedo, Consuelo Sanchez, Magaly Sanchez, Luis Sanipatin, Lucy Santacruz, Karina Sarmiento, Mark Sawyer, Adam Sheingate, David Shenk, Beverly Silver, Richard Snyder, Courtenay Sprague, David Steinberg, Patricia Sullivan, Kellee Tsai, Marcela Vasquez-Leon, Pedro Velasco, Egle Verseckaite, Darshan Vigneswaran, Juan Wang, Wendy Wong, William Zartman, the UMass Boston IR Faculty Group, the Junior Faculty Writing Group and Junior Faculty Research Seminar, my colleagues in the UMB Department of Conflict Resolution, Human Security, and Global Governance, my political science and global studies colleagues at Providence College, students in my graduate seminars who read early versions of this work, the *International Migration Review* editors and anonymous reviewers who significantly strengthened my related article, my talks at the United Nations, Brown University, Johns Hopkins, the University of Arizona, Universidad de las Americas (UDLA), Universidad Politécnica Estatal del Carchi (UPEC), Facultad Latinoamericana de Ciencias Sociales-Ecuador (FLACSO), the University of Georgia, and the participants in numerous conference panels over the years where my ideas were presented in preliminary form.

I appreciate research assistance from Tim Adivilah, Ruth Álvarez, Luz Marina Caicedo, Sergi Cardona, María Paz Dávila, Monica Freire, Magaly García-Pletsch, Ethan Gentes, Emily Ginsberg, Lizeth Gonzalez, Uluc Karakas, Rachel Koepsel, Bettina Latuff, Jessica Losier, Indira Martinez, Sharon McCoy, Maribel Melo, Christopher Monteiro, Daniela Moreira, Julie Moreno, Jennifer Moya, Jefferson Nazamues, Ana Oña and *Opinión Pública Ecuador*, Carlos Perez, Yifan Ren, Adriana Rincón, Julie Rodríguez, Andrea Rojas, Emily Schkeryantz, Martin Secaira, David Sulewski, Safiya St. Claire, Fernando Tatés, Casondra Turner, and Michael Zhang. Thanks to Steve McAvene for superb indexing. This book has benefited tremendously from the research support and assistance provided by the staff and volunteers of the Center for Mediation, Peace, and Resolution of Conflict in Ecuador, especially Omar Rodriguez, Diana Palacios, Jeffrey Akomah, Lana Balyk, Kristen McCaskey, Tatiana Fontalvo, Casey Morrison, Karoline Popp, Jack Rodriguez, Liz Valverde-Bartlett, Alexandra Visser, and Katie Windle.

I am grateful to my family for years of supportive understanding through triumphs and challenges. My parents and sister have provided a lifetime of loving support and patiently tolerating my nerdy conversations. I thank my wife Ling Chen for her patience, skill in clarity and organization, all-around support, and partnership. Most importantly, my daughter Sophie has brought so much light and joy to my life that every day is better because she is in it. For that reason, I dedicate this book to her.

Portions of chapters 2 and 6 were previously published in article form: Jeffrey D. Pugh, "Negotiating Identity and Belonging through the Invisibility Bargain: Colombian Forced Migrants in Ecuador," *International Migration Review* 52, no. 4 (2017): 978–1010.

Abbreviations

AAE/ASELER	Asylum Access Ecuador
ACEREX	Asociación de Colombianos Emprendedores Residentes en el Exterior
ALBA	Bolivarian Alliance for the Peoples of Our America
ARCOE	Asociación de Refugiados Colombianos en Ecuador
ASOREC	Asociación de Refugiados Colombianos
CEDHU	Comisión Ecuménica de Derechos Humanos del Ecuador
DPE	Defensoría del Pueblo / Human Rights Ombudsman
FARC	Fuerzas Armadas Revolucionarias de Colombia
FAS	Fundación Ambiente y Sociedad
FENARE	Federación Nacional de Refugiados
FEPP	Fondo Ecuatoriano Popularum Progressio
FFLA	Fundación Futuro Latinoamericano
FLACSO	Facultad Latinoamericana de Ciencias Sociales
HIAS	Hebrew Immigrant Aid Society
INREDH	Fundación Regional de Asesoría en Derechos Humanos
IOM	International Organization for Migration
ISAMIS	San Miguel Church of Sucumbíos
JRS	Jesuit Refugee Service
MIES	Ministry of Socioeconomic Inclusion
MMRREE	Ministry of Foreign Relations
MNS	Migrant Networks Survey
MOS	Migrant Organization Survey
NRC	Norwegian Refugee Council
OAS	Organization of American States
PUCE	Pontifica Universidad Católica del Ecuador
RET	Refugee Education Trust
RIS	Race and Immigration Survey
SENAMI	Secretaría Nacional del Migrante
SENPLADES	Secretaría Nacional de Planificación y Desarrollo
SJRM	Jesuit Refugee and Migrant Service
UASB	Universidad Andina Simon Bolivar
UDENOR	Unit for Development in the North

UNASUR	Union of South American Countries
UNDP	United Nations Development Program
UNHCR	United Nations High Commissioner for Refugees
USAID	US Agency for International Development
WFP	World Food Program

Chronology

Year	Event
1999	Economic crisis in Ecuador leads to hyperinflation, emigration of more than 10% of population.
2000	Plan Colombia escalates violence in Colombian countryside, increasing displacement to Ecuador.
2002	UDENOR is established to coordinate northern border development.
2003	President Gutierrez places visa/police record restrictions on Colombians; Kofi Annan visits.
2004	UN assessment team visits northern border.
2005	Lucio Gutierrez leaves presidency amid national protests.
2006	Rafael Correa is elected to presidency on platform of human security / Plan Ecuador.
2007	UNHCR's main partner changes from Catholic Church to HIAS.
2008	New constitution enshrines "universal citizenship," nondiscrimination by migratory status; Colombia bombs FARC camp at Angostura; UNDP begins Peace in N Border Zone program.
2009	UNHCR / Foreign Ministry Enhanced Registration joint mobile brigades initiative begins, doubling the number registered refugees.
2010	Convivir en Solidaridad anti-xenophobia campaign starts; Foreign Ministry opens more field offices.
2012	Correa issues Decree 1182, abandoning Cartagena Declaration criteria for Refugee Status Determination, establishing fifteen-day eligibility period to apply for refugee status upon arrival.
2013	Mercosur visa is introduced.
2014	Asylum Access and Universidad San Francisco de Quito win partial victory in case when Constitutional Court nullifies parts of Decree 1182.
2016	FARC signs peace agreement, begins demobilizing.
2017	Lenin Moreno becomes the new president; Human Mobility Law is signed into effect.
2018	FARC splinter cell in Esmeraldas province kidnaps, kills journalists.

Year	Event
2019	Mobs attack Venezuelans in Ibarra; Moreno imposes visa rules on Venezuelans; in October there are indigenous protests in Quito and a national strike (Venezuelans were accused of being "agitators").
2020	Moreno imposes curfew and closes borders due to COVID-19; Ecuador is one of the hardest hit Latin American countries in deaths per capita.

1

Introduction

How do forced migrants access the protections and rights that they are guaranteed in international and domestic law but often denied in practice? Under what conditions do nonstate actors develop and adapt institutions to protect security and build peace within a country whose state is unable to provide these functions effectively in the face of the conflicts raised by becoming a major recipient of international migrants? Political discourse in response to mass refugee and migration movements from conflict hot spots like Syria, Afghanistan, or Colombia often portrays newcomers as potentially threatening components of a "wave," "invasion," or "swarm." Different groups within the receiving country may frame the relationship between migrants and the host society in terms of humanitarian solidarity, economic contribution (or threat), or security fears, which in turn influences the informal expectations of migrants and the formal migration policy responses adopted by the state. The new relationships being negotiated by citizens and foreigners may threaten existing social hierarchies and exacerbate tensions between citizens and the migrant population in ways that lead to xenophobia and conflict. In the case of forced migrants, for whom return to their country of origin is not a realistic option because of security threats to their lives, it is particularly disconcerting to flee from one conflict only to confront a new one in the country of refuge. At the same time, states, which have the primary obligation to provide security within their own borders, often have inadequate capacity or political incentives to extend this protection to nonvoting newcomers, even those that international refugee law and domestic migration legislation obligate them to protect.

This book develops the argument that an unwritten set of expectations of migrants and refugees serve as a powerful set of norms conditioning their precarity, the ability (or not) to access in practice the formal protections and rights that are guaranteed in formal law and international treaties, their social relationships and ability to build social capital, and the possibilities and forms of political participation that they can pursue to have a say in decisions that affect them. Under this "invisibility bargain," the host community accepts,

The Invisibility Bargain. Jeffrey D. Pugh, Oxford University Press (2021). © Oxford University Press.
DOI: 10.1093/oso/9780197538692.003.0001

or at least tolerates without active persecution, the presence of migrants to the extent that they are perceived as *contributing value* to the host country and they remain *socially and politically invisible*. The intersectionality of race, ethnicity, gender, social class, and nationality structures the ways that multiple forms of difference make particular migrants more or less visible, more or less desirable for inclusion in the "community of value" that is constructed by powerful actors in society, and more or less able to maintain secure livelihoods and peaceful relations with citizen neighbors. The paradox of this bargain is that the more pressure or leverage that migrants attempt to employ in order to make demands and claim rights that are guaranteed them by the state, the more politically visible they become, and thus risk triggering a backlash from the host community that might actually make them less secure and more at risk.

With a keen awareness of this complexity, migrants often are confronted with a choice among competing strategies: (*a*) embrace invisibility and live in the shadows, minimizing interactions with law enforcement and other agents of the state and even informal social relationships in order to reduce the risk of backlash and potential harm or deportation; (*b*) build coalitions with a diverse set of nonstate actors and other allies who can act as brokers, articulating the interests and grievances expressed by migrants to state decision-makers while encouraging migrants to take advantage of spaces for dialogue, organization, and participation that are created by these organizations; or (*c*) make visible demands on the state while simultaneously trying to reframe the narrative to emphasize the legitimate basis of their claim-making by employing discourses of human rights, cosmopolitanism and universal citizenship, reciprocal obligation, empathetic solidarity, or other narratives. My research with Colombian refugees in Ecuador shows that the first of these strategies tends to be the most common, the second tends to be the most successful, and the third is frequently counterproductive when employed directly by migrants without brokerage via nonstate allies.

Although 86% of the world's refugees live in the Global South, according to the UNHCR, most of the resources for effective integration of migrant populations are concentrated in industrialized countries, which have also been the subject of the overwhelming majority of scholarly work on integration of migrants (both forced and economic migrants). The traditional assumption embedded in the national security literature was that the path to greater security in the face of increasing migration flows was to develop greater state capacity to impose border controls, expel potentially threatening outsiders, and enforce immigration laws with greater efficiency (Weiner 1995; Adamson 2006). This can be seen in most host countries, as illustrated by the US response to the 2015 Syrian refugee crisis that included congressional proposals to deny entry to all Syrian refugees because of fear of potential security threats. In states in the Global South with weak governance institutions, these fears can be magnified by the recognition that the institutional capacity to impose border restrictions and block migrants from entering the territory is often much lower. More coercive state capacity may not lead to greater peace and human security for residents of migrant-receiving areas, however, as the perverse political incentives and multiple sources of authority in border regions can lead to invisible migrant populations, greater victimization without effective institutional remedies, and escalating insecurity for all residents (d'Appollonia 2012).

Ecuador, the main empirical case examined in this book, is one such country. Ecuador was the largest recipient of refugees and asylum seekers in Latin America for most of the past two decades and also has been a major sending country of emigrants following an economic collapse at the turn of the twenty-first century (UNHCR 2016), many of whom have gone to Europe and the United States (Kyle 2000; Alvarez 2020). Approximately sixty thousand registered refugees and an estimated 150,000 people in need of international protection live in Ecuador, of whom more than 95% are from Colombia, most having entered since 2000, when Plan Colombia escalated the violence and displacement in their home country. Relatively open and progressive formal institutions exist in Ecuador to facilitate the integration of significant new migrant populations, and the country has been a laboratory for political innovations seeking to translate the concepts of open borders and universal citizenship into policy and embed them in its 2008 constitution (Pessina 2011). There is a significant divide, however, between the formal state policies designed to integrate migrants in a way that ensures human security and peace and the actual practice of migrant reception as experienced by migrants and their hosts. The capacity of formal state institutions to provide security, a core sovereign function, in migrant-receiving areas of Ecuador (especially those outside of the major cities) has been quite weak. At the same time, however, migrants in Ecuador enjoy greater protections and live in conditions of greater human security than in many other host countries, including those with stronger governments and more resources, such as South Africa, where migrants have been targeted by periodic waves of xenophobic violence (Misago 2017).

This study seeks to explore how Ecuador, a country with traditionally weak state institutions, has nonetheless been able to provide security and promote peace in some areas with large populations of citizens and foreign migrants coexisting in the same geographic territory, and to explain variation across different migrant-receiving localities. This puzzle emerges from the expectation in traditional security literature that stronger states (i.e., those with greater capacity to defend against external threats and control migration into their territory) are more secure states (Solomon 2003). In contrast to the enforcement and control policies that states employ as guarantors of national security, the book examines ways in which human security is provided through networks of nonstate actors. These institutions, which often do not start off with the explicit purpose of taking on security or peacebuilding functions, adapt to gaps in formal state institutions and intervene to protect rights, develop resources, or promote mutual recognition within migrant-receiving communities. The institutional governance networks that connect state and nonstate actors increase access to rights, resources, and recognition by all residents (migrants and citizens) while being sensitive to the unwritten demands that are sometimes imposed on migrants by the host population to remain politically and socially invisible while contributing economically to the host society. Through this process of institutional adaptation, nonstate actors create networks of security governance that complement, negotiate with, and sometimes substitute for the state at the local level. The formation of these networks can alter the relationship between the state and society in areas of the country where a mixed population of migrants and citizens challenges the state's ability or willingness to fulfill its core function of protecting human security for everyone living under its authority.

This book draws on a wealth of data from approximately fifteen months of fieldwork spanning eight years in Ecuador. The book draws on more than 170 interviews with officials in governments, nongovernmental organizations (NGOs), and international organizations, as well as Colombian migrants living in Ecuador. It also relies on an original survey of more than 650 foreign migrants (95% of whom were Colombians) living in the six provinces in the northern border zone of Ecuador with the largest populations of foreign migrants and refugees. This survey provides rich insights into the experiences and attitudes of migrants in Ecuador, particularly their trust in and access to institutions, their experience with human security outcomes, and their relations with Ecuadorians. Through network analysis, I am able to trace relational ties through which governance networks influence human security in migrant-receiving communities, allowing for systematic comparison of localities. The key finding is that localities with more dense networks composed of more diverse actors (including the state, nonstate actors, and international organizations, rather than only one of these types) tend to produce greater peace and human security for the citizens and migrants who live in them than other localities. Historical process tracing of institutional development in Ecuador over the past decade and a half and discourse analysis of media stories and presidential rhetoric also allow me to trace the evolving social and political context in which the integration and political participation of Colombian migrants has been negotiated, highlighting the interplay of structure and agency.

The book challenges the conventional understanding of the relationship between migration and security, and provides a fresh approach to the negotiation of authority between state and society in migrant-receiving countries. Its willingness to trace the production of human security through governance networks at multiple levels dismantles the false dichotomy between international and national politics, and exposes the micropolitics of institutional innovation and adaptation. By focusing attention on the practical implementation of migration policies and the levels of protection experienced by migrants as a result of their access to institutional governance networks, the book's policy-relevant findings shed light on the formal and informal political structures that produce effective peace and human security in migrant-receiving countries.

Contributions to an Evolving Field

The book makes four primary theoretical contributions and two major empirical contributions to the understanding of nonstate actors as providers of human security in Latin America. The collective theoretical contributions include the development of the invisibility bargain, the emphasis on institutional relations and networks rather than characteristics and policies, the analysis of distinct political realities of informal institutions in the Global South, and the rethinking of familiar concepts of populism and clientelism through the lens of brokering networks that include transnational and nonstate institutional authorities and collective negotiations of belonging in *el pueblo*.

Theoretical Contributions

First, the introduction of the invisibility bargain concept and the employment of network theories provide an intellectual framework for understanding how nonstate actors broker access to resources and participation in negotiations among states, migrants, transnational actors, and the citizen population (Hellgren 2011; Koinova 2014; von Bülow 2010; Cooley and Ron 2002; Keck and Sikkink 1998; Granovetter 1973). In this process, migrants often gain access indirectly through brokers that connect them to the rights, resources, and recognition that they need, while shielding them from the backlash and social sanctions that migrants might incur from the host population if they made these demands directly on the state. This argument extends the literature on invisibility as a strategy and migrants' innovative approaches to political participation in a context of uncertain belonging in the political community (Coutin 2003; Mas Giralt 2011; Das Gupta 2006; Okamoto and Ebert 2016), highlighting both the constraints and the possibilities for creative agency that influence the negotiation between migrants and their host societies.

Second, it brings the study of the *relationships* among state, nonstate, and international institutions into the foreground of explaining the political and social structures that produce the highest levels of peace and human security for migrants and the host population with whom they live. A growing literature has underscored the formal and informal ways in which governance is produced by state and nonstate actors, especially in parts of the world where formal state institutions are weak (Risse 2011; Helmke and Levitsky 2006; MacLean 2010). There is a recognition among many scholars that global institutions can and do penetrate into national and local political spaces, interacting with domestic actors to influence the way that human security protections are designed and implemented in practice through dissemination of international norms, sharing of expertise and technical assistance, and channeling of international pressure that raises the costs of "noncompliance" with international treaties and norms (Dai 2007). The actors and institutions that possess the most salient "practical authority" to get things done in a particular place and issue area may not be those with formal titles or jurisdiction, but may be nonstate actors with other types of resources or legitimacy (Abers and Keck 2013; Hancock and Mitchell 2018). Building on important macrotheoretical work by others that exposed the way in which state and nonstate actors contribute to global structures of authority that influence security and migration policies and can result in the expulsion of certain populations from the political community (Sassen 1999, 2014; Betts 2011), the book contributes to the cluster of scholarship that traces the social and political negotiation of participation and identity by migrants at the ground level (Anderson 2013; Coutin 2003; Zolberg and Woon 1999; Theiss-Morse 2009; Hochschild et al. 2013; Ambrosini 2013).

Previous work on governance related to security in migrant-receiving countries often focused on the *capabilities* or *characteristics* of different institutions, such as state capacity to enforce laws and protect borders (Adamson 2006; Weiner 1995), or the ways in which NGOs are incentivized, structured, and funded (Wong 2012). This book seeks to refocus attention on the *channels* and *relationships* through which these state and nonstate institutions interact, arguing that a robust and diverse network structure that connects NGOs and intergovernmental organizations (IGOs) with the state may be more important in providing access to human security and peace in migrant-receiving areas than the mere presence of strong state institutions (Cox 2009; Landau and Duponchel 2011; Wilson et al. 2016). By elaborating a detailed examination of the ways in which state and nonstate actors mobilize and use authority to produce security outcomes, the book offers a useful treatment of sovereignty as an empirical practice with microlevel manifestations rather than an organizing assumption about international politics.

Third, the book tackles head-on the distinct factors that influence migrant integration, participation, and conflict resolution with the host population in receiving countries of the Global South. In the past decade, the reasons behind xenophobia, anti-immigration attitudes, and other forms of conflict between migrants and citizens have motivated a compelling line of systematic empirical research (Danzygier 2010; Hainmueller and Hopkins 2015; Okamoto and Ebert 2016). A robust literature has argued that migrants exercise agency in negotiating access to resources and political participation (Jacobsen 2002; Hochschild et al. 2013; Ambrosini 2013), but most of this work has focused on migrant integration in industrialized societies, especially Europe and the United States (Ellerman 2010; Engbersen and Broeders 2009; McIlwaine 2011; Andreas and Snyder 2001). UNHCR figures show that 86% of refugees live in the Global South, and the International Organization for Migration (IOM) reports that South-South flows make up a larger component of the global migrant population than migration from developing countries to industrialized countries. Despite this fact, the Global

North has received the vast majority of the scholarly attention on migrant integration and social negotiation. Conventional studies showed how conflict in the developing world could produce refugee and migration flows (Zolberg et al. 1989; Lischer 2006), but only relatively recently have some scholars taken on the important task of examining social conflict resulting from integration attempts within migrant-receiving host countries in the Global South (Adida 2014; Landau and Duponchel 2011; Polzer 2009; González-Murphy 2013; Lawrence 2015; Korovkin 2008; Gottwald 2004). Given the importance of national identity in shaping the possibilities and boundaries for the political and social integration of migrants, the literature on populism in Latin America also provides a theoretical foundation for the ways in which migrants are defined as insiders or outsiders, either complicit/potential threats as outsiders or sympathetic victims deserving of protection. The migration approach of the populist regime in Ecuador contributes to the development of the literature by highlighting the articulation of internal or external enemies, the identification of the "real" *pueblo*/people versus those who threaten them, and the uneasy coexistence of nationalism that excludes migrants and antihegemonic populist discourses that include them in performative solidarity against exclusionary traditional receiving countries in the Global North (de la Torre 2017, 2020; Pugh 2017; Ulloa 2013). In this context, migrants have an unusual possibility for inclusion in *el pueblo* in a way similar to the community of value, if they "play by the rules" for expression and participation set out by the leader, but there are fewer checks on arbitrary redefinitions of the boundaries that could exclude them from participation or even from physical presence.

The book's focus on Latin America as a host region is important because of the combination of relatively long-standing postcolonial democratic political institutions and persistent economic underdevelopment and inequality in the region, which have led to significant differences between the promise of formal democratic institutions and the lived experience of the population in marginalized regions where the state has been absent or weak. Through careful attention to the *implementation* in practice of migration and security policies, the book contributes a more nuanced understanding of the way in which informal institutions and nonstate actors can be key contributors to the state's provision of human security in the Global South. Furthermore, the fragmented clientelistic networks of political authority and the multiple regional authorities that make competing claims for citizens' loyalties in "brown areas" at the margins of the state in Latin America (O'Donnell 2004;

Das and Poole 2004) provide unique potential points of access for migrants to negotiate resources and political participation that may not be available in receiving states in the Global North. The book highlights the networks that link migrant beneficiary "clients" and patrons, which can be state, nonstate, or international actors. It compares these actors' brokering relationships that exchange political support, economic resources, and normative legitimacy with traditional electoral clientelistic relationships connecting state and society in Latin America (Hilgers 2012; Fox 1994). By doing so, it brings fresh ideas to old debates on clientelism, representation, and democratic legitimacy in Latin America, adding nuance and transnational analysis that better align with the political realities of the region today.

Empirical Contributions

Empirically, the book makes two main contributions. It has at its foundation the most comprehensive data collection efforts in the past fifteen years to be published in English on migrant integration, human security, and institutions in Ecuador (see Bilsborrow 2006 for the last major effort). Drawing on approximately 170 interviews with migrants and officials of NGOs, state agencies, and international organizations conducted during fifteen months of fieldwork over the course of eight years, and more than 650 surveys of migrants in six provinces, the book rests on a solid empirical core. Despite excellent Spanish-language contributions by Ecuadorian scholars (Moscoso and Burneo 2014; Ortega and Ospina 2012; Zepeda and Carrion 2015; Santacruz 2013; Rivera et al. 2007), the current book is the only systematic study of this topic to span all six of the provinces in the northern border region with the largest populations of refugees, and to capture fine-grained organizational network patterns that allow for comparison across localities. In this way, I am able to compare migrant integration and human security pathways and networks in rural provinces near the border that have an active presence of irregular groups and a weak presence of the state with those in the capital city and other more highly developed provinces along the Pan-American Highway in the Andes mountains. In an era in which the UNHCR and other international organizations are struggling to recalibrate their understanding of refugee integration from camps to urban settlement, the ability to compare outcomes across localities, and across different types of intervening organizations, provides fruitful insights into questions of human security and governance provided by nonstate actors as well as policy-relevant findings about the most effective institutional structures.

The second major empirical contribution is a result of the mixed-method approach that combines rich data from interviews, participant observation, surveys, network analysis, and discourse analysis collected over the entire ten-year period of Rafael Correa's presidency (2007–2017). Ecuador represents a unique laboratory of migration policy, as simultaneously a major sending, receiving, and transit country (Alvarez 2020), and one in which the president during the main period of study rested his election and policy platform on open borders and universal citizenship, which were then codified in a new constitution. This study, which traces the political, institutional, and social changes in host-migrant relations in Ecuador over this time period, illuminates the formal and informal processes by which migration policy and its application in practice lead to more or less human security experienced by migrants and citizens. This empirical contribution promises to uncover potential pathways and expose potential pitfalls that would be useful for other migrant-receiving states in the Global South, as well as illuminating aspects of integration and migration governance that are transferrable to the Global North, but might otherwise be missed in those contexts.

Methods and Data Sources

This book draws on a wealth of data collected in Ecuador. I conducted more than 170 interviews with migrant leaders and officials of NGOs, state agencies, and international organizations (plus two focus groups of forced migrants in Quito) during fifteen months of fieldwork spanning 2007 to 2017 (and several follow-up interviews later) in six provinces that compose the northern border and surrounding region in Ecuador. Throughout the text, I refer to these interviews with simple code numbers in order to ensure anonymity and human subjects protections while giving at least basic information about the category and location of the interviewee I am referring to.[1] To complement these qualitative data, I draw on data from the five

---

[1] Interview codes follow a simple formula of the interview number followed by a letter to denote the locality in which the interview took place (Q for Quito, S for Sucumbíos, E for Esmeraldas, I for Imbabura, C for Carchi, D for Santo Domingo) and a letter to denote the category of interviewee (M for migrant, N for NGO or nonstate actor, S for state, I for IGO), and the year in which the interview took place.

surveys summarized in Table 1.1, two of which were carried out by others and three of which were conducted by my research team. The combination of different data sources—multiple surveys of Colombians and Ecuadorians plus interview and focus group responses—provides empirical richness and depth complemented by more systematic evidence of how broadly these attitudes and experiences about migration apply within the two populations. Because working with hard-to-reach populations involves trade-offs in data-gathering strategies, and because the complexities of identities, informal

Table 1.1 Survey data sources

Year	Name[a]	Explanation
2007	Latinobarometer (Latinobarómetro 2007)	Nationally representative survey with Ecuadorian sample size of 1,200. Four-stage modified probabilistic sample, with quotas in final stage, sampling error of +/− 2.8% at 95% level of confidence.
2015	The Americas and the World (Zepeda and Carrion 2015)	Nationally representative survey with Ecuadorian sample size of 1,800. Cluster sampling of census units selected by probabilities proportional to size. Multistage probabilistic sampling frame stratified by geographic region, urban/rural locality, and socioeconomic level.
2008	Race and Immigration Survey[b] (RIS 2008)	131 Ecuadorian respondents in five distribution sites outside of high-traffic public transportation stations selected through a judgment sampling frame in different parts of Quito.
2009–2010	Migrant Organization Survey[b] (MOS 2010)	130 Colombian migrants in Quito. Distributed using a snowball sample with migrant-serving organizations and key informants as starting points to identify respondents.
2013–2015	Migrant Networks Survey[b] (MNS 2016)	678 foreign migrants (99% Colombian) in six cities—Quito, Lago Agrio, Esmeraldas, Ibarra, Tulcán, and Santo Domingo, selected via geographically segmented quota sampling in migrant neighborhoods and through snowball sampling with migrant-serving organizations and key informants as starting points to identify respondents (see Pugh 2015).

[a] The form in which the survey is cited is given in parentheses.

[b] Survey was conducted by the author's research team.

institutions, and intergroup relations are difficult to reliably capture using only one method, triangulation emerges as a way to offer a more convincing base of evidence. My constructivist approach uses survey data to systematically compare experiences and perceptions and to visualize institutional networked relationships (and multiple surveys that are geographically disaggregated allow me to show dynamic changes across time, space, and population). Interviews help illuminate *why* respondents have particular views, or why institutions took particular actions, especially over time periods that my survey data do not cover. Discourse analysis of speeches and news media help to capture the way narratives about migration are advanced and accepted (or not), how they influence the collective understanding, and whose narratives prevail. These multiple data sources together reveal a fuller truth that might otherwise be missed, especially in reflecting voices of both Ecuadorians and Colombians over time and across populations and geographic space.

The large national surveys conducted by Latinobarometer (2007) and Zepeda and Carrion (2015) offer snapshots of Ecuadorian public opinion. Both surveys are conducted regularly, but these specific years were selected because of the number and relevance of immigration-related questions asked. My Race and Immigration Survey (2008)[2] of Ecuadorian respondents is limited by a small sample size and implementation only in Quito, but it asked questions that allow for deeper engagement with race and identity than either Latinobarometer (2007) or Zepeda and Carrion (2015), allowing us to disentangle the influence of multiple markers of difference on migrant experiences.

My original Migrant Networks Survey (MNS) in 2015 provides detailed evidence about the self-reported attitudes and experiences of a larger sample of migrants in Ecuador, at least 95% Colombian. The MNS was carried out in field visits of one to two weeks each in the capital cities of six provinces in Ecuador's northern border region: Quito, Lago Agrio, and Esmeraldas in 2013, Ibarra in 2014, and Santo Domingo and Tulcán in 2015. The questions were developed and validated with feedback from refugees, NGO leaders, and other stakeholders.[3] Based on planning meetings with key informants and a review of published lists, I developed a comprehensive database of 112 organizations and other stakeholders relevant to the migration field, which

---

[2] Conducted together with Casondra Turner, Sharon McCoy, Michael Zhang, and Martin Secaira.
[3] The original MNS is included as an appendix to this book.

served as a contact list for in-person interviews in each locality. Migrant and refugee respondents were then recruited in each town to complete the MNS with the help of these local organizations and stakeholders, as well as by identifying the neighborhoods with high concentrations of migrants.

Evidence from the MNS and interviews in the provinces provide a more complete picture of migrant integration in both Quito and smaller border towns than do national aggregate data, since the social and political expectations can differ among these localities. The 2010 Migrant Organization Survey[4] was implemented only in Quito and has a small sample size, but it forms a useful baseline (with some questions that are the same as those asked in the MNS) for measuring change in time between 2009 and 2013, especially regarding migrants' trust in various Quito organizations and their experiences with different political strategies. It also contains a useful item on location of migrant interactions with Ecuadorians. The data on Colombian migrant perceptions are much harder to collect than Ecuadorian attitudes, so drawing on multiple sources compensates for some of the limitations of any one survey, particularly small and nonrandom samples resulting from the trade-offs involved in surveying difficult-to-reach populations under the constraints of limited resources (Bloch 1999).

Key Concepts and Definitions

Human Security

There is an increasing disjuncture between the tools for ensuring security and peace that are available through the traditional national security conceptualization of the state and the new transnational and networked threats that have arisen over the past two decades (and the more complex limitations on state action represented by increased salience of international organizations and globalization). As a result of a "crisis of confidence" in the ability of formal state institutions of national security to provide meaningful protections for people, Robin Luckham argues that the human security perspective provides a framework for thinking about the prevention of violence and conflict that is more relevant to the fears of everyday people (see also Lipschutz 1995; UNDP 1994). "This crisis of confidence has in turn inspired

---

[4] Conducted together with Emily Ginsberg.

a number of alternative conceptualizations of security, challenging state-centered paradigms, and beginning to re-center security around the safety and welfare of citizens and human beings" (Luckham 2007: 685). Beginning with its 1994 *Human Development Report*, the United Nations Development Program (UNDP) codified this new approach with a clear definition, emphasizing "safety from the constant threats of hunger, disease, crime and repression" and "protection from sudden and hurtful disruptions in the pattern of our daily lives—whether in our homes, in our jobs, in our communities, or in the environment" (UNDP 1994: 3). In doing so, the report called on the UN system and member states to prioritize *human* security in the nexus of promoting both security and development. This approach takes a broader view of who should be protected, but it also argues that we need a deeper appreciation for the kinds of threats against which people need to be protected, recognizing that nonmilitary and nonstate actors (and even the state itself) are often greater threats to people's lives than traditional enemies in the form of armed foreign state aggressors (Andersen-Rodgers and Crawford 2018; King and Murray 2001; Murphy 2013). It also argues that people are more vulnerable to violence when they are deprived of the means of survival, access to rights, and secure legal status, and thus structural violence must be taken into account in the provision of security as well (Jacobsen 2002). Human security approaches are often organized around the twin goals of "freedom from fear" and "freedom from want" (UNDP 1994), emphasizing the interrelated nature of violence and economic deprivation.

Abello Colak and Pearce contrast the human security explanation's approach to preventing violence with that of the national security approach, focusing on the inadequacy of the latter in providing security for mobile, organic units like individuals and communities, in contrast to the static territorial units of states:

> The crisis in security provision makes more problematic the lack of connection between the State's objectives and local communities' needs. In contexts of violence, communities need to be protected and helped to build more secure environments. However, public security provision tends to focus on eliminating enemies or competitors to their territorial control and not on mitigating the perverse effects of insecurity and violence on people's lives. That is why sometimes the methods used by the police and military forces cause more unrest, fear and insecurity amongst the local population. (Abello Colak and Pearce 2009: 16)

This recognition of the limitations of the state in providing security in many of the areas that need it most (such as migrant-receiving communities where intergroup tensions can escalate to violence) has led scholars to identify the important role of nonstate actors and informal institutions in offering protection for individuals and communities, although there is some disagreement over the legitimacy or desirability of this phenomenon. According to Donna Lee Van Cott's analysis of Latin American informal institutions, "In parts of the Andes in which state legal institutions either do not exist or are widely viewed as corrupt or ineffective, informal systems of justice such as indigenous law, *rondas campesinas* (community patrols; Peru) and *juntas vecinales* (neighborhood juntas; Bolivia) have been used to resolve disputes, provide security, and dispense justice. Where they are effective, informal justice systems may offer some partial remedies for low-intensity citizenship" (2006: 12). Baker and Scheye (2007) argue that security provision by nonstate actors is not a bad thing, and that the focus of human security should be on maximizing the quality of the service for the end user, regardless of what type of institution provides it, whether state, nonstate, formal, or informal. Abello Colak and Pearce disagree, however, arguing that only the state can ensure that security as a public good is enforced as a right and not distributed privately according to wealth or status: " 'Security from below' has nothing to do with vigilantism or de facto civilian responses to their insecurity" (2009: 12).

The analysis in this book draws heavily on the human security literature, since migrants are excluded from both the territorial protections of their own state borders and are often prevented from integrating into the receiving society or gaining access to state protections because of their precarious status under the invisibility bargain. The human security explanation provides an underlying theoretical approach for understanding why institutions that are often informal and developed by nonstate actors are essential to building peace where the absence or weakness of the state has left marginality and vulnerability to violence. It broadens the scope of intervention from a narrow, instrumental attempt to stop violence by defending against threats to the creation of structures that increase access to justice and rights, and thus decrease the vulnerability of people to violent threats. Expanding on this last point, the next section makes the case that all of the security approaches outlined here tell only part of the story. Security is necessary in preventing violence in migrant-receiving communities, but a deeper peace is needed to ensure that the relationships among migrants, citizens, and societal structures are transformed to ensure mutual recognition and access to basic rights, which allow for a more sustainable coexistence.

Ensuring Security, Building Peace

A narrow focus on security is insufficient for understanding the ways in which institutions seek to prevent and mitigate violence in migrant-receiving communities. Because tensions exist between neighbors, coworkers, and classmates whose lives are intermingled and to some extent interdependent, preventing this conflict from escalating to violence involves transforming the relationship between citizens and migrants from a threatening one to a harmonious one, rather than simply controlling or excluding one group in order to shield the other. This is known as peacebuilding, a process that John Paul Lederach describes as transforming "deeply divided, hostile, and violent relationships into a peace-system characterized by just and interdependent relationships with the capacity to find nonviolent mechanisms for expressing and handling conflict" (1997: 84).

Security is a key component of peacebuilding, since people who are insecure have an incentive to increase their own protection at the expense of others, including by violence if necessary. Conversely, sustainable and meaningful peace is important in order to ensure that security will last. People who do not perceive other groups a threats to their well-being, and people who believe that there are well-established mechanisms by which conflicts can be resolved peacefully, have less to fear and are thus more secure. In contrast, those who feel vulnerable because of a group's hostility may fear that it could result in harm to themselves, and in the absence of effective institutions to facilitate cooperation or mitigate violence, they are less secure (Galama and van Tongeren 2002). These connections between peace and security build upon seminal works by Johan Galtung (1969) and Kenneth Boulding (1978) that argue that security is an essential part of peace, but also that a sustainable peace makes violence less likely to recur, which means that everyone is more secure. Elaborating on the point, Bjørn Møller argues, "For 'security' to be meaningful and durable, it would have to amount to a positive or stable peace structure. This would imply considerably more than negative peace equated with an absence of war, as merely one particular form of 'direct violence.' Genuine peace and security would presuppose an elimination of, or at least a reduction of, 'structural violence,' i.e. the relative deprivation of large parts of the world population" (2000). Because they are grounded in the same communities that are affected by host-migrant hostility, nonstate institutions have the potential to drive this peacebuilding process in ways that the state cannot do alone.

It is important to recognize here that not all nonstate institutions are benevolent or "good." Nonstate actors have also taken advantage of or adapted to weak penetration of state authority in order to facilitate the economic enrichment or violence capacity of private actors, thus decreasing security for many who live in their areas of influence (Briscoe 2008; Idler 2019). According to Ivan Briscoe, "The combination of non-state armed groups and trafficking networks operating along various poorly policed Latin American borders raises intense concerns that these frontiers have become the focal points for organized crime and non-state powers, displacing instability, institutional malaise and civil violence from one country to the next" (2008: 8). It is this phenomenon that Abello Colak and Pearce were concerned about in arguing for the importance of state involvement in security provision as a public good. My argument is not that nonstate institutions will always build peace in a way that increases security for everyone; rather, it is that they have different incentives than the state, and a governance network that links nonstate and international actors whose mission includes migrant protection with the state increases possible access points for the production of human security for everyone in migrant-receiving communities. In chapters 3 and 7, I will trace the ways in which networks of state, IGO, and nonstate actors increase human security for migrants and citizens in Ecuador by improving access to four major components of human security: the protection against violent threats, protection of rights, development of resources and livelihoods, and the promotion of mutual recognition between groups.

Distinguishing among Refugees, Immigrants, and Migrants

In laying the groundwork for the rest of the book, one additional note is in order. In this book, I am most interested in the building of peace among the host population and forced migrants, as these persons fleeing violence in their home country had little choice in their exodus, they represent both consequences and causes of conflict, and they have more universally recognized rights than other types of migrants, making it more interesting to examine the gaps between the formal guarantees of these rights and the empirical denial of them. However, limiting the scope of the analysis specifically to *refugees* raises more problems than it solves, and so I include other categories of migrants as subjects of analysis as well. It is important for theoretical utility to be clear in defining and specifying the key concepts that I use in my analysis. When I talk specifically about refugees, I am referring to those persons who are fleeing persecution in their country of origin and who have been recognized by the receiving country's government as meeting the criteria established in international law, and specifically the 1951 Convention on the Status of Refugees and the 1967 protocol, in order to receive protection by the host state.[5] When I use less specific terms, such as "forced migrant," I am referring more generally to any person who has fled his or her country of origin because of fear of violence, whether or not the host state has given formal recognition as a refugee. Some policymakers and practitioners (especially within the UN system) have begun increasingly to refer to "persons living in a refugee-like situation" or "persons in need of international protection," so when I quote these formulations, I interpret them, like "forced migrant," to mean a person who is fleeing violence in his or her home country, but who for whatever reason has not formally applied for refugee status in the receiving country. Finally, my use of the term "asylum seeker" refers to a forced migrant who has applied for refugee status from the host government, but has not yet received this recognition.

The definition I use for migrants refers to those persons who have moved their primary residence to a country other than their country of birth. With this definition, I include economic immigrants and refugees, both of whom leave their country of origin to live in a different country for the purpose of improving their quality of life. I exclude transient population groups, such as tourists, students, and business travelers, as these groups travel to other countries without moving their primary residence, and with the expectation that they will return home to their country of origin relatively soon. I also exclude later generations who are the offspring of immigrants. Especially in cases where the state's legal definition of citizenship is based on birth (as opposed to blood ancestry), these later-generation persons are no longer

---

[5] The Refugee Convention definition defines a refugee as a person who, "owing to a well-founded fear of being persecuted for reasons of race, religion, nationality, membership of a particular social group or political opinion, is outside his country of nationality and is unable or, owing to such fear is unwilling to avail himself of the protection of that country; or who, not having a nationality and being outside the country of his former habitual residence as a result of such events, is unable or, owing to such fear is unwilling to return to it." The 1967 protocol extends this definition to persons meeting the criteria in the future and in locations beyond only Europe.

immigrants, but rather represent a subgroup of citizens, even when they maintain strong identity affiliations with an "imagined homeland" as part of a diaspora (Graham 2019; Telles and Sue 2019).

Refugees and immigrants who move for economic reasons are not the same, and it is important to recognize that the "push factors" and "pull factors" that influence the decisions of each group to migrate and determine the host state in which they settle are often quite different (Moore and Shellman 2007; Weiner 1996; Hollifield 2008). When it becomes necessary to distinguish the two populations (for example, in the legal rights and the sources of these rights that are available to refugees vs. economic immigrants), I will use the more specific terms for each group. Through much of the book, however, I combine both refugees and economic immigrants together under the same analytical category of "migrants." I am focusing much of my analysis on the perceptions and reactions of the host population to the migrant population, and conflict that emerges between migrants and citizens represents a relational phenomenon, meaning that the mutual perceptions of both groups is fundamental for constructing their relationship, whether conflictual or peaceful. I argue that there is frequently very little distinction made between different classes of migrants in the perception of most of the Ecuadorian host population and their openness to full integration of migrants into society. In the words of one NGO worker in Ecuador, "Refugees are seen by everyday people merely as immigrants with sadder stories."[6]

Perhaps more importantly, the negotiation of criteria for who is a refugee, an immigrant, an "illegal alien," or a member of another category is frequently contested and negotiated at both formal and informal levels in different ways depending on the context (Sajjad 2018), so I would lose any analytical ability to examine this negotiation if I assumed away by definition the fuzzy border that exists between several of these categories. Lacey Andrews argues that the frequent use of the term "refugee" as a bureaucratic category by national governments, international institutions like the UNHCR, and to a lesser extent, NGOs, in order to determine eligibility for particular services, benefits, and legal status, is counterproductive for scholars and thinkers attempting to understand migration and integration processes. "UNHCR and humanitarian agencies commonly use the category of 'refugee' in order to determine the population eligible for aid or resettlement. However, for understanding . . . how the displaced themselves negotiate their survival

---

[6] Interview 110QN 2007.

with their hosts, this demographic category obscures more than it reveals" (Andrews 2003: 1). In the context of South Africa, Michael Neocosmos has noted,

> The distinction between "economic migrant" and "political migrant" or "refugee" is a legal distinction which was developed in Europe relatively recently for the purpose of restricting access to Western economies by job seekers. The fact that the South African state has emulated this distinction does not mean that it is a real one for migrants who may lose their jobs at home for political reasons. One needs to critique and transcend such state categories if one wishes to provide a coherent explanation of a xenophobic discourse which by most accounts originates from the state itself. (2006: 6)

I believe that it is important to have analytical clarity around the concepts that I employ, such as refugee, forced migrant, economic immigrant, and migrant, but at the same time, in this study I will refer most frequently to the broader category of "migrants" in order to be able to examine the hazy border between these different categories, and the impact that this blurring has for host-migrant conflict resolution.

Potential Extension to Other Excluded Groups within Societies, Not Only Migrants

At countless conference and workshop presentations and invited talks that I have given on the research presented in this book, a perennial comment that emerges is this one: "This sounds really interesting! The invisibility bargain framework seems like it could apply quite well to [insert marginalized domestic group here]." It is certainly the case, as Bridget Anderson (2013) argued in her book, that many populations—migrants as well as domestic minorities—struggle to be included in the "community of value," and sometimes their coping strategies include scapegoating and "othering" even more marginalized groups in order to secure their own acceptance and reduce social sanctions targeting themselves.

Sometimes, historically marginalized domestic minority populations have confronted similar expectations of invisibility, in which their visible presence in social spaces, or their overt political activism, incurs a racist or discriminatory backlash from the dominant majority population of their own country. The backlash against the Black Lives Matter movement, the public apathy over, and impunity of, police officers' extrajudicial killing of unarmed black men in public spaces, and the active persecution and smear campaign against Colin Kaepernick and black NFL players protesting this police brutality by kneeling during the national anthem at football games in the United States are examples of how the invisibility bargain can be extended to explain insecurity for domestic minority groups as well. Black people as well as immigrants were exploited for their labor, deemed "essential" workers, and put at greater exposure during the COVID-19 crisis at the same time they were labeled thugs and terrorists and their lives and safety were deemed disposable when demanding protections in visible political protest against police brutality or when their trip to work exposed them to deportation authorities (Jordan 2020). Likewise, coalitions of allies that cross racial, social, and political groups, and meaningful interaction toward shared goals to increase peaceful coexistence may offer promising avenues for addressing these conflicts (Mundt et al. 2018). In the Americas, indigenous and Afro-descendent populations are also often excluded from spaces of political participation and social integration, with acceptance being premised on depoliticization and adapting to majority norms/expectations.

Despite these similarities, I have chosen in this book to focus exclusively on migrants rather than include other minority groups as subjects of their own invisibility bargain. One major reason for this is that, despite frequent social discrimination and inadequate implementation of formal protections for such groups, domestic minority groups still have the basic privilege of having been born in the country, which in the vast majority of *jus soli* countries means that they are not at risk of being deported or returned to a country where they might be killed, with a few exceptions like the case of descendants of Haitians born in the Dominican Republic (Kushner 2012; Murray 2020). Thus, the stakes of the backlash accompanying the invisibility bargain, and the strength of the underlying norms offering protection, are different for migrants than for other minority groups. That said, additional theorizing and thoughtful cross-population comparative research could expand the conceptual boundaries of the invisibility bargain (while maintaining its analytical cohesiveness and rigor) and spark creative new thinking on inter-group relations. For example, the backlash that occurs against the social and political visibility of minority groups might include the acceptance or promotion of violent repression, economic precarity, and mass incarceration that is parallel to or worse than deportation from the country; rather, these can involve the threat of expulsion from dignified and secure forms of life *within* the country (Sassen 2014).

Brief Historical and Political Context of Ecuador and Colombia

Ecuador is a South American country of seventeen million people that is classified by the World Bank as a middle-income economy. Heavily dependent on agriculture, especially bananas and cut flowers, and since the 1970s on petroleum, which is now its leading export, Ecuador has two large cities and many smaller towns in the more rural provinces. Quito, the capital city in the Andes mountains, and Guayaquil, the large port city, have historically maintained something of a regional rivalry between the mountainous sierra and the coast, with the Amazon jungle, Ecuador's easternmost third region, being relatively isolated until the discovery of oil in the 1970s led to colonization and increased infrastructure. Ecuador is a heavily Catholic country, with about 80% of the population reporting a Catholic identity.

In addition to the mestizo majority of people with mixed European and indigenous ancestry, indigenous people represent a significant and politically vocal proportion of the population, although the exact number is subject to debate, with estimates ranging from 7% to more than 25% (and up to 40% claimed by the Confederation of Indigenous Nationalities of Ecuador). The indigenous movement succeeded in pushing through constitutional reforms that included progressive group rights and the establishment of Ecuador as a "plurinational" country (Van Cott 2005; Yashar 2005). Through a series of mass mobilizations, indigenous people were key actors in the overthrow of multiple Ecuadorian presidents during the ten-year period from 1996 to 2007, an inchoate decade that saw ten different people serving as president of the country. Most notably, they led a national march and protests that (in cooperation with junior military officers, who reinforced the role of the military as an arbiter and "veto player" in Ecuadorian politics) ousted President Jamil Mahuad. This president was forced to leave office after an economic crisis in 1999–2000 that led to hyperinflation, a freeze on bank accounts combined with corrupt bailouts for banks, and eventually dollarization that led to skyrocketing prices (Gerlach 2003). As a result of this economic crisis, more than 10% of the Ecuadorian population emigrated abroad, mostly to Spain, Italy, and the United States, where they sought job opportunities, and the remittances they sent home in the years that followed represented the second largest source of foreign income after oil.

Ecuador's relationships with its neighbors—Peru and Colombia—have ranged from close to very tense over the years. A simmering border dispute with Peru led to armed combat in 1941 and again in 1995, culminating in a peace agreement in 1998, which has been preserved with relative stability between the two countries since then (Herz and Pontes Nogueira 2002). Ecuador and Colombia, which share a 365-mile border that spans the three regions from the coast through the Andes mountains and into the Amazon jungle, have a long and closely interlinked history dating back to their joint membership in Gran Colombia after independence from Spain. During the 1990s, Ecuador had a self-image as an "island of peace" between Peru, which was roiled by the violent Shining Path insurgency, and Colombia, which confronted a decades-long internal conflict involving the Fuerzas Armadas Revolucionarias de Colombia (FARC), other leftist guerrilla groups like the Ejército de Liberación Nacional and Ejército Popular de Liberación, right-wing paramilitary groups, transnational narcotraffickers, and the Colombian state, among other actors. In 2000, the United States and Colombia agreed on an aid package with some humanitarian but mostly military assistance, which significantly increased the equipment and capacity of the Colombian military to confront FARC and other groups in the countryside, where they had previously exercised de facto control. The size of the Colombian armed forces increased by 60% between 1998 and 2002. As a result, intergroup clashes and the number of people killed and displaced skyrocketed, at the same time that FARC's number of fighters was decimated (ICG 2012).

In the face of such threats and violence, Colombians began fleeing the country, seeking refuge in neighboring countries, and since Panama had restrictive entry requirements and Venezuela allowed people to enter but recognized few with formal refugee status, Ecuador with its relatively open borders and scant visa requirements was the primary destination for thousands of forced migrants. Figure 1.1 shows the number of refugees registered in Ecuador during the time period between 2000 and 2019.

In the decade and a half following Plan Colombia, Ecuador was the leading recipient of refugees and asylum seekers in Latin America according to UNHCR, and its political response varied from open reception to tighter visa restrictions to quite progressive solidarity policies beginning in 2007. In this year, Rafael Correa, a former economics professor and minister of economy, began his presidency after winning a

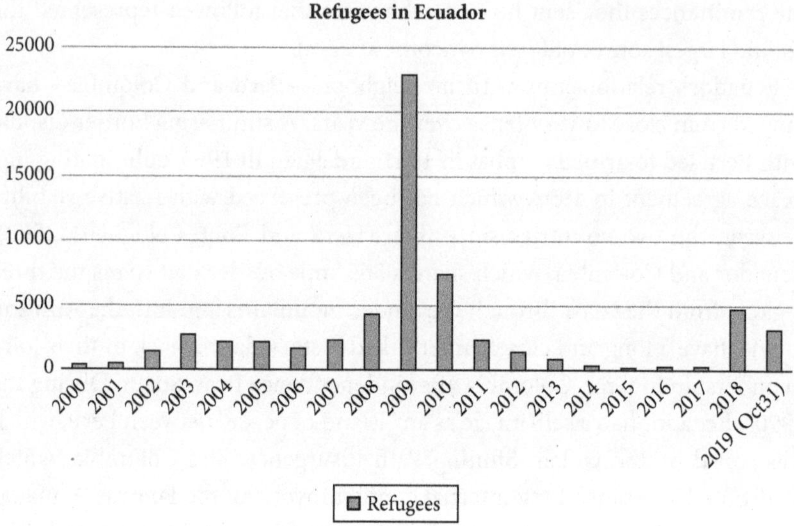

Figure 1.1 Registered refugees in Ecuador, 2000–2019

Source: Ministerio de Relaciones Exteriores, "Estadísticas de refugiados (histórico)," updated November 5, 2019.

dark-horse campaign. His political agenda was based on the promise of a leftist "citizens" revolution that would involve increasing social spending, decreasing foreign debt service, renegotiating state revenues from oil revenues, and rewriting the constitution through a constituent assembly that resulted in greater centralization of power in the presidency as well as codification of a range of progressive rights protections. Importantly, one of Correa's central campaign promises was to enact what he called "Plan Ecuador" as a response to the migration flow and underdevelopment of the northern border with Colombia. In contrast to Colombia's militarized Plan Colombia (and the critique that it followed US hegemonic intentions in the region), Correa, who allied himself with Venezuela's Hugo Chavez and the Bolivarian Alliance for the Peoples of Our America (ALBA) alliance in support of "twenty-first-century socialism," promised an integral, developmental, rights-based approach to refugees and migration that would enshrine the concept of "universal citizenship" and position Ecuador as a country of solidarity and welcome for immigrants. He argued that the statebuilding era he envisaged would counteract the decade preceding his administration, which he frequently referred to as the "long neoliberal night." Correa ultimately ended the era of inchoate leadership turnover, serving a full ten years, the longest continuously serving constitutional president in Ecuador's history.

Since Colombia's population as well as GDP are both about three times as large as Ecuador's, and it received much larger amounts of US foreign aid (often ten times as much as Ecuador from 2000 to 2009), there was some resentment from Ecuador because of the perception that Colombia was off-shoring its problems onto Ecuador, which had far fewer resources to deal with them (Poe and Isaacson 2009). Colombia for its part accused Ecuador of allowing FARC a degree of impunity to operate in the Ecuadorian border region, and suggested that there were political and economic alliances between elements of FARC and elements of the Ecuadorian government and President Correa's political party.

In 2008, the Colombian military penetrated at least a mile into Ecuadorian territory in Sucumbíos province in the Amazon to carry out "Operation Phoenix," bombing and raiding a FARC camp in Ecuadorian territory at Angostura, killing two dozen people, including an Ecuadorian, four Mexican students, and nineteen Colombian guerrillas. One of those killed was a top FARC commander, Raul Reyes, whose laptop computer was seized as evidence and confiscated by the Colombian military, and the Truth Commission that Correa later appointed to investigate alleged that the operation was carried out with US intelligence support based in the Manta US military base on Ecuador's coast (Huerta Montalvo 2009).[7] In response to this attack on Ecuadorian sovereign territory, President Correa cut off diplomatic relations with President Alvaro Uribe of Colombia, the two countries accused each other of hostile actions and of insufficient efforts to control FARC insecurity, and Ecuador and Venezuela both mobilized additional troops to the border region as a warning to Colombia. Finally, Track II dialogue efforts led by the Carter Center helped to restore relations (UNDP and Carter Center 2011). The Angostura episode led to greater ongoing militarization of the northern border region even after relations were restored.

A 2010 protest by police in Quito (who were complaining about a proposed law that would change rules for promotion, pay, and other benefits) escalated to the point that airports and TV stations were occupied, protesters stormed the National Assembly, and the police held the president hostage in a military hospital until loyal troops rescued him in a shootout. The president denounced this incident as an attempted coup, accused his predecessor

---

[7] Interview 112QN 2015.

and political opponent, Lucio Gutierrez, of helping to orchestrate it, and used the incident as an excuse to crack down on the police. The incident further consolidated Correa's control over the security forces of the country as it led to a purge of the police and greater control by the president over security policy (Becker 2016).

Ecuador and Colombia developed more constructive cooperative relations under Colombian president Uribe's successor, President Juan Manuel Santos, whose leadership resulted in the signing of a peace agreement in 2016 between the Colombian government and FARC, which agreed to disarm and demobilize in exchange for the possibility of political inclusion and some limits on punitive action toward lower-level former FARC members (Rincón et al. 2019). Although the peace agreement was initially rejected by a razor-thin margin in a national plebiscite in Colombia, it was later revised and ratified by Congress (Pugh 2016b). The signing of the peace agreement held the promise of a more peaceful Colombia and the eventual return of refugees from Ecuador, but nearly five years later, the border region was still confronted with criminal armed groups and narcotrafficking, and most Colombian refugees in Ecuador do not consider that it will be safe to return home anytime soon (Pugh et al. 2020). Finally, the humanitarian, economic, and political crisis in Venezuela has led to a mass exodus from that country, with the largest number of displaced Venezuelans hosted in Colombia. Ecuador is the third-largest recipient, and this led to a new round of restrictive policies and securitizing messages targeting Venezuelan migration in the country under President Lenin Moreno, who was elected in 2017 to take over from his mentor-turned-adversary President Correa (Selee and Bolter 2020; Pugh and Moya 2020).

Plan of the Book

The first three chapters of this book introduce and develop my theoretical argument. This introductory chapter has previewed the main argument and laid out the scope of the book, defined several of the key concepts that will be used throughout the book (including justifying the usage of the term "migrant" and making explicit the interlinking relationship between human security and peace), provided a brief historical context of the case study, and presented a rationale for the significance of the project. It also previewed the remaining chapters and the key points made in them in order to sketch the progression of the core argument that will be developed throughout the book.

Chapter 2 introduces the concept of the invisibility bargain in order to explain how the informal strategies chosen by migrants to resolve conflicts, participate politically, and gain access to resources respond to the unwritten expectations within the host society that govern social relations between migrants and citizens and establish the "rules" by which the host population will accept the physical presence of migrants. It traces how the perception of migrants' valued contribution, combined with their social and political invisibility, is often the price of the host population's acceptance of their physical presence, and argues that violation of these expectations may lead to social sanctions and a hostile backlash against migrants by the host population. The invisibility bargain lays important conceptual groundwork for the main argument of the book, to be developed in chapter 3.

Chapter 3 lays out the main argument of the book, that in the context of the invisibility bargain, a democratic government has a political incentive to prioritize the interests of citizens over migrants (even when formal institutions promise protections for all residents), and as such may be less than ideal as the primary guarantor of security in migrant-receiving areas. This leads to gaps in the formal protections offered by the state, and further vulnerability of migrants, which can escalate conflict between migrants and citizens. In areas with a robust presence of nonstate actors and international institutions, but with a weak state presence, networks that connect all three types of institutions can emerge and adapt innovative forms of governance that complement, substitute for, or compete with state authority and security provision. The fact that nonstate actors have different missions, accountability structures, incentives, and levels of trust than the migrant population means that a diverse and well-coordinated network that includes these organizations as well as state agencies may counterbalance the limitations of a governance structure that only includes one type of organization. More diverse and dense networks also provide a greater number of potential access points through which migrants might gain the resources they need or establish social relations that contribute to their resiliency and ability to thrive in the host community. The chapter provides a theoretical framework for understanding the role of these governance networks in host-migrant human security provision and peacebuilding.

Chapters 4–7 represent the empirical core of the book. Chapter 4 introduces the context of the northern border region of Ecuador and the six provinces in which I conducted subnational comparative research. Drawing primarily on my MNS data of foreign migrants, the chapter maps the institutional network structure of six major migrant-receiving provinces, including capital cities of Esmeraldas, Tulcán, Lago Agrio, Ibarra, Quito, and Santo Domingo. The chapter compares the institutional relations and the level of coordination in each locality with the human security and peacebuilding outcomes experienced by the migrants who live there. It provides evidence for the claim that state capacity and economic development level are not as persuasive, in explaining the human security experienced by migrants, as network density and diversity.

Every network has key central actors through which information passes to other actors, and who exercise greater influence than the other actors on the agenda, goals, and inclusiveness of the network. Chapter 5 takes a closer look at three of the most important sets of actors involved at a national level in defining the agenda for migrant integration in Ecuador: the Ecuadorian state (especially the Ministry of Foreign Relations and Plan Ecuador), the United Nations system (especially UNHCR and UNDP) in Ecuador, and the Catholic Church. This case study illuminates how three categories of institutions contribute to security provision and peacebuilding in migrant-receiving communities, and illustrates how institutional adaptations developed by UNHCR and the church challenge and reinforce each other and interact with the authority of the state. By tracing the institutional development and interaction of these three broad organizations, the chapter seeks to understand how the differing political incentives and institutional missions and structures of different components of the migration governance network have developed across localities in Ecuador, and what factors have impeded or promoted effective peacebuilding and coexistence. The chapter identifies trust, mission, capacity, and transnational linkages as key factors influencing the difference in institutional strategies, cooperation versus competition among the different institutional actors, and peace and human security outcomes in migrant-receiving communities. Recognizing the importance of change over time, the chapter traces the evolution of the institutions in the critical period from 2000 to 2017, which represents the most important period of forced migration into Ecuador, and particularly focuses on Rafael Correa's administration from 2007 to 2017. It traces three distinct phases within this time frame: absence, coordination, and regression. In doing so, the chapter shows how the evolution of state capacity and political will has interacted over time with the adaptation of civil society and the international community to shape the possibilities for migrant integration and coexistence in Ecuador.

Chapter 6 illustrates the empirical application of the social invisibility component of the invisibility bargain in Ecuador, showing how race, gender, and other markers of difference structure host society expectations of who belongs in the "community of value." Using an intersectional lens, it teases apart the overlapping structures of exclusion that affect indigenous and Afro-Colombians, other Colombian migrants, and Afro-Ecuadorians quite differently in their access to human security and social integration in Ecuador. The chapter highlights accent as the primary marker of difference that heightens the social visibility of Colombian migrants, and it traces the coping mechanisms—including minimizing difference, reducing social distance, and informal negotiation through intermediaries—that migrants use to avoid the social sanctions of backlash under the invisibility bargain.

Chapter 7 illustrates how the invisibility bargain has shaped the opportunities and limitations constraining Colombian migrants in Ecuador, and how they have responded to pursue access to the rights, resources, recognition, and protection that they need. It shows that the strategies that migrants pursue most often are those that are individual and do not require collective action, but that the most effective strategies are those (both individual and collective) that do not require overt, visible, public demand-making on institutional actors that would invoke a backlash from the host population. Instead, informal negotiation at the local level, adapting cultural practices to better "fit in" with Ecuadorian society, and intentional, meaningful, task-oriented interaction between Ecuadorians and Colombians were all associated with better access to the governance network, and as a result, better peace and human security outcomes. This chapter draws on the empirical cases of the 2008 constitution, Enhanced Registration, and the Interagency Peace and Development Program in the northern border zone to show the mechanisms through which networked governance has led to greater peace in migrant-receiving communities of Ecuador, as well as the limitations and risks that have sometimes impeded human security.

I conclude the book in chapter 8 by elaborating a number of concrete policy implications of the findings for migrant-serving NGOs, international organizations, and state agencies tasked with human security and peacebuilding in migrant-receiving countries, especially in the Global South. I also suggest directions for further research and explore the future applicability of this research more broadly for migrant-receiving democracies, especially in other parts of the developing world.

2

Understanding the Invisibility Bargain

> Colombians have started getting involved in politics, because they are smart and well prepared. Not too long ago, one even ran for prefect of Esmeraldas, despite being in this country for only five years or so. I think they are ungrateful, coming to our country, being welcomed, and then taking over. We as Ecuadorians are the ones who have the right to decide how we will be governed.
>
> —Local government official in the border region of Ecuador

Among 195 countries in the world from which the International Organization for Migration (IOM) reports data, 62% of governments in 2011 had adopted policies to promote the integration of foreigners into their society. There is a difference by socioeconomic level and region, with 91% of developed countries and 47% of developing countries having adopted such policies, but in both cases, integration policies are becoming more common, having expanded from 44% to 62% of governments between 1996 and 2011 (IOM 2014). In many migrant-receiving countries, the government has a set of laws, policies, and institutions that establish formal rules and procedures for the types of migrants that receive legal recognition to resettle in the country, as well as the criteria and process for this acceptance to occur.

In practice, fewer people are allowed in through these formal channels than there is demand for, and a large number of migrants exist within the territory without formal recognition from the state. This raises a dilemma, as the presence of these migrants satisfies the interests of some constituencies within the host population—most notably, businesses that benefit from low-cost labor, or political parties or ethnic kinship groups that would benefit from influence over a larger political constituency. Maurizio Ambrosini points out "the widespread tolerance of certain types of irregular migration among broad sectors of the receiving society, street-level bureaucracy, and the control apparatuses themselves. . . . The social construction of the danger of irregular immigrants

The Invisibility Bargain. Jeffrey D. Pugh, Oxford University Press (2021). © Oxford University Press.
DOI: 10.1093/oso/9780197538692.003.0002

consequently proves to be very selective: very harsh for some, more tolerant for others" (Ambrosini 2013: 12). It is costly and sometimes not feasible for the state to identify undocumented migrants and coercively remove them from the country, especially while upholding commitments to democratic pluralism and human rights (Ellerman 2010). Quite often, the response is a de facto scenario that allows for practical coexistence, even when the terms violate the formal laws and institutions of the country.

Under these conditions, an informal understanding emerges in the form of a set of unwritten expectations that I call the *invisibility bargain*. The physical presence of large numbers of migrants in the host country is tolerated and not actively persecuted as long as the migrants in question abide by three key expectations: (*a*) they are perceived to be making a *valued contribution* to the host society, especially bringing economic benefits, (*b*) they remain *socially invisible*, meaning that ascriptive and cultural differences that challenge the host population's expectations of acceptability are minimized, and (*c*) they remain *politically invisible*, meaning that they are not engaging in overt, public contestation and claim-making on the government. Integrating the findings of Sullivan (2004), the valued contribution requirement includes not only economic benefits, but any publicly valued contribution to the host society, including military service and sacrifice, a long period of living and working in the country as an upstanding member of the community, and so on, although the value of each of these contributions is socially constructed and will vary across local contexts.

When the conditions of the invisibility bargain are perceived to be violated, a backlash against migrants on the part of the host population is a common response. The accusations by the Tea Party in the United States against "undeserving" immigrants freeloading off welfare, straining public services, and taking jobs from native-born citizens provides an example of a backlash against perceived violations of the valued contribution argument (Williamson et al. 2011). The salience of this perceived violation is reinforced by previous scholarship on economic threat arguments related to immigration (Citrin et al. 1997; Olzak 1992). The "burkini" ban at certain beaches in France and English-only ballot initiatives in the United States provide examples of native perceptions that the social invisibility demand has been violated by immigrants who are making insufficient effort to conform to host-country cultural norms and logics of appropriateness (Saas 2001; Zolberg and Woon 1999). This perception, in reaction to immigrants who are visibly/audibly different from the dominant in-group in these countries, confirms the expectations of the group threat hypothesis (Olzak 1992). The backlash is likely to be stronger when the violation of the invisibility bargain is taken to signify migrants' refusal to conform to the expectations of the dominant group, or to undermine the authority of their group norms (Thomsen et al. 2008). In subsequent sections, I further develop the theoretical foundations and assumptions underlying each of the components of the invisibility bargain.

Valued Contribution

The economic threat argument is one of the most prominent explanations for xenophobia and anti-immigrant attitudes on the part of host populations (Citrin et al. 1997; Malhotra et al. 2013). This theory says that immigrants are more likely to spark xenophobic responses to the extent that they are seen as competing with the host population for jobs or economic resources, especially when their economic success is seen as "unfair" or the result of "undeserved" advantages. According to Citrin et al., "Surges in anti-immigrant sentiment . . . have followed sharp economic downturns, partly in response to the tendency of politicians and labor union leaders to blame foreign workers for unemployment and downward pressure on wages" (1997: 859). Olzak's model of ethnic competition predicts that an influx of migrants, especially low-skilled workers, will lead to a tighter job market for native citizens, which in turn leads to greater perception of threat and suspicion of foreigners (Olzak 1992).

Drawing on the idea of relative deprivation, a key argument is that the gap between the economic level that people believe they should be able to achieve when comparing themselves to others around them (value expectations) and the level that they personally have achieved (value capabilities) leads to frustration, and ultimately aggression toward the group that they blame for this disjuncture (Gurr 1970). In other words, if the host society's citizens expect that they should be enjoying economic prosperity but are not, or if they expect that their economic level should be higher than that of entering migrants because of assumed social hierarchies, but they do not maintain their relative economic advantage, they are likely to develop (and potentially act upon) negative attitudes toward migrants. Most of these arguments focus on native citizens' perceptions of aggregate economic harm to society, rather than on calculations of likely or actual individual economic harm to themselves as a result of migration. In fact, the evidence shows that one's individual economic situation and the fear that immigrants will represent a direct threat to one's own job or financial well-being is not directly correlated with one's attitudes in general or policy preferences regarding immigrants (Hainmueller and Hiscox 2010). Rather, a general perception that immigrants will create a general burden on society (i.e., cost resources for services while not contributing taxes) is more strongly correlated with anti-immigrant attitudes, including in Latin American receiving contexts (Meseguer and Kemmerling 2018).

The implication on the flip side of the economic threat argument is that those migrants who are seen as contributing something of value (especially economic) to the host society by providing needed services, labor, skills, or drawing international assistance or investment are less likely to be seen as an economic threat, and thus less likely to provoke anti-immigrant backlash.

The fact that migrants can bring economic benefits to their receiving communities, in addition to the challenges they raise, has been noted in both policy and scholarly circles. Karen Jacobsen argues that migrants (whether they are fleeing violence or economic hardship) can bring with them valuable resources that can be traded in exchange for political tolerance and/or local political, social, and economic resources. These resources may include transnational capital such as remittances and migrant networks that enable greater information flows and trade; needed skills that are not found in the host community; and access to humanitarian assistance in the case of refugees, to name a few. As Jacobsen points out, "Many of these resources are traded or exchanged in the local community as a way to gain access to local resources" (2002: 5).

Migrants, because of their geographic mingling with the citizen population and because of many receiving countries' economic dependence on their labor, represent a special category of subjects. When their presence creates within the host society the perception of a threat to national unity, stability, and order, the pressure to exclude them from the protections and benefits of the state (or to exclude their presence completely through deportation) clashes with pressures from interest groups seeking to benefit from their labor, skills, or other resources.

These competing pressures, combined with the realization that migrants are likely to stay in the country with or without permission because of the desperate conditions in their country of origin, are frequently balanced through the acceptance of an informal status that allows de facto presence while denying formal status or entitlements to migrants. Sergio Diaz-Briquets and

Sydney Weintraub note that even in the United States, competing political pressures can lead to a dual system of formal and informal institutions:

> U.S. immigration policy has long been ambivalent and often incoherent, reflecting in large measure public sentiment on the subject. If our laws closed the doors to some immigrants, our legal system assured there were always cracks that others could slip through. If it was illegal to enter without proper documentation, it was not illegal for employers to hire un-documented workers.[1] Inconsistency is constantly reflected in U.S. foreign policy decisions that are driven by considerations often at odds with immi-gration concerns, and this sends a host of contradictory signals to actual and potential migrants. (1991: 278)[2]

In countries (like Ecuador) where the state has less capacity to enforce formal laws, or even to extend its presence into some regions of the country, there is even greater opportunity for informal arrangements to arise.

Social Invisibility

Social invisibility refers to the expectation that migrants' characteristics and practices that are distinct from the rules of appropriateness defined by the dominant host society, including language, religion, and customs (or even visible racial differences), should be minimized or hidden in public. A vio-lation of the social invisibility expectation is likely to result in greater hos-tility and sanctions on migrants from the host population. The controversy over the public wearing of headscarves by Muslim schoolgirls and teachers from North Africa in France is an obvious example of this phenomenon (Saas 2001). The more visible are the markers of difference that set migrants apart from the host population and that contradict "acceptable norms of be-havior,"[3] the more likely their presence will be used to rationalize social or physical exclusion from the host society.

---

[1] Note that significant changes accompanied the Patriot Act and other post-9/11 legislation, which placed new restrictions on employers who hire migrants.

[2] See also Andreas 2000.

[3] These sociotropic and normative factors indicating perceived ability to contribute to the country and integrate into its norms and values are more important explanations for attitudes toward the type of migrant who is perceived to be desirable than the individual economic situations of native citizens, according to Hainmueller and Hopkins (2015).

This observation draws upon the "group threat" and "cultural threat" arguments found in the literature on migrant integration, which argue that immigrants are likely to receive a more hostile reaction from the host society when they form a large, ethnically distinct out-group (especially during a time of economic scarcity), and when native citizens fear that their relative size threatens the dominant position in the hierarchy of the in-group (Quillian 1995; Blumer 1958). A "threshold of tolerance" may be informally understood as a collective understanding of the percentage of immigrants that is too many, or, as in the case of some German municipal housing and educational policies, it may be a specific formal quota for the ratio of immigrants to native citizens that is allowed (Kastoryano 2002). The underlying logic of group threat suggests that an immigrant population that exceeds this threshold risks undermining the capacity of the host society to absorb those who are different, and threatens the unity of the dominant group. Sides and Citrin (2007) found that social and "symbolic" preferences (like a desire for cultural unity) were stronger predictors of anti-immigrant attitudes than economic anxieties. The response by the host population to the influx of migrants depends in part on who the migrants are, and on the ethnic and racial group cues that native citizens associate with them, which may be based on emotional triggers more than cognitive evaluations of threat (Brader et al. 2008). Some observers worry that immigrants who are more visibly different on cultural dimensions will be less likely to assimilate or integrate into the host society. They may remain in ethnic enclaves that reinforce incompatible "foreign" values and relieve pressure to learn the host society's dominant language or form interdependent economic ties through trade with members of the host society (Huntington 2004). This fragmentation of society along nationality and ethnic lines could threaten the cohesion of the host country's national identity, leading to lower levels of social trust, less civic engagement, and more social conflict, among other ills that these scholars fear (Schlesinger 1992).

In the face of these cultural fears on the part of the host society, and the social sanctions that go with them, "immigrant others" who do not conform to the cultural norms of the host society, or whose ethnic, linguistic, or religious characteristics are constructed as threatening by their native citizen neighbors, may confront a choice. On the one hand, they may seek to minimize these forms of difference by assimilating, changing those traits that they can (or at least not practicing them publicly) in order to adapt to the expectations of the dominant culture and making invisible the markers of their previous (or true) cultural identity. On the other hand, they may continue to practice or display these markers of difference and risk increased social conflict or violence. When this happens, survival instincts lead to selective invisibility—reducing contact with elements of the host society (such as police, or in some cases members of the dominant group) that might be likely to enforce social sanctions, or remaining hidden in informal spaces that do not require immigrants to disclose their full true identities (Cebulko and Galvão 2016). The potential pathways to social integration do not represent a straight-line choice for migrants; rather, "segmented assimilation" offers a bumpy path to adaptation and integration, depending on the characteristics, history, and social construction of the group that particular migrants belong to. Depending on these social and historical characteristics, the ease of integration and the welcome offered by the host society may be easier or more difficult, even across multiple immigrant generations (Portes and Zhou 1993; Portes and Rumbaut 2006).

Engberson and Broeders (2007) propose the concept of "foggy structures" to describe the types of informal social institutions that immigrants and their allies in the host society construct in order to facilitate their existence, and sometimes their selective invisibility, while minimizing their vulnerability to state identification and enforcement. In these underground spaces, social relationships and friendships can be essential lifelines, but they can also be fragile and vulnerable, as the stakes of betrayal or trusting the wrong person are not only hurt feelings, but physical incarceration or ejection from the country (Meloni 2016). Immigrants are physically present in the host country, but undocumented migrants are legally absent, and even immigrants with legal documentation may be socially invisible in order to survive and avoid social sanctions. In both cases, migrants occupy an ambivalent liminal space of nonexistence or vulnerability (Coutin 2003). The identity that the occupants of this space adopt is a negotiated construct between their own group, their collective goals, the host state, and the host society, and their sense of belonging (or lack thereof) as valued members of the host society is the product of this negotiation (Meloni 2016). Particularly when the categories of identity that certain immigrant groups use to define themselves do not correspond with the salient identity categories within the host society, the social existence of these immigrants is "invisible" to their native citizen neighbors (Naber 2000).

In place of the social contract of citizenship, the informal contract that connects migrants to the state where they reside affects their safety, livelihood, and acceptance as members of the political community (Bosniak 2006). Susan Coutin observes,

> According to this implicit contract, when migrants contribute to a society through their labor, the society incurs certain obligations to them, such as the obligation to recognize them as full social and legal persons. Through various forms of social participation (going to school, having a family, obtaining an address, working), migrants "imitate citizens" and thus act on the rights that this implied contract promises. (2003: 189)

By *performing* the actions expected of valued members of the political community, migrants seek to gain full membership in this community, or at least to gain an approximation through de facto acceptance by the host population that does not expose them to active persecution or expulsion (Anderson 2013). These actions have sometimes legitimated the presence of migrants (Coutin 2003), but have often resulted in a backlash from the host population and a hardening of the social boundaries between insiders and outsiders (Bosniak 2006; Adida 2014). Immigrants are not passive recipients of host society actions to define, include, or exclude them, but rather exercise agency in negotiating the boundaries of belonging, social inclusion, and value (Anderson 2013). Douglas Massey and Magaly Sanchez argue,

> Whatever labels a society imposes on immigrants, whatever boundaries natives erect to exclude them, and whatever meanings natives attach to people from different lands, immigrants nonetheless are always active agents in negotiating, constructing, and elaborating their own identities. . . . As they encounter actors and institutions in the receiving society and learn about the categorical boundaries maintained by natives, they *broker* those boundaries and try to influence the meaning and content of the social categories defined by those boundaries. We thus conceptualize immigrant assimilation as a process of boundary-brokering in which immigrants, encountering categorical boundaries that separate them from natives, do whatever they can to challenge, circumvent, or accommodate those divisions to advance their interests. (2010: 16)

The intersectionality of overlapping forms of difference can multiply the marginalization of certain immigrants when their presence threatens to complicate social hierarchies of power (Crenshaw 1991; Collins 1990; Hancock

2016; Hankivsky and Jordan-Zachery 2019). Choo and Ferree understand intersectionality to contain three major dimensions: "the importance of including the perspectives of multiply-marginalized people, especially women of color; an analytical shift from addition of multiple independent strands of inequality toward a multiplication and thus transformation of their main effects into interactions; and a focus on seeing multiple institutions as overlapping in their co-determination of inequalities to produce complex configurations from the start, rather than 'extra' interactive processes that are added onto main effects" (2010: 131). All of these dimensions are relevant for the analysis of social invisibility and conflict in migrant-receiving communities. For example, a woman of color migrating from a poorer country who does not speak the language of the host society and whose dress reflects religious convictions that the dominant culture views as reflecting opposing or threatening values may experience much higher levels of discrimination than someone with fewer forms of difference. Not only does she face the sum of racial, gender-based, xenophobic, and religious discrimination from the host society, she may also face pressure from those sharing one or some of her identity groups to prioritize that group at the expense of other overlapping groups, with intersecting forms of social rejection from those whose expectations are violated by her presence or behavioral choices. This intersectionality affects both her experiences of marginalization and the type of agency and resistance that she may pursue to achieve her goals despite the barriers (Peñaranda and Sulewski 2018; Caldwell 2006).

These social hierarchies, present even in the most mundane practices of social interaction, clothing choices, and family activities, reproduce the power structures that privilege the dominant group and the state and social institutions that they control (Enloe 2011; Rigoni 2012). A Muslim migrant woman who decides to wear a burkini to the beach in France may then be labeled as a threat to law and order in a society that has securitized Muslim immigration and associated public practice of Islam with terrorism risks. An Afro-descendent woman who speaks with a Colombian accent in Ecuador may be labeled as a prostitute by a society that has constructed a *machista* collective understanding of sexualized and commercialized social roles for foreign women and women of color.[4] Their acceptance in society is a

---

[4] While these are obviously distinct types of differences, both represent a discernible marker of difference that can stigmatize migrants as suspect others. In both cases, the migrant has some agency in deciding which forms of difference to present publicly (i.e., whether or not to wear hijab or burkini, whether or not to speak audibly in public), but there are identity and safety trade-offs involved in this decision.

transactional function whose price is the normalization of their availability (real or imagined in the collective understanding) as providers of sexual services (the "valued contribution" on which their compliance with the invisibility bargain might hang). At the same time, however, this constructed understanding may offend collective moral values to the extent that the mere public presence of migrant women of color triggers social sanctions. Since state institutions often establish an easier path to legal immigration status for those who are married to a native citizen, an immigrant woman may choose a transactional sexual or marriage relationship with a member of the host society as a survival strategy, but this choice in turn increases her vulnerability to exploitation or abuse because of the power imbalance it introduces into her social relationships (Camacho 2005).

Connecting this argument to the "valued contribution" expectation discussed earlier, we can observe that host society expectations sometimes result in the social presence of particular migrants in public being very visible while their labor and economic contribution that occurs in informal or domestic spaces is invisible, and thus not valued. Examples like migrant women who are domestic workers in Malaysia (Chin 2003) or who care for the elderly as providers of "invisible welfare" in Italy "perform work perceived as useful for households and persons in need of assistance . . . [and] the social alarm diminishes while acceptance increases" (Ambrosini 2013: 12). This tentative and provisional acceptance, however, is contingent on these migrant women publicly conforming to in-group social expectations.

The social invisibility argument claims that migrants, who are discernible from the host population by markers of difference that include accent/language, race, cultural practices, or other characteristics, face informal expectations in the host society that attempt to separate their productive capacity from their humanity. National difference intersects with race, class, and gender to intensify the stakes of this separation for migrants' human security. Faced with this reality, migrants minimize or hide the markers of difference that set them apart in order to integrate more easily into the "community of value," which facilitates access to rights, protection, and resources. They may also try to reduce social distance between themselves and the host population in order to improve personal relationships and curb intergroup dehumanization (Pugh 2018). Alternatively, they may negotiate indirectly with the state and dominant social groups through NGOs and allies in the host society who can broker access to rights, resources, and protection while avoiding an antimigrant backlash from the host society. These dynamics of political negotiation are the focus of the next section.

Political Invisibility

Political invisibility refers to the expectation that migrants are not full, participating members of the host polity, and rather than citizenship, their relationship to the state is more like subjects or denizens—subject to the decisions and the authority of the state within the territory it controls, but not full participants in the collective decisions that affect their lives (Hammar 1990; Park and Gleeson 2014; Lori 2019; Pedroza 2019; Walzer 1983). A guest in someone's home would be expected to abide by the rules of the owner and not make overt demands or contest the norms of the household (and would be judged negatively if the guest did so). Likewise, immigrants are expected not to make direct claims or demands on the state, because their status in the receiving country is provisional and not situated squarely within the political community. This assumption has been justified because of the liminal, "in-between" stage that immigrants are assumed to occupy, with full access to a firm political status and a set of rights being at both the beginning and end points of this transition (Walzer 1983; Bosniak 2006; Cebulko 2014). Migrants are assumed to have had a set of rights and to have been full participants in the politics of their country of origin, and upon naturalization as full citizens of their receiving country, they will gain full access again, so the contingency of their rights and political participation during the transition phase is justified as merely temporary (Walzer 1983). This, of course, ignores the multiple future aspirations that migrants may have, the protracted time in which they may remain in this limbo stage, and the standards of basic human dignity that international norms require states to uphold for all people, even noncitizens (Bosniak 2006; Lori 2019).

Like the social invisibility expectation, political invisibility also builds on the group threat hypothesis (Quillian 1995). The basic argument here is that the more visible and salient the presence of immigrants in the country becomes, and the more "different" and threatening particular groups of migrants are perceived to be, the higher the expected level of native xenophobia and support for restrictivist policies will be. Since fear of a loss of political influence and power by the dominant group is one of the primary pathways for this threat perception (Thomsen et al. 2008; Dancygier 2010), host-population attitudes about migrant political participation are a manifestation of the group threat logic. Anti-immigrant sentiment is often expressed as hostility toward foreign others who are perceived to be taking what rightfully "belongs" to the host society, whether these are resources like government benefits, employment and housing, or the power to dominate political decision-making and the outcomes of collective choices (Williamson et al. 2011). Such an ownership paradigm establishes native citizens on the societal inside, as deserving participants in decision-making and rightful recipients of collective goods. Immigrants may be allowed physical entry, but their access to rights, resources, and status are contingent on the permission and invitation of host citizens, not on inherent rights of their own, which remain territorialized in their country of origin (Benhabib 2004).

Donald Kinder and Cindy Kam suggest that this hostility toward migrants is rooted in ethnocentrism, or the in-group favoritism that privileges one's own group's way of doing things as the normative center against which out-groups are measured and judged: "The issues provoked by immigration lend themselves readily to ethnocentric framing and ethnocentric understanding. Should we allow them to come in? Should we tighten our borders to keep them out? If we allow them in, should they be able to enjoy the same rights and privileges as we do?" (Kinder and Kam 2010: ch. 6). Host population perceptions of migrants are tempered at least in part by the degree to which migrants' political behavior and activism conform to the host society's "logic of appropriateness," which often is the expectation of political invisibility, especially when the group boundaries between immigrants and native citizens are activated and made politically salient by political entrepreneurs. The group characteristics and behaviors of specific migrant populations also influence the host population's willingness to accept activism and political claim-making of group members in comparison to native citizens, and in comparison to other migrant groups.

Bridget Anderson offers a helpful framework for understanding the internal boundaries that societies and states produce to separate those members of a receiving society who do not "count" from those who do, those who share a collective understanding of "us" as distinct from "them": "Borders are not simply territorial, but they reach into the heart of political space. Together with their associated practices, and in particular, laws and practices of citizenship, they may be more usefully analyzed as *producing* rather than reflecting status" (2013: 2). She argues that the legitimacy of the state, the social hierarchies that hold the host society together, and the aspirations and strategies of migrants are all tied up in the negotiation of the "community of value": "Modern states portray themselves not as arbitrary collections of people hung together by a common legal status but as a community of value, composed of people who share common ideals and (exemplary patterns of behaviour expressed through ethnicity, religion, culture, or language—that is, its members have shared values. They partake in certain forms of social relations, in 'communities'" (Anderson 2013: 2).

Related to Benedict Anderson's (1983) classic notion of the "imagined community" to describe nations, the community of value seems more dynamic and porous, shifting as different categories of people fight their way in and try to protect their position against others they seek to push out. It not only establishes boundaries around a common national identity, but can be constructed differently at multiple local or national levels of society. Rather than being defined simply by essential traits like language, ethnicity, or shared history, the community of value is constantly constructed in the practices and relationships of its members. These social relations are reproduced and reinforced through mundane practices, informal relationships and networks, and conversations that disseminate the norms and values that define the community of value and that must be protected from outsiders who might threaten it. Bridget Anderson argues that such outsiders are defined not only by legal status, but by the social construction of categories that are laden with worth, honor, or rejection, with the noncitizen, the criminal, the benefit scrounger, the failed citizen, and the good citizen (among other archetypes) variously being lumped together, or seeking to define themselves in contrast to one another:

> Migrants and their supporters are usually eager to differentiate themselves from failed citizens with whom they are often associated. Assertions that refugees are not criminals, or that migrants do not claim benefits, are attempts to counter these associations by affirming the community of value. Migrants and refugees are fit to belong because they have the right kinds of values, unlike criminals and benefit scroungers. Similarly, citizens at risk of failure may seek to dissociate themselves from non-citizens in order to bolster their claim to rights. . . . Contingent acceptance turns tolerated citizens, who must often struggle for acceptance into the community of value, into the guardians of good citizenship. Because these categories and boundaries are constructed, even though they are often imagined as real, they easily collapse into one another, legally and metaphorically. Those who are not

> firmly established in the community of value, must endlessly prove them-
> selves, marking the borders, particularly of course by decrying each other
> to prove that they have the right values. (2013: 6)

This negotiation of which groups belong in the "community of value," who is deserving of full participation in the collective decision-making of the country, is a key part of the logic underlying the invisibility bargain and in identifying the types of social and political visibilities that are viewed as violating in-group norms and values, and thus subject to social sanctions and antimigrant backlash.

An abundance of scholarship has emerged on activism and political agency by immigrants and refugees and the innovative ways that these political actors negotiate their relationship with the state (Das Gupta 2006; Zepeda Millan 2017; Hoschild et al. 2013; Silber Mohamed 2017). Political inclusion of migrants is often resisted by constituencies within the host society, and the state may deny formal citizenship to newcomers because of this political pressure. At the same time, however, Nyers and Rygiel argue that migrants find indirect and less visible ways to engage politically, which in effect represent a form of practical citizenship: "Through various strategies of claims-making, non-citizen migrant groups are involved in practices and ways of engaging in citizenship even when lacking formal citizenship status" (2012: 2). Migrants are one of many marginalized groups that must fight for inclusion and citizenship and perform it through everyday practices (Caldwell 2006). This applies both to migrants and to other marginalized populations who are "contingently accepted" in the community of value, showing that this community is not coterminous with birth citizenship. The degree to which migrants conform to host society normative expectations seems to be influential in openness toward greater acceptance and political inclusion of such migrants in the community of value (Anderson 2013; Hopkins 2015).

In particular, the politics of gratitude seems to privilege those migrants who are seen to have contributed to or sacrificed for the host country, while those who are seen to be making presumptuous demands or violating the expectations of guests are subject to greater social sanctions (Moulin 2012). The widespread backlash against Donald Trump's attacks on the Pakistani immigrant family of a deceased Muslim American soldier who made critical public remarks at the 2016 Democratic National Convention in the United States, and the dramatic 2016 rejection of a bill in the US House of Representatives to ban undocumented immigrants from military service, indicate that sacrifice and military service are pathways to recognition of belonging and political inclusion (Sullivan 2014). This type of "valued contribution" earns such migrants greater legitimacy as political participants and greater acceptance in the community of value. As Michael Sullivan (2019) puts it, migrants can sometimes "earn" greater acceptance and perceptions of deservingness for citizenship by providing valued contributions that are costly to themselves, for public benefit, and involve caring or sacrifice for the host country.

In Latin America, foreign migrants who played prominent roles in independence struggles sometimes helped to craft a national imaginary that included the meaningful social integration of their group because of their valued contribution. For example, Chinese migrants in Cuba were valued both for their loyalty and for playing a key supporting role in the independence struggles against Spain in the late nineteenth and early twentieth centuries: "Daily interactions with Cubans, participation in ethnic networks, and the making of legal claims facilitated the Chinese transition out of indenture. But it was their participation in the struggles for independence from Spain that enabled Chinese inclusion as an integral component in the public discourse on the Cuban nation" (López 2014: 185). Thus, Chinese migrants' military sacrifice superseded even their economic contribution through their labor to earn them a position more securely within the Cuban community of value, despite distinct markers of difference (Young 2014).

The evaluation of political activism by migrants is not purely a function of considering the specific claims they make, or the characteristics of the people and groups making such claims. Rather, the intensity of a potential backlash is often magnified or mitigated by the salience of the immigration issue in national and local political discourse, especially as framed by political leaders and the media (Zepeda Millan 2017). A number of studies have found that anti-immigration attitudes are stronger when they resonate with political rhetoric that is widely disseminated by recognized figures, blaming immigrants for problems that the host society views as major threats (Hopkins 2010; Brader et al. 2008). Ideological framing of the immigration issue to fit within the worldview and expectations of particular political beliefs has been shown to be a key predictive factor in the likelihood of local implementation of anti-immigrant policies (Ramakrishnan and Wong 2010).

Andrea Bohman argues that "political factors may influence anti-immigrant attitudes. For example, if issues of immigrant presence are highly salient in the national political arena, this entails a kind of priming . . . that is likely to increase immigrant visibility and thereby trigger feelings of threat among the native population. Also, as people who hold negative attitudes will be more likely to speak them out loud, as well as to advocate or act on their beliefs, if they resonate with views and interpretations conveyed in rhetorical frames, political actors may enhance anti-immigrant attitudes through legitimizing such views" (2015: 12–13 n. 3). The articulation of security threat narratives about Mexican and Muslim immigrants by Donald Trump, for example, raised the salience of immigration in national political discourse in the United States and emboldened those groups who shared these views to advocate and act on their beliefs by supporting more extreme policies to ban categories of migrants than would have been previously possible. The effect of this political priming of migrant threat, however, can be mitigated or reduced by extensive intergroup contact between migrants and members of the host population (Bohman 2015). The suggestion here is that social sanctions against visible migrant political activism are most likely and most intense when political leaders frame immigrants as threats to native citizens' enjoyment of privileges or domination of decision-making institutions, and when native citizens have few direct personal experiences with actual immigrants that would produce competing narratives or cognitive dissonance.

Since the state in a democratic polity is politically accountable primarily to citizens (those who vote) and not to migrants (who often do not vote), there are political incentives to ignore elements of formal institutions that extend protections to foreigners if sufficient antimigrant sentiment is expressed by citizens (Hopkins 2010). Scapegoating migrants by blaming foreigners for the problems of society can be a convenient diversionary tactic for a government that wishes to avoid critical scrutiny of its own performance while responding to constituent anger and pressure for action. As a result, migrants may pursue a different response: using informal networks and nonstate actors in the host society who ally with them to broker access to protection rather than risk violating the invisibility bargain by directly demanding rights from the government themselves.

Because of their contingent acceptance into the community of value (or their exclusion from it in the context of racialized invisibility expectations under the invisibility bargain), the pathways to political participation and incorporation for migrants can be perilous and respond to socially constructed rules of appropriateness. At the same time, the strategies employed by immigrants to apply leverage and participate in the decisions that affect them may use social-electoral coalitions based on ideological or ethnic allies in the host society or organized communities that link migrant groups with advocacy resources to respond to injustices and demand rights. In both cases, there is an insulating intermediary within the host population that allies with migrant activists, provides political cover for claim-making, and acts as a broker between migrants and the state. In this way, the likelihood of triggering a xenophobic backlash because of a perceived violation of the invisibility bargain is mitigated somewhat. Such coalitions that rely largely on allied nonprofit organizations and other nonstate actors play a key role in migrant political activity, given the frequent unavailability of electoral possibilities for noncitizens, and the fact that state agencies may have political incentives not to protect migrant interests, or even basic rights (de Graauw 2016; Zepeda-Millan 2017; Silber Mohamed 2017).

Exit and repatriation to their country of origin is sometimes an option for migrants facing increased discrimination or persecution, such as Zimbabweans in South Africa or Mexicans in the United States. In the case of Ecuador, however, Colombians who have fled the violence in their own country (who comprise the majority of the Colombian migrant population in the country) have little choice but to remain abroad for the foreseeable future, as the Colombian conflict has been ongoing for some fifty years, with few prospects for a meaningful shift from violence to safety in the near future, despite the 2016 peace agreement (Pugh et al. 2020). This illustrates the problematic dilemma of "choice" in the invisibility bargain. Both parties are generally aware of the rules (or are alerted through social sanctioning if they break the rules). The exchange of tolerance of migrant presence for economic contribution and social and political invisibility involves some degree of agency from both parties to the extent that the host population can withdraw its implicit tolerance if it perceives the invisibility bargain to be broken, while migrants can physically leave the country. The dramatic power imbalance and the very constrained set of options that many migrants face, however, mean that, like a Faustian bargain or the gangster's offer you can't refuse, the invisibility bargain is often rather one-sided in its distribution of benefits and in the degree of meaningful choice exercised by each party.

In the face of this dilemma, migrants and other nonstate actors in the host society who ally with them may pursue a different response: developing new (often informal) institutions and adapting existing ones to provide the public goods of security and peace in migrant-receiving areas in ways that allow migrants to avoid directly violating the invisibility bargain by demanding protection from the government themselves. These institutions exercise "practical authority" to help migrants and citizens who construct them to achieve common goals and legitimize their vision for a collective future. They may be driven by nonstate actors and are often informal, and they emerge through processes of adaptation in response to gaps in the formal state institutions that provide security and peace in migrant-receiving areas. In the next chapter, I explore how these institutions come into being: the ways in which international organizations, other nonstate actors, and the state form governance networks as a response to the challenge of providing peace and security for migrants and citizens in the context of the invisibility bargain.

3

Adaptive Institutions and Networked Governance

Along the way I understood that the voices of many of the refugees, forced migrants or other victims of the Colombian conflict needing international protection, build channels with international organizations or other third sector organizations, and it is these groups who often try to advocate to affect government agendas, who represent or accompany [migrants'] complaints and requests for change in the public policies that affect them both as migrants in terms of the role of the Ecuadorian State and as victims of the conflict in terms of the role of the Colombian State.

—Maritza Palma, Colombian migrant in Quito (Palma 2017: 13)

Taking the invisibility bargain concept developed in the previous chapter as a starting point, this chapter lays out the main argument of the book. Governance networks composed of state, nonstate, and international institutions that share information, balance power and political incentives, and negotiate the framing of shared migration challenges offer indirect access points for migrants seeking to coexist in peace and participate in decisions that affect them while not violating political invisibility by making overt collective demands on the state. In the context of the invisibility bargain, a democratic government has a political incentive to prioritize the interests of citizens over migrants (even when formal institutions guarantee protections for all residents), and therefore may be less than ideal as the primary guarantor of security in migrant-receiving areas. This leads to gaps in the formal protections offered by the state and to further vulnerability of migrants, which can escalate conflict between migrants and citizens.

In areas with a robust presence of nonstate actors and international institutions, but with a weak state presence, networks that connect all three

The Invisibility Bargain. Jeffrey D. Pugh, Oxford University Press (2021). © Oxford University Press.
DOI: 10.1093/oso/9780197538692.003.0003

types of institutions can emerge and adapt innovative forms of governance that complement, substitute for, or compete with state authority and security provision. The fact that nonstate actors and IGOs have different missions, accountability structures, incentives, and levels of trust from the migrant population means that a diverse and well-coordinated network that includes these organizations as well as state agencies may counterbalance the limitations of a governance structure that includes only one type of organization.

Of course, there is also overlap among the different organizational types—NGOs can be politicized, UN agencies can offer political cover to legitimize policies while not incurring a constituency cost because of their "democratic deficit," influential state officials may have worked previously for NGOs and rely more on their personal credibility and relationships than on formal state chains of command, and so on. There is also quite a lot of variation and debate within each type—the state is not a unitary actor, and turf battles among state agencies as well as within different international organizations are common.

Despite all this, diverse actors tend to produce a less exclusive network than a homogenous governance structure. More diverse and dense networks provide a greater number of potential access points through which migrants may gain the resources they need or establish social relations that contribute to their resiliency and ability to thrive in the host community. The chapter provides a theoretical framework for understanding the role of these governance networks in host-migrant human security provision and peacebuilding.

Societal Responses to Human Security Challenges from Migration

Nonstate institutions that take on state-like functions to provide security that extends beyond citizens who are bounded by the "national security" protections of the state play an important role in working toward peace for everyone who inhabits the territory of the country. Although these institutions are developed and promoted by nonstate actors, they often involve the state either as partner in implementation and enforcement of the (sometimes informal) institution, or as the target of a desired change that the institution seeks to facilitate. In areas where state capacity and authority are weak and formal state institutions are poorly enforced or unstable, institutional adaptations by local, nonstate actors often seek to fill the void in security provision for migrants and citizens alike. It is possible in these areas to have the paradoxical situation in which more inclusive security is being provided through nonstate actors than would be provided if the state alone were the only actor responsible. Figure 3.1 illustrates the logic of this argument.

This is not an entirely new idea. Recent literature on complex structures of globalization and privatized security has recognized the diffusion of security provision functions across a range of state and nonstate institutions and actors. Saskia Sassen, for example, proposes the concept of global assemblages as a way of thinking about the multi-stakeholder institutional clusters that take on security functions, often with the full knowledge and cooperation of the state. She claims that "the marking features of the new—mostly but not exclusively—private institutional order in formation are its capacity to privatize what was heretofore public and to denationalize what were once national authorities and policy agendas" (Sassen 2006: 222–23). Abrahamsen and Williams take this idea a step forward to identify networks of private security provision, which they associate with neoliberal analyses of politics, in order to understand the diffusion of sovereignty through public/private governance structures: "Neo-liberalism promotes a form of networked governance and involves a shift toward a new model of government less involved in direct service provision, and more focused on managing and organizing devolved centers and resources" (Abrahamsen and Williams 2009: 4).

Applying this idea of networked governance and collections of formal and informal institutions (within and outside of the state) to the area of security and control of violence, David Garland argues that these arrangements represent a "third sector" of security service provision—not necessarily implying a degradation of state capacity, as it has become fashionable to assert within the globalization literature. He claims that these structures of

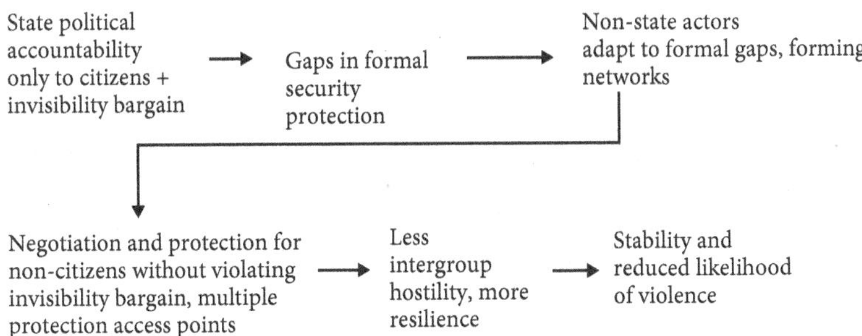

Figure 3.1 Nonstate institutional adaptation to provide human security under the invisibility bargain

governance form "an enhanced network of more or less directed, more or less informal crime control, complementing and extending the formal controls of the criminal justice state. Instead of imagining that they can monopolize crime control, or exercising their sovereign powers in complete disregard of the powers of other actors, state agencies now adopt a strategic relation to other forces of social control. They seek to build broader alliances, enlisting the 'governmental' powers of private actors, and shaping them to the ends of crime control" (Garland 2001: 124). This is a key point to emphasize, that the diffusion of sovereignty into a more complex constellation of actors involved in governance does not necessarily mean the "erosion of the state." In fact, it may be a way of leveraging the capacity of the state to provide public goods that are expected of it in order to increase domestic security and peace, and thus ultimately the political stability of the country. Sometimes, however, this proliferation and empowerment of a larger range of nonstate actors may reduce the flexibility or control of the state in certain policy areas. Nonstate institutions, for example, may constrain, enable, or substitute for state action in the provision of human security within migrant-receiving regions.

Due to the mutually constitutive nature of state and society, the development of nonstate institutions often produces a symbiotic rather than zero-sum relationship with state institutions. Joel Migdal's "state-in-society" approach is helpful in understanding this process. For Migdal, the state in practice engages with societies through numerous ties, and the interaction of the state and society can transform both sides, producing complementary and mutually empowering outcomes (Migdal 2001). This idea pushed others to think more deeply about the interconnections and interdependence of the state with the social organizations over and through which states enforce rules that govern people's behavior. As part of this conversation, a growing number of studies have examined the governance role of nonstate actors, and the ways in which both formal and informal institutions within and outside of the state have an active role in political decision-making, as well as the actual extension of authority at the level where it affects the actions of individuals and communities (Hyden et al. 2004; MacLean 2010). In addition to the diffusion of governance functions that are being implemented by a wider range of nonstate actors, recent studies have explored the ways in which institutions other than the state have been involved in creating and enforcing rules and standards that supplement, complement, or compete with formal state laws to address social and political problems (Peters et al. 2009; Helmke and Levitsky 2006).

Consistently with these studies, the comparison between state and nonstate institutions in this chapter shows that in the face of migrant vulnerability and conflict between migrants and citizens, the advantages of nonstate institutions in geographical presence, contact, and credibility with migrant populations, and the flexibility to provide services with fewer political restrictions can offset the disadvantages of state institutions. Table 3.1 summarizes advantages and disadvantages of state and nonstate actors at local and international/transnational levels in promoting effective human security for migrants and host communities. As the next section describes, state institutions face significant obstacles in providing effective human security in migrant-receiving areas of the country, including a lack of resources, geographical penetration, institutional cohesion and continuity, and the dilemma of attempting to perform dual roles as both enforcer and service provider.

Nonstate Actors in Networked Governance: Navigating Informal Institutions

Nonstate actors adapt as they identify gaps in formal state institutions, and their own purpose and structure may be changed along with resulting political outcomes as a result of this institutional adaptation, by which I mean the development or change of a set of durable norms, practices, and/or organizations in response to challenges and inadequacies of existing formal state institutions. The resulting institutions may include activities that are officially sanctioned or not, they can structure the interventions of formal organizations, or they can reflect regularized but unwritten patterns in social network and community activities. In the case of human security in particular, institutional adaptations often arise out of necessity and survival in response to failures of formal state institutions to prevent violence and offer protection. In contrast to David Garland's "third sector" structures of security governance, these institutional adaptations to take on security functions are not limited to protection through control of crime or violence. They may seek to mitigate overt violence directly, meaning physical attacks perpetrated by a human actor upon another, or indirectly by reducing structural violence, meaning the social structures that cause harm to come to some people more than other people (Galtung 1969).[1]

---

[1] Galtung elaborates on the difference between direct and structural violence: "When one husband beats his wife there is a clear case of personal violence, but when one million husbands keep one million wives in ignorance there is structural violence. Correspondingly, in a society where life expectancy is twice as high in the upper as in the lower classes, violence is exercised even if there are no concrete actors one can point to directly attacking others, as when one person kills another" (1969: 171).

Table 3.1 Comparative advantages of state versus nonstate interaction

	State advantage	State disadvantage	Nonstate advantage	Nonstate disadvantage
Promoting interaction	State participation can help to signal/strengthen norms of tolerance and pluralistic acceptance within the host society.	Especially in rural areas, reach is limited, and it may be unable to identify or bring together key actors on both sides; dehumanization of out-group may contribute to unifying narrative / political stability of regime agenda.	A nonstate actor often has credibility and contact with both groups through location and work in the field; may be better able to reach and convene with informal status.	A nonstate actor may be perceived as not neutral, may have an agenda that interferes with true sharing of experiences and an interaction of viewpoints.
Protecting human rights	It may have greater leverage and clout against other agencies of the state to hold accountable by law.	As primary target of HR complaints, the state may lack credibility or political will to change.	Independence allows criticism of or advocacy against state.	Asymmetric power relations may limit efficacy in achieving state change.
Promoting economic/ community development	Sometimes a state may have more resources available, an administrative capability to coordinate initiatives across regions.	It may be subject to differential political pressures/ incentives to use development money only for citizens, which may not reach those in need because of their fear of state's enforcement role.	A nonstate actor may have fewer internal competing interests to decrease effectiveness and may have lower perception of corruption, attracting external donors.	Donor structure may incentivize short-term (one- to two-year) projects showing "deliverables" more than long-term results and effectiveness; localized focus may duplicate efforts of others.

Table 3.1 *Continued*

	State advantage	State disadvantage	Nonstate advantage	Nonstate disadvantage
Providing protection	It has enforcement capability, coercive technologies, and legitimacy, based on preset rules/ expectations (law).	Its dual role of enforcement and service provider / dispute resolver can prevent access for those without legal recognition because of eligibility requirements or fear.	A nonstate actor may be able to deal with unexpected situations not contemplated in law; negotiation rather than enforcement can overcome legal inequities to provide nonviolent alternatives to all sides; presence and trust among migrants can lead to early warning / greater awareness of security threats.	A lack of capability, legitimacy, and agreed-upon standards may lead to favoring only certain groups; a nonstate actor may apply standards/practices inconsistent with law, and generally has very limited capability to offer physical protection/security against violent threats; it may sometimes have profit motive that relies on violence (i.e., armed groups / drug traffickers).

Another distinction is that the privatized security that is the focus of Garland's analysis converts protection from violence into a commodity that can be bought and sold for the benefit of particular people or groups. Since money is distributed unequally, privatized security maps the social and economic hierarchies and exclusions of society onto protection from violence. Nonstate institutions may also adapt to protect particular groups, but to the extent that they seek both security and peace, these goals are treated as *public* goods that benefit everyone. Since migrants are often prevented by the invisibility bargain from accessing rights and protections through formal state institutions, the public good characteristic is important in understanding the key role of nonstate institutions in extending and enabling security for everyone living in the receiving country. Nonstate institutions are often informal, and in isolated migrant-receiving communities of countries with weak states, nonstate actors working through these institutions may in fact be the only meaningful source of security and protection (Baker and Scheye 2007). Through a combination of coercion and service provision, even violent nonstate actors can exercise a type of authority, developing relationships with society that take the form of "shadow citizenship" (Idler 2019). According to Donna Lee Van Cott,

> Informal institutions often emerge in the vacuum created by weak formal institutions. In Latin America, formal institutions may be weakest with respect to the rule of law. For centuries, segments of Latin American geography and society have existed outside the reach of the state. . . . Large swaths of Latin America may be considered "brown areas," in which most citizens are not protected by the courts and police. In the absence of judicial control, corruption and impunity are endemic, and conflicts are resolved and order maintained through extrajudicial means. (2006: 249)

In my treatment of nonstate actors and institutional adaptation, I build upon the definitions proposed in earlier work on informal institutions, which represent the best scholarship on ways in which nonstate actors provide services at the local level in response to widespread recognition that the formal institutions of the state are not working. Helmke and Levitsky define *informal institutions* as "socially shared rules, usually unwritten, that are created, communicated, and enforced outside officially sanctioned channels." The authors propose a typology of informal institutions in the context of Latin America, categorizing them in relation to formal institutions (Helmke and Levitsky 2006). This typology divides institutions by whether the intended outcomes of the informal institution are convergent (shared goals) or divergent (different goals) from the intended outcomes of formal institutions, and whether the formal institutions themselves are effective or not. The four resulting categories of complementary (convergent/effective), substitutive (convergent/ineffective), accommodating (divergent/effective), and competing (divergent/ineffective) institutions gain significant ground in understanding the various possible relationships between the formal institutions of the state and informal institutions, which may challenge or reinforce the formal rules.

The Helmke and Levitsky understanding of informal institutions is limited, however, by the definitional question of what represents "officially sanctioned channels." Does this represent the written laws of the state, or the intended outcomes of the governing regime, or the practices of state agencies in charge of particular policy areas, all of which might express different manifestations of "officially sanctioned channels"? Given the limitations of the unitary state myth, the political interests and packets of authority within the state are already more fragmented than a monolithic "official channels" label would imply, and it is difficult to know when political factions and turf battles between "street-level bureaucrats" end and a division between formality and informality begins. Also, do large and elaborate nonstate institutions count as formal or informal institutions? Considering that they often contain defined sets of written rules and are supported by a constellation of organizations with budgets, buildings, and staff, one assumes that they would represent formal institutions. If that is the case, however, it is unclear how one determines which referent formal institution is "official," and thus has the power to approve of a set of rules or not. In the face of this issue, it may be more enlightening to analyze institutions in terms of their purpose (which may adapt over time) and relationship to the state rather than their constitutive nature. Defining an institution as informal requires one to make a judgment about whose approval matters in giving it the stamp of formality or not; referring to its nonstate, adaptive characteristics, in contrast, merely requires a recognition that it is designed to compensate for a shortcoming in the institutions of the state.

It is also important to recognize that there is not always a clear distinction separating state and nonstate, formal and informal, actors. Formal agencies can carry out policies that appear to be grounded in law but are manipulated systematically by internal factions to accomplish some divergent goal, from extrajudicial assassinations by police in Brazilian favelas (Van Cott 2006) to "lawfare" attacks by government agents to harass and silence critics, which rely on alliances that blur the boundaries of state and nonstate actors.

Kellee Tsai, writing on informal banking and economic practices in China, refers to *adaptive informal institutions* as "everyday interactions between economic and political actors at the grassroots level. Even though these interactions are typically informal, they may be highly institutionalized and carry more relevance than the formal rules that are supposed to govern the political economy" (Tsai 2007: 202). She also notes that informal practices often create feedback loops that may shape and influence the formal institutions and rules that they were created to subvert or work around.

In an earlier article, Tsai argues that "the etiology of formal institutional change lies in the informal coping strategies devised by local actors to evade the restrictions of formal institutions." These formal institutions

> comprise a myriad of constraints and opportunities that may motivate everyday actors to devise novel operating arrangements that are not officially sanctioned. With repetition and diffusion, these informal coping strategies may take on an institutional reality of their own. In contrast to deep-rooted, "primordial" informal institutions, which tend to resist change, the resulting norms and practices can be called *adaptive* informal institutions because they represent creative responses to formal institutional environments that actors find too constraining. Widespread use of adaptive informal institutions may then motivate—and, indeed, enable—political elites to reform the original formal institutions. (Tsai 2006: 117–18)

I embrace Tsai's recognition that many nonstate institutions emerge as "coping strategies devised by local actors" when the formal institutions of the state are perceived not to be serving the needs of these local actors. This same logic can apply to social practices reproduced through informal social networks and relationships, or through the enforcement and promotion of formally constituted nonstate institutional actors such as the UN or the Catholic Church, so instead of labeling one concept with the characteristics of the institutions I want to describe, I refer instead to what these nonstate institutions do, and how they adapt to accomplish goals in new ways.

The need for this shift is reinforced by the realization that the strength of an institution is often related to the capacity, resources, and legitimacy of the organizations that embody and promote it. Often, institutional adaptations bind together a combination of actors in order to provide particular services or functions, especially in the absence of effective responses by the government. These actors may include domestic nonstate actors (NGOs, firms, networks, etc.), local government agents, and international or transnational actors interacting in complex structures of governance. The institutional adaptations that emerge from the interaction and mutual reaction among these actors (as well as the social construction of norms) may reinforce existing formal institutions, or they may exist outside of, and even undermine, the formal institutional structure within a particular state or community.

These institutional adaptations may also involve violent and/or illicit actors. Annette Idler (2019) argues that especially in transnational spaces and borderlands, violent nonstate actors leverage jurisdictional flexibility and thus impunity that the state does not have, low-risk/high-opportunity environments, and sometimes overlapping interests with state authorities to produce murky, partially illicit forms of governance. "The resulting institutional pluralism contradicts conceptions of borderlands as ungoverned or ungovernable spaces; borderlands transform into illicitly governed spaces" (266). When citizens have greater confidence in the capacity and reliability (and violent consequences) of long-term deals with illicit armed actors than with the state, and when the political economy favors it, the relation between local inhabitants and informal institutional sources of authority can take the form of a "shadow citizenship." Idler (2019) argues that "an ideal-type shadow citizenship hinges on a recursive relationship in which violent nonstate groups provide public goods and services—including the provision of security—and define the rules of appropriate behavior while people socially recognize the illicit authority, consent to these rules, and participate in shaping them" (59). It is important to realize that such areas of shadow citizenship do not necessarily imply the *absence* of the state, but rather, configurations and relationships between elements of the state and nonstate actors (both legal and illicit) that produce authority, services, and resource extraction in informal ways that complement or contradict formal institutional structures (Ballvé 2020).

Having laid the conceptual groundwork to think about nonstate actors and informal institutions in response to gaps in formal state protections, I turn now to the ways in which the different types of institutional actors form new structures of governance that rely on the strength and diversity of their relationships. This analysis, which focuses on the distribution of power, information, relational position, and trust across state and nonstate actors within domestic and transnational political spaces, reveals that providing security and fostering peace in migrant-receiving areas of the Global South often mobilizes coalitions of overlapping, cooperating, and competing actors. While a straightforward review of legal and organizational protections may hide many of the important actions and the pathways through which migrants and their citizen counterparts experience human security in practice, a network analysis approach promises to provide a more nuanced understanding of how migrants circumvent the exclusions inherent in the invisibility bargain to negotiate access to protections, rights, and the resources needed for their livelihood.

Governance Networks Providing Protection
through Relationships

Migration is a complex and fluid phenomenon, and it presents different sorts of policy challenges for governments than other issue areas. Migration governance involves providing services and security, and ensuring compliance with laws and norms within a population that often moves back and forth across territorial borders through both formally controlled and informal crossings. This population may include those who have documentation that they have been legally approved to come into the country, as well as others that do not have such a status, and are existing in the shadows. Some migrants are fleeing threats to their lives and have refugee status, others are in need of this protection but for a variety of reasons have not received recognition of refugee status, and others have come to the country in search of economic opportunities. There is often overlap among these categories, and both migrants and the state may have different incentives to prefer one category over another, regardless of the individual facts of a person's case. In this context, the hierarchical bureaucracy of state agencies, which are bounded by territorial jurisdictions and organized into distinct issue-specific bureaus, may struggle to effectively exercise authority and achieve their goals and policy outcomes.

In response to this type of complex, "twenty-first-century challenge," states have shifted from a hierarchical bureaucracy model to mobilizing networks of providers, leveraging a range of providers that includes private sector firms, NGOs, and international organizations, as well as multiple levels of state agencies. Previous work on networked governance emphasizes the use of contractors and outsourcing to accomplish specialized and technically complex tasks while maintaining flexibility and cost efficiency (Donahue and Zeckhauser 2011). Going beyond the need for more flexible network structures, Leon Churchill (2011: 225) argues for a duality of hierarchical and network functions: "The primary challenge of network and hierarchy relationships is connectivity. The network has to bring its findings, goal consensus, and aspirations back to the hierarchy and effect the necessary change so the change can be routinized in the updated hierarchy."

Such networks can be mapped onto an array of existing institutions and informal actors in society. Xiang and Lindquist (2014) claim that migration is not merely the consequence of individual actors with outcomes determined by a receiving state's policies, but instead is an intensively mediated phenomenon that is influenced by the overlapping institutions, actors, technologies that form a "migration infrastructure" spanning sending and receiving countries. This infrastructure, which has commercial, regulatory, technological, humanitarian, and social dimensions, can be dense, multifaceted, even contradictory in its effects, but it universally shapes the experiences and interactions of migrants and their receiving communities (Xiang and Lindquist 2014).

Networked Governance Producing Human Security and Peace

Ensuring the security of those living within its territory is a core function traditionally associated with the sovereign state. Control over who enters the country across territorial borders and the resolution of disputes within the country also both represent core sovereign functions. In countries with a sizable migration flow, however, even these core state functions require a networked governance approach. The hierarchical structure of state agencies may make it difficult to address effectively the cross-cutting challenges of migration, such as the intersection of legal rights with economic livelihoods, or of social integration and coexistence with protection from violence and discrimination.

Given the importance, well -established in the peacebuilding and humanitarian assistance literature, of programs and interventions that are developed with buy-in and local ownership (Mac Ginty 2011; Autesserre 2017; Honig 2018) and integrate fully into existing political and social institutions, governance networks can help to legitimize actions and build trust, pool knowledge and resources, and provide more horizontal structures for coordination and collective action (Pugh 2016a; Balyk and Pugh 2013; Lederach 2005). In border regions where migration and other transnational phenomena present challenges to the jurisdictional authority of the state and there is not a clear single dominant source of "practical authority" (Abers and Keck 2013), governance assemblages link the state with international organizations and local nonstate actors in "shifting networks of alliances" (Johnston 2006: 34). In such areas of "limited statehood" (Risse 2011), some institutions may be more powerful than others and may exercise different sorts of influence, but it is not necessarily the state that is the predominant holder of influence or authority (O'Donnell 2004; Baker and Scheye 2007; Abers and Keck 2013). In fact, local outcomes can depend even more on the actions of NGOs, the church, or external actors, including UN agencies or representatives of foreign governments like USAID. Along with the potential for constructive outcomes that these arrangements offer, however, Schneckener warns that "transnational and nodal governance also implies a sharing of costs and responsibilities that usually generates tensions and disappointments, in particular between international actors who invest resources for state building and local elites who want to secure their dominant position in state and society" (2011: 252).

The state's political incentive structure may also create a power inequality between migrants and citizens that can result in uneven enforcement of laws governing migrants, or it may even lead to scapegoating and blaming migrants for the problems of a country as a diversionary tactic. Especially in democratic countries with relatively recent migration flows and few migrants who have become naturalized citizens, the state is likely to respond to and take more seriously the interests of citizens, who vote, rather than migrants, who do not. In countries where state capacity is limited, especially outside of the capital city, states that seek to address livelihood and resource concerns of migrants may confront critical pressure from citizens who see this as undermining their own economic interests, or placing additional economic burdens on citizens.

Exercising "Practical Authority" in Networked Governance within the Global South

Previous works recognize the role of informal and more flexible governance arrangements that link state and nonstate actors (Helmke and Levitsky 2006; Baker and Scheye 2007). They pay insufficient attention, however, to the agency and independent forms of "practical authority" of nonstate actors in the network, meaning the "capabilities to solve problems and recognition by others [that] allows an actor to make decisions that others follow" (Abers and Keck 2013: 7). Nonstate actors such as NGOs, private firms, and international organizations have their own agendas that also influence the types of policy goals being pursued, the way that governance is produced, the legitimizing discourses that are employed, and even the structure and goals of the government agencies themselves. Less formal structures like networks do not exist solely to increase the efficiency and flexibility of government service provision. Rather, the different nonstate actors in the network can complement, legitimize, compete with, or undermine the state agencies that are operating within the same issue area (Helmke and Levitsky 2006). Abers and Keck (2013: 7) argue that "although organizations sometimes gain the capacity to influence behavior through formal dispensations emanating from state power, they also can, and often do, gain that capacity by other means, such as by garnering social respect, acquiring new technical skills, and taking advantage of private resources. . . . state institutions often develop authority less through their formal attributions and more through such relational mechanisms. Non-state organizations also do so."

The migration literature has long recognized the importance of social networks for migrants' ability to access resources, respond with resilience to challenges, and integrate into their host society (Portes 1995; van Meeteren 2010; Ambrosini 2013). Even those works that complicate this insight with skeptical nuance, recognizing that the potential of these networks is influenced by external and structural factors like migration laws, the host economy, and political narratives in receiving societies, still recognize the fundamental importance of relational connections to migrants' success (Menjívar 2000; Landau and Duponchel 2011; Hopkins 2010). These networks can provide access to a diverse set of institutions and actors with significant "practical authority" to provide protection and resources or defend the rights of migrants when the state is unable or unwilling to do so. The resources and capabilities that become available through these connections to other people and institutions are often referred to as social capital (Putnam 2000), which is an important explanatory factor in good governance and economic development (Woolcock 1998). Applying the concept to peacebuilding, Susan Allen Nan argues that "social capital in networks can also support conflict resolution by creating cross-cutting ties engaging in constructive conflict resolution processes. Those networks which include both intra-group ties and inter-group cross-cutting ties are those which support peacebuilding. These conflict-resolving networks appear to be more inclusive" (2009: 173). Networks can help build resilience and conflict resolution capacity most obviously at a local level, but the networks that connect conflict resolution organizations across borders can also act as channels for information and norms dissemination and embed states within cooperative structures that lead to less armed and political violence at national and international levels (Wilson et al. 2016; Ohanyan 2015; Pugh and Ross 2019).

In the fluid spaces of coexistence within cities in the Global South that bring together migrants from various countries and their host society counterparts, politics is the result of a confluence of interests, informal and formal institutional spaces, and competing sources of authority in the "urban estuary" (Landau 2015). Formal institutions organized around hierarchical decision-making and distributions of power may be poorly adapted to providing security or governance that is effective in these transitional zones where the acceptance of many of the participants is not rooted in any formal legal status, but in the contingent expectations of the invisibility bargain, their precarity, and their economic contributions:

> The diversity and mobility of people works against the consolidation of unified and state-centered patterns of authority and power that are likely to be internalized and linked to an overarching teleology or political metanarrative. But while these point to a kind of fragmentation and anarchy, these places are not bereft of order. Instead, in the absence of strong and shared formal or social institutions that regulate interactions of people, property, or production, other kinds of highly socialized, contextualized, and decentered politics are emerging. These are at once geographically specific and deeply networked across space through residents' social and economic ties. (Landau 2015: 219)

In these complex political and social spaces of the Global South, those studying only the formal institutions and legal status that govern immigrant rights and political participation may miss the most important parts of the story in explaining the lived experience and strategies used by migrants to survive and thrive. In a survey of migrants in four cities of Africa, Landau and Duponchel found that "legal status is neither consistently associated with particular migration histories nor a reliable predictor of effective protection: receiving refugee status is not a good indicator of someone's substantive experience nor does it have a strong effect on welfare or security. Rather than claiming status, invisibility and a form of silent integration is often a conscious and more effective protection strategy" (Landau and Duponchel 2011: 2).

Brokering, Clientelism, and Patron-Client Networks

Understanding the political dynamics of this sort of political capital and brokering activity, which often has greatest salience at a local rather than national level, involves producing and legitimizing power and authority by a range of formal and informal actors that include state and nonstate institutions as well as networks and informal institutions (Helmke and Levitsky 2006). In Latin America, political relationships that facilitate brokering through networks of unequal power have traditionally been captured through the concept of clientelism. This idea referred to politics that involved long-term, unequal relationships built on an exchange of political support for material economic favors and patronage. Often, this exchange involved political leaders providing jobs, economic benefits, and favored policies to key power brokers, which enabled the brokers to provide tangible benefits to their network of "clients" who voted according to the preference of the "patron" so that the benefits would continue. According to Hilgers (2012), "In addition to being an exchange in which individuals maximize their interests, clientelism involves longevity, diffuseness, face-to-face contact, and inequality. That is, it is a lasting personal relationship between individuals of unequal sociopolitical status" (162). Jonathan Fox (1994) further notes the subversion of democratic quality and political agency of poor and marginalized citizens, saying that such states "oblige the poor to sacrifice their political rights if they want access to distributive programs" (152). This structure, which melded the political and social, was compatible with a hacienda economy and with the importance of personal relationships in business and political transactions and trust in the region. Rather than programmatic preference, ideological alignment, or sectoral corporatism, political structures in much of Latin America—certainly including Ecuador—have relied on this brokerage of electoral/political support for economic and employment benefits through personalistic relational networks. Clientelism is a dynamic and resilient type of political relationship that has adapted to many political contexts and regime types (Hilgers 2012).

Just as nonstate actors and institutions exercise "practical authority" beyond elected office, in the context of Latin America, these actors' attempts to broker representational voices and performative participation in exchange for beneficial policies for their "clients" and increased program budgets for themselves may sometimes emulate the patterns of clientelism. Especially with transnational NGOs, IGOs, and other international actors working in local spaces, the "patrons" (or indeed sometimes the clients) may move or be based across borders (despite maintaining bonds cemented in personal relationships and unequal status), so this observation promises to complicate the hyper-local focus of traditional electoral clientelism. State policymakers, UN officials, and other national-level actors may seek the appearance of "representation" and "participation" from migrants and refugees and instead use migrant-serving NGOs or migrant association leaders as proxies for inclusion in discussion forums since they are more convenient and accessible. In this way these groups play the role of brokers, speaking on behalf of their "clients" and trying to negotiate benefits or narratives that are favorable to them and the migrants they work with from "patrons" above them with power or resources that can be distributed. In less ideal situations, such brokering in a context of unequal power relations has resulted in some migrants feeling used as "poster children," having their stories and photos of their hardship used by IGO and NGO brokers to increase donations and justify their work, and sometimes not allowing the migrants to feel meaningfully included in any decision-making processes or to see any direct benefits.[2]

In both traditional electoral clientelism and the type of brokerage that takes place through migrant governance networks, the degree of exploitation versus autonomous participation is dynamic, and those on the less powerful end find coping strategies that can eventually shift the system. Fox (1994) argues that transition to greater associational autonomy and political agency is possible, and that clientelistic brokerage networks are not necessarily irredeemably authoritarian. He details the possibility of a "process by which poor people gain access to whatever material resources the state has to offer without having to forfeit their right to articulate their interests autonomously" (153). Likewise, the current study seeks to expose the mechanisms of brokering and mediation that take place through formal and informal networks of state, nonstate, and international actors, and the way that migrants can move from being acted *upon* or manipulated by these networks to actively selecting coping strategies that allow them to use the networks to access protection and spaces of political participation.

Networked Governance in Action: Responding to the Political Invisibility Expectation through Intermediaries

The actors and institutions in the governance networks that migrants rely on fulfill several key functions that are critical to the livelihood, social integration, and sometimes the very survival of migrants, especially those who are more vulnerable because of undocumented status or victimization

---

[2] Interview 102QM 2009.

as refugees. Ambrosini (2017) proposes a categorization of the types of functions that intermediaries in the host country perform, which they might do for profit or moral reasons, within the scope of legal actions or not. He argues that the primary types of intermediation that such brokers offer migrants are connection, provision of services, immediate help, tolerance, and political pressure. This typology provides a helpful way to organize this section's analysis of governance networks and their relationship in linking migrants with state and nonstate actors in the host society, and eventually in facilitating migrants' access to rights, resources, recognition, and protection. At the same time, it is important to recognize that these different categories of intermediation overlap, and sometimes a strategy that is most obviously about connection or provision of services may be part of an indirect polit-ical pressure strategy designed to circumvent the political invisibility expec-tation. Likewise, a strategy that emphasizes host society tolerance toward migrants may, if successful, make it easier to provide services, connect pre-viously segregated communities, or delegitimize policies that rely on xeno-phobic prejudices for their political viability.

Immediate Help and Provision of Services

Given the legal precarity of some migrants without documentation, the social precarity of other migrants because of the invisibility bargain, and barriers of distrust or lack of orientation that may confront newcomers to a country, many of the institutions that native citizens rely on for help, security, mo-bility, and other services may not be as available to migrants. Banks often re-quire a permanent address and ID number to establish an account or access credit, and potential employers—through which health insurance is often obtained—may require employees to have a bank account and an ID number (and in some countries, permanent resident status). Instead, migrants may rely on loan sharks or family loans, NGO microcredits, and community/tra-ditional healers for economic livelihood and health services.

Migrants may be afraid of or distrust police, courts, and other state agents, making them less likely to appeal to these agencies for protection. In addi-tion to increasing their vulnerability to victimization, this situation may also incentivize migrants' use of neighborhood watch groups, private security, or even linkages with illicit armed groups from their country of origin as ways to prevent intimidation by threatening actors in the host society. Travel in some countries makes migrants' exposure to such state agents more likely as they cross borders and confront border agents, pass through police checkpoints on highways, and face the possibility of being stopped while driving or being detained in public spaces if they do not have a permanent home. Therefore, migrants often rely on the services of coyotes, or illicit guides, to navigate cross-border travel and settlement into a new location. Most of these alternative service providers are nonstate actors, and many are informal or even illegal. Identifying and accessing them requires word-of-mouth and social networks. Trust and accessibility are primary deciding factors that influence whether migrants are able to find and use services and emergency help through formal institutional channels (including from state agencies), or through indirect relationships, networks, and nonstate actors.

Connection and Tolerance

Human security and peaceful coexistence in migrant-receiving communities is stronger or weaker depending on the connections that exist between migrants and the host society (and within the migrant community itself). Not only is a sense of connection and community cohesion important to help migrants respond with resilience to challenges and ensure their livelihoods, but more meaningful interaction is also correlated with higher levels of tolerance (Bohman 2015; McLaren 2003; Pugh 2017). It is difficult to justify the denial of rights and dignity of people one knows personally and has interacted with in meaningful relationships, in contrast to broad dehumanizing categories of people. Two types of problems create challenging disconnects between recently arrived migrants and others living in the host society who might help them: intergroup prejudice, fear, or distrust between native citizens and migrants can make it more difficult for migrants to access resources and develop social and friendship networks (Ager and Strang 2008; Ryburn 2018). At the same time, a sense of connection and solidarity cannot be assumed between recently arrived migrants and their ethnic kindred in the host society or migrants who have lived there for a longer period of time (Menjívar 2000; Bloch and McCay 2016).

A key dilemma posed by the invisibility bargain is that positive social relationships between migrants and native citizens can be important sources of information and positive affect that provide access points to the governance network for migrants and mitigate citizen prejudice; however, the social invisibility expectation makes migrants whose cultural or ethnic characteristics are visibly different more likely to withdraw from social spaces in order to protect themselves from social sanctions (Pugh 2017). Here the role of intermediaries is critical, as they can help forge useful relationships in a context where the potential value of a new connection must be weighed against the possible risk of being betrayed, exposed, or having one's own interests harmed (Bloch and McCay 2016; Menjívar 2000). Intermediaries can reduce the likelihood of betrayal by guaranteeing the personal relationship, or offer an avenue of redress if the new contact does not fulfill promises. This form of informal social insurance helps to address fears and make it more likely that migrants will take the risk of building new relationships across nationality groups that help facilitate further integration and offer protection.

Political Pressure

Political activism is one of the most important ingredients in migrants' efforts to go beyond individual survival strategies and have a collective voice in the decisions that affect their livelihoods, security, and access to basic rights. Because of the political invisibility expectation, however, direct, visible mobilization that makes overt claims on the state is likely to trigger a host society backlash that actually undermines migrants' goals. In that context, intermediaries offer a channel for migrants to negotiate their claims indirectly, often through broader coalitions. Such coalitions that rely largely on allied nonprofit organizations and other nonstate actors play a key role in migrant political activity, given the frequent unavailability of electoral possibilities for noncitizens, and the fact that state agencies may have political incentives not to protect migrant interests (or even basic rights). Examining the case of nonprofits in San Francisco, California, in the United States, Els de Graauw (2016) proposes a tripartite model of advocacy strategies to promote immigrant rights and integration. She argues that these NGO allies sought to influence local government agencies to promote migrant integration through (*a*) administrative advocacy, (*b*) cross-sectoral and cross-organizational collaborations, and (*c*) strategic framing.

Rather than large visible protests aimed at elected officials, more effective interventions often involved working with local bureaucrats, providing technical support and political legitimacy for the implementation of more constructive policies. Coalition building with similar organizations as well as unions, state agencies, and other types of institutions helped to pool resources, take advantage of complementary restrictions on political activity for different types of organizations, and provide trusted access to information about the migrant population for decision-makers who might lack it. Issue framing was critical given the earlier observation of how political elite framing influences host-population attitudes toward migration. Migrant-serving nonprofits and allies coordinated to adopt a strategic framing of the issue in question, often choosing to emphasize issues like human rights or economic justice that would include host-population beneficiaries as well as immigrants, in order to avoid characterizing the issue as a competition of us versus them, and to avoid triggering native backlash against migrants perceived to be undeserving beneficiaries of special assistance (de Graauw 2016).[3]

In addition to forming coalitions and brokering their political claim-making through NGO allies, migrants may sometimes wish not to engage in collective decision-making, but instead to avoid involvement in politics altogether. This is a common response by refugees, undocumented immigrants, and others whose precarity and past negative experiences with state agents (or in a few cases, nefarious motives) causes their primary concern to be making themselves illegible to the apparatus of the state. Such migrants may pursue strategies that make them difficult to identify, and thus to persecute or deport, by remaining in the informal sector, reducing contact with the state, and/or fulfilling their basic needs through "foggy social structures" that allow them to evade state surveillance and tracking and also to avoid violent social coercion (Engbersen and Broeders 2012). States can be quite limited in their incentives and capability to actually implement migration controls while maintaining a commitment to liberal democratic order (Ellerman 2010). This phenomenon produces gray zones in which migrants are physically present but legally, socially, and politically absent.

Finally, migrants as strategic political actors pursuing their interests realize that while overt visible contestation may trigger a backlash from native citizens, and hiding may keep them in a vulnerable and precarious situation, they can achieve many of their goals through relationship building and negotiation with individual local power brokers. This phenomenon is particularly

---

[3] However, Voss et al. (2020) find that human rights frames can be less effective in changing attitudes and policy preferences toward migrants (especially undocumented immigrants) than values frames.

important in the Global South, where central state institutions may have less capacity and legitimacy for control and implementation of policy, especially in remote territories and border regions. Tara Polzer (2009) argues that migrants and refugees in South Africa negotiate local integration, and the types of resources, rights, and political spaces to which they can gain access, with a range of power brokers that have the capacity or influence to provide what they need, not only elected state officials. They employ a range of legitimizing discourses and forms of exchange, since making claims based on the protection of their own rights may not resonate with a host population that views them as only contingently accepted in the community of value. Polzer also argues that those within the host society who engage in this negotiation with migrants and who provide certain resources or access to rights or a voice in collective decisions do so for a variety of reasons and to satisfy diverse interests, not only (and perhaps not primarily) because of a principled or altruistic concern for migrant rights (Polzer 2009).

The specific strategies employed by transnational migrants and their allies to produce desired political outcomes within the constraints of the political invisibility expectation are similar in many ways to the strategies that scholars have long associated with other types of transnational advocacy networks (TANs). One of the classic works on networks of nonstate activists that operate transnationally, Keck and Sikkink's *Activists beyond Borders*, argues that networks influence the governance process through four strategic processes that contribute to achieving the activists' political goals while not relying on citizenship-based territorial rights claims:

> (a) *information politics*, or the ability to move politically usable information quickly and credibly to where it will have the most impact; (b) *symbolic politics*, or the ability to call upon symbols, actions or stories that make sense of a situation or claim for an audience that is frequently far away; . . . (c) *leverage politics*, or the ability to call upon powerful actors to affect a situation where weaker members of a network are unlikely to have influence; and (d) *accountability politics*, or the effort to oblige more powerful actors to act on vaguer policies or principles they formally endorsed. (Keck and Sikkink 1998: 95)

Many of these same forms of influence pursued by TANs to achieve a domestic change in a specific country can also be used to understand the political and social strategies of transnational migrants and their allies trying to mobilize networks of state, nonstate, and transnational institutional actors to achieve a change in domestic policy or practice. To be sure, these parallels are not exact, as TANs traditionally were focused on coalitions focused on specific issue campaigns, rather than around specific populations seeking greater participation. In both cases, though, the political actors in question find that they are not able to access state protections or political participation in the country where they live through traditional "vectors of contestation" like electoral politics and interest intermediation through political parties (Pugh 2008). Instead, they strengthen relationships with a diverse set of political actors within and outside of the state that can contribute leverage and resources in ways that their own direct political action has been unable to accomplish. The effectiveness of the networks on which they draw to accomplish their goals helps to explain when and whether they are able to accomplish their goals. Whether it is a community of activists from multiple countries trying to accomplish a policy change through social movement strategies and advocacy, or a community of migrants from multiple countries and their allies trying to accomplish a policy change within a host country, networks offer a helpful explanatory framework for understanding how these groups apply "practical authority" within state and nonstate institutions to achieve change.

Political Alliances and Coalitions as Key Links in the Peacebuilding Network

Traditional political participation in different sectors of democratic societies has tended to emphasize organizing and building party coalitions and structures that facilitate the exchange of electoral support for favorable policy outcomes and patronage (Roberts 2002). Alternatively, organized sectors of society that do not have a winning electoral coalition, or who do not trust parties or formal state institutions as intermediaries that will work in their interest, have applied political pressure through social movements that seek change from the outside by taking advantage of political opportunities and mobilizing resources strategically to change the perception of decision-makers about their key interests and the costs of denying the proposed outcome (Tarrow 1998; Mouly and Hernández 2019). These two channels are not mutually exclusive, and political actors often play them off each other, choose between them based on changing power configurations, or pursue them simultaneously (de Leon 2013; Pugh 2008). However, both channels are facilitated to some extent by the degree to which political actors "belong" as members of the community of value. Electoral politics in particular is most readily employed by full members of the political community, that is, citizens, especially those in groups with relatively more power and privilege (Dancygier 2010). Although social movements often serve as vehicles through which marginalized groups mobilize collective action for change, they are more effective when key allies in the coalition enjoy unquestioned belonging in the community of value that give them credibility and leverage to contest policies and apply pressure for change (Ackerman and Merriman 2015). Partly for this reason, regimes confronting social movements often try to portray their opponents as foreign, subversive security threats, deviant, lazy dilettantes, or all of these negative labels (Chenoweth 2015). For example, during the US civil rights movement, business owners, students, and churches represented important allies applying pressure in solidarity with the activists in the South.

One of the functions of such insider allies is to convince state decision-makers that their political and economic interests would be better served by making accommodations and allowing (at least limited) reforms desired by constituents and potential electoral challengers than by opposing them. When such challenges come from people whose status is not firmly established within the community of value, however, they may have the opposite effect, pushing state leaders to double down on policy resistance and justify the "violent othering" of protestors, portraying their actions as a threat to the group identity and/or safety that the political leaders are tasked with protecting. This is the logic through which the xenophobic backlash against perceived violations by migrants of the political invisibility expectation can be understood. Especially in countries where large migrant populations are relatively recent and thus few are likely to vote (as is the case in Ecuador), large mobilizations of migrants making direct claims on the state through protest are less likely to persuade decision-makers that they will increase their electoral strength by acting to protect the rights or consider the interests of such migrants (Moulin and Nyers 2007). In fact, state leaders may see demonization and scapegoating of migrants as an opportunity to transfer blame for problems onto distrusted outsiders, or to weaken political opponents who can be accused of betraying the national interest of citizens. This position, however, may actually exacerbate intergroup distrust and cause an escalation of conflict as migrants become less willing to cooperate with law enforcement to maintain public order, preferring to withdraw from public spaces and minimize contact with the state. Despite evidence that first-generation immigrants are much less likely to commit crimes than native citizens (Ewing et al. 2015; Bersani et al. 2014),[4] denying protection to migrants may reduce social trust, disrupt community cohesion, and strengthen illegal actors who enforce protection rackets in ways that harms the security of all residents, citizens and migrants alike (Ochoa 2016).

While the political incentives of government officials in a democracy can render the state a flawed protector of peace and security in migrant-receiving localities, nonstate actors and informal institutions that might take on this role have potentially problematic limitations as well. Questions of legitimacy, representation, and "democratic deficit" are all relevant when international organizations, NGOs, and informal institutions and actors offer protection or seek to influence collective decisions about migration. Informal security providers may employ extreme or violent methods, target particular minority groups, or act in the primary interest of particular local economic or political power brokers, with little accountability for their actions (Abello and Pearce 2009; Baker and Scheye 2007). Examples include vigilante gangs and neighborhood watch groups in South Africa that killed or expelled dozens of refugees and migrants, or the Minutemen who hunt migrants in Arizona, sometimes with tacit acceptance by local law enforcement agents (Misago 2017; Sang et al. 2009). The danger for human security of a "strong state control" policy that emphasizes coercive exclusion of migrants emerges in part because the informal, nonstate organizations that emerge to fill the gap in state protection could (and sometimes are) nefarious, and could threaten the security of all who live in the receiving community. Julie Murphy Erfani makes this point in the context of the US-Mexico border:

> Paradoxically, federal immigration enforcement policies aimed at increasing governmental control over people crossing the southern border of the United States have actually inspired a complex array of informal networks, both legal and criminal, that exercise increasing control

---

[4] In the United States, native citizens are four times more likely to commit a violent crime than first-generation immigrants (Ewing et al. 2015). Similar findings have been found in other receiving countries, both in the Global North and in the South (Vaughn et al. 2014). Precisely because of their uncertain status within the community of value, migrants often seek to strengthen their contingent acceptance by adhering carefully to laws and rules (Anderson 2013; Bloch and McKay 2016).

over everyday life and movement through US-Mexico border regions. . . . Current US border-security policy and practice have also helped to trigger crime waves associated with human and narcotics trafficking, which have in turn diminished the personal security of people who live in and transit though the borderlands. (2007: 41)

Even when the nonstate organizations and informal actors that take on protection and service provision functions are well intentioned, they still are constrained by donor-driven missions and the need to show short-term success stories and measurable indicator changes that fit within a delimited one- to two-year project cycle, often a difficult prospect for complex processes of peace and integration (Wong 2012; Pugh 2016a). International organizations are sometimes criticized for a democratic deficit—referring to their being led by nonelected officials—that call into question the legitimacy or representativeness of their actions, especially when they oppose an action carried out by an elected sovereign government (Moravcsik 2004). They also face concerns that their missions and agendas—devised by faraway leaders who may not know much about the contexts in which they seek to intervene—respond more to donor preferences than to actual needs identified by those with a local stake in the problem (Autesserre 2017; Campbell 2018). While their independent mission based on international norms and laws provides a useful counterpoint to state laws that are oppressive or unfair, they also have been accused of imposing "foreign," and especially Western, values from the Global North to countries in the Global South that may have significantly different values and culture (Salem 1993).

Because of these observations, the point of the argument being advanced here is *not* that nonstate actors are always better providers of security and promoters of peace in migrant-receiving areas than states. Rather, I argue that states are not reliable providers of peace/security in areas with large migrant populations because of their political and electoral incentives, and that a dense and diverse network that *includes* state agencies, international organizations, and nonstate actors provides multiple access points for protection, service provision, and political articulation. The network structure allows for a balance in the strengths and weaknesses of each organizational type, while allowing for referrals and cooperative action. Taking into account the different levels of trust that migrants and citizens are likely to have in state, nonstate, and international actors, a network that links them increases the potential spaces where migrants may establish social relations that contribute to their resiliency and ability to thrive in the host community.

In the next four chapters, I will develop the theoretical argument presented in this chapter and the conceptual framework of the previous chapter through the empirical case of Ecuador and the Colombian forced migrants who live there.

4

Comparing Governance Networks and Human Security Outcomes in Six Ecuadorian Provinces

The empirical section of this book comprises the next four chapters. It begins in this chapter by laying out the subnational context and comparison of the governance networks and human security outcomes in the six provinces of the northern border area in which I conducted research. I will also draw on some of the survey data described in the methods section of the introduction to build an evidence base for my arguments about how social and political invisibility shape access to governance networks, and how these networks are key channels through which migrants access rights, resources, and protections that they need to ensure their human security, even (or rather, especially) in areas where state presence is historically weak. Chapter 5 will analyze the three core actors within the national-level migration governance network in Ecuador and how they have evolved over time. Then a detailed examination of the evidence from Ecuador will show the dynamics and effects of the social invisibility expectation (chapter 6) and the political invisibility expectation, as well as the ways that migrant participation, rights, resources, and protections have been increased (or not) through adaptations of the governance network (chapter 7).

Even a small country like Ecuador has significant subnational variation, and the diversity of its regions offers promising opportunities for comparative research that hold national conditions constant as a control. This chapter compares the six provinces in the northern part of Ecuador that receive most of the Colombian migrants and refugees coming into Ecuador: "Zone 1," directly on the border, which includes the provinces of, first, Esmeraldas on the coast, second, Carchi in the Andes mountains, and, third, Sucumbíos in the Amazon jungle, plus, fourth, the next Andean province down the Pan-American Highway from Carchi, Imbabura. It also adds, fifth, Pichincha, which is home to the capital city of Quito, and, sixth, Santo Domingo,

The Invisibility Bargain. Jeffrey D. Pugh, Oxford University Press (2021). © Oxford University Press.
DOI: 10.1093/oso/9780197538692.003.0004

located between Quito and the coast, and an important trading stop between the two regions. Officially named Santo Domingo de los Colorados, it has earned the less formal moniker Santo Domingo de los Colombianos for the number of migrant tradesmen who settled there. For the quantitative part of this comparison, I draw on surveys carried out with migrants in all six of these provinces, and include network analyses for each province as a point of comparison. I also construct a deeper qualitative comparison based on interviews in all six provinces.

This research design follows Richard Snyder's (2001) proposition that subnational comparative methods have three key advantages in increasing the validity of inferences made through small-N studies. These include increasing the number of observations, which helps to facilitate controlled comparisons; increasing the accuracy of case coding through greater sensitivity to variations within countries; and better capturing the spatially uneven impact of complex phenomena (Snyder 2001). Moncada and Snyder (2012) point to a first generation of such subnational comparative research that emphasizes subnational authoritarian regimes that can undermine national democratization projects, and subnational variations in social capital that can result in uneven consolidation of democratic structures across territories. In contrast, this chapter, and some of the other work done in the "second generation" of subnational comparative research, highlights the ways in which subnational variations in political interests, institutional networks, social capital, and migration patterns can show the contribution of local and regional actors and innovations to national policies and discourses, and to the scaling up of local policy innovations. The next section introduces the six provinces and their capital cities in order to facilitate comparison.

Snapshot of the Northern Provinces

According to the UNHCR, 30% of Colombian migrants live in rural communities along the Colombian border, with the remaining 70% concentrated in cities (UNHCR 2016); 34% live in Quito, the capital city of Ecuador (Ortega and Ospina 2012). In order to compare the different contexts in which networked governance plays a role in the lives of Colombians in Ecuador, I carried out more than 650 surveys of migrants in six capital cities of six different provinces with large concentrations of foreigners. This chapter compares them: Esmeraldas and Santo Domingo in the coastal region,

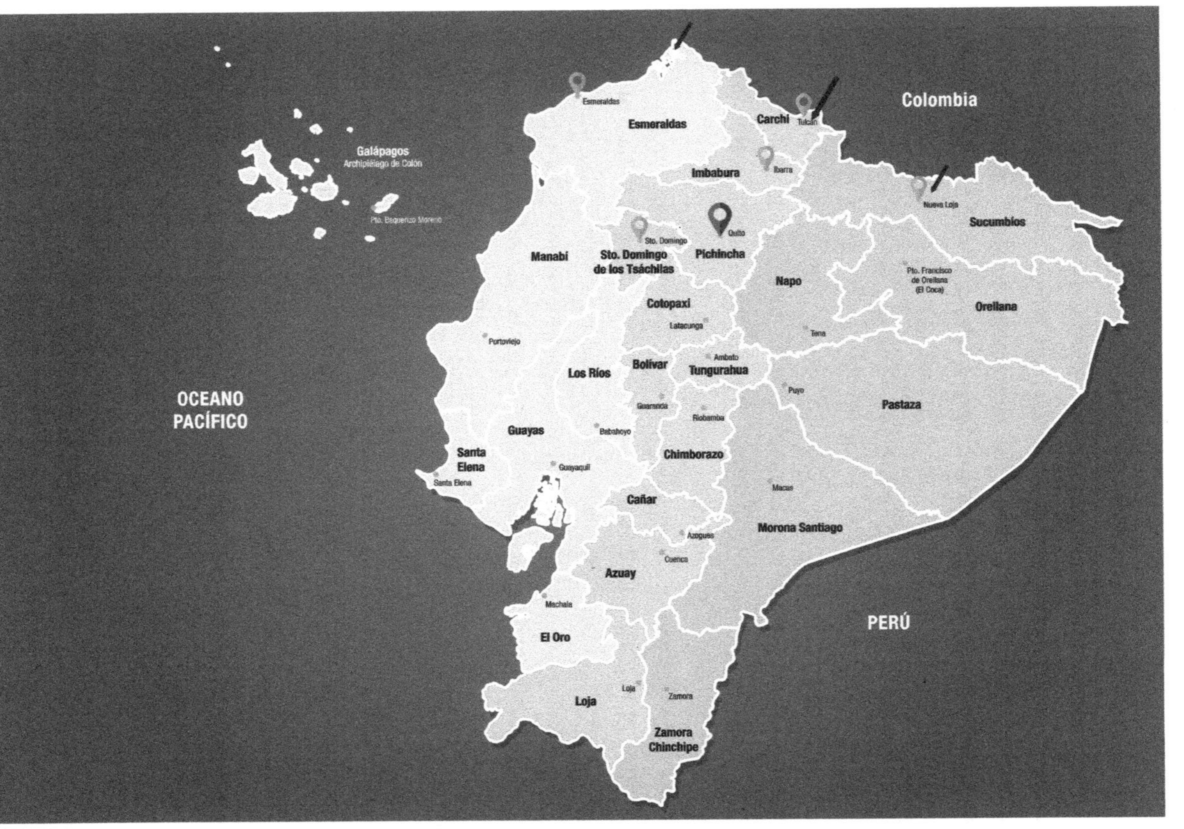

Figure 4.1 Map of study provinces in the border region: Carchi, Esmeraldas, Sucumbíos, Imbabura, Pichincha, Santo Domingo

Source: Map created by author.

Tulcán (Carchi province), Ibarra (Imbabura province) and Quito (Pichincha province) in the Andes mountain region, and Lago Agrio (Sucumbíos province) in the Amazon jungle region. Each of these cities is marked on the map of the border region in Figure 4.1. There are two formal crossings for migration from Colombia to Ecuador (in addition to more than fifty informal crossings, or *trochas*, that facilitate unauthorized, unregulated, and sometimes illicit flows of people). Indicated on the map in Figure 4.1, they include the Rumichaca bridge across which the Pan-American Highway connects Ipiales in Colombia to Tulcán in the northern Andes region of Ecuador, and the bridge connecting San Miguel, Colombia, and Lago Agrio in the Amazon region (Idler 2019). There is a third major route in the Pacific coastal region though which many Colombian displaced persons enter Ecuador, by land and in small boats along the water. This route, connecting Tumaco in Colombia with San Lorenzo and Esmeraldas in Ecuador, is one of the most complex, given the multiplicity of armed actors with presence in the area, and less regulated than the other two.

The border provinces of Esmeraldas and Sucumbíos suffer from greater economic deprivation, unsatisfied basic needs, and a weaker state presence (and more fluid family and social ties across both sides of the border) than the Andean provinces along the Pan-American Highway, which have benefited from better transportation and trade infrastructure and more state presence. Santo Domingo is a gateway city between the coast and the Andes, and the migrants who have moved there and given it the nickname "Santo Domingo de los Colombianos" tend to be involved in commercial trade activity. The brief snapshot that follows sketches the comparisons among these diverse localities on a range of relevant dimensions, including social structure, size and geography, race/ethnicity, and economic activity, before delving into more detailed comparisons of their security contexts, politics and governance, and the relationship between nonstate actors and migration governance networks.

Entrenched Social Structure

Both Santo Domingo and Lago Agrio are relatively new cities, having expanded their populations mostly with internal migrants from other parts of Ecuador who came for economic reasons. Quito and Ibarra both trace their roots to the colonial era. This is important, as the social hierarchies and established power families are more firmly entrenched in Quito and Ibarra, so newcomers may have a harder time integrating and gaining acceptance than in Santo Domingo and Lago Agrio, where few families have lived for more than a couple of generations. In the words of an NGO official in Ibarra,

> Since everyone arrives there [in Lago Agrio] poor, they understand the needs of their neighbors. So you feel the need, you open up and look for people. Here in the Sierra region, we are with our nuclear family, our social circle, and we don't feel the need to open up to more people. That is a positive characteristic of the people in Lago Agrio. . . . They say, "We are all colonists," meaning that we are all migrants. If Colombians come there, they say, "How cool they are!" They are more of *us*. But, in contrast, here they are more of *the other*. So I think that is a very positive and very open characteristic to take people in there, not only Colombians, but everyone who is in a condition of mobility.[1]

Likewise, the Colombian consul in Santo Domingo mentioned that in the thirteen years he had lived in the city, discrimination against Colombians had decreased, in part because the city had grown into a trading hub where commerce brought people from all over together, and nearly everyone was from somewhere else. With few lifelong Santo Domingo natives, Colombians became ingrained in the culture and society, and their entrepreneurship helped give them a relatively positive reputation among Ecuadorians.[2] As explained by a local government official in Santo Domingo, "This is a city of transit. You ask, 'Who was born here?' It is a tiny percentage. The majority of us were born somewhere else. We come from Loja, from Quito, from everywhere—so that is part of the special characteristic of this city, where no one says to you, 'You are not from here.' But that doesn't always work with the refugee population." She is alluding here both to Santo Domingo's relative openness to outsiders compared to other localities, and also to the fact that discrimination against refugees (who might be associated more with conflict than economic migrants are) still does occur.[3]

---

[1] Interview 61IN 2014.
[2] Interview 32DS 2013.
[3] Interview 31DS 2015.

Size and Geographic Distance

Some of the most significant factors that affect the way migrants interact with Ecuadorians and how they experience integration involve the size and characteristics of the population where they live, and their geographic distance both from the border and within the locality from each other and from institutions. In this sense, it is helpful to compare cities with similar population sizes, border provinces versus nonborder provinces, and to pay attention to the percentage of migrants as a proportion of overall population that live in each province. Within the cities being studied, it is important to recognize that social distance and geographic distance are related. It is easier to develop dense social and governance networks, and to integrate migrants into these networks, when the organizations and agencies in the governance network are less geographically distant from each other and from where migrants actually live. For example, Quito stretches north to south in a long narrow valley, and most state and nonstate institutions that work on migration issues are located in the modern north/center part of town, while two of the neighborhoods with the largest concentrations of Colombians are located in Comité del Pueblo in the extreme northeast periphery of the city, and in Solanda in the southern periphery. The distance between Solanda and Comité del Pueblo is twenty-two kilometers, and the distance from either to the modern north part of the city is over an hour using public transportation. In Lago Agrio, in contrast, most of the institutions serving migrants and refugees are within walking distance of each other in the main downtown area of the city.

Distance from the border and the geographic origins of Colombians living in the different Ecuadorian cities also vary. Unlike Quito, Ibarra, and Santo Domingo, which have a more diverse population of migrants from various parts of Colombia who now live far from the border, Esmeraldas and Lago Agrio are dominated by migrants originating in the Colombian department directly on the other side of the border from where they now live—some two-thirds of Colombians living in Esmeraldas originate from neighboring Nariño department, and over half of Colombians living in Lago Agrio are from the immediately adjacent Putumayo department (Santacruz 2013). This means that cross-border fluidity and maintenance of ties with family and friends in Colombia are more prevalent in the border region than in the inland provinces of Ecuador (Méndez 2013).

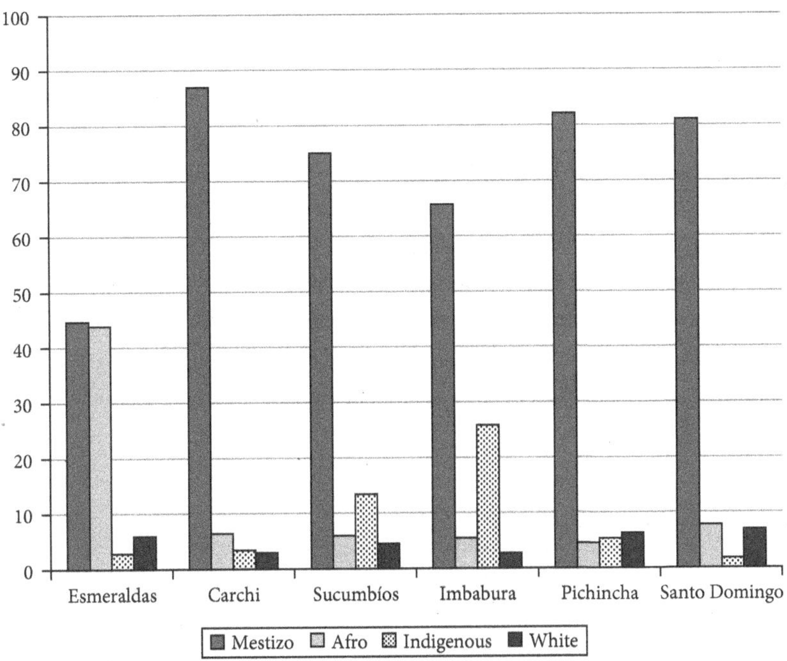

Figure 4.2 Racial composition by province
Source: INEC 2010.

Race and Ethnicity

Given the importance of visible differences between migrants and their host population in the invisibility bargain, it is important to note the baseline racial/ethnic concentrations in the different provinces. Figure 4.2 summarizes the racial/ethnic composition of the six provinces under study. Esmeraldas has the highest population of Afro-descendants, with just over 40% each mestizos and black people. Imbabura in the Sierra and Sucumbíos in the Amazon both have significant indigenous concentrations.

These characteristics of racial and ethnic composition are significant for several reasons. The border region includes several binational indigenous populations, such as the Cofan in the Amazon and the Awa and Epera on the coast (Becker 2019; Zaragocin 2019). On the one hand, their large and rural zones of presence and territorial mobility mean that the geographic border separating the country holds little meaning and is not demarcated nearly as meaningfully (given the relative absence of state authorities from either country) as identity and group-based markers like language, clothing, customs, and shared knowledge. There have been cases in which a Cofan child born in Ecuador was baptized and registered by a Colombian priest, as the only institutional authority anywhere nearby, and for this reason was later considered to be Colombian and was treated as a foreigner by his own government.[4] While the territorial border may have a peripheral meaning in the lives of some transborder indigenous groups, identity is often used as a defensive shield for group protection, which can result in (nonindigenous) Colombians being treated with suspicion. Given the history of territorial conquest and settler colonialism that has forced indigenous groups—especially in the Amazonian and coastal regions—to defend against outsiders seeking to exploit, buy, or steal their land in ways that would change their livelihoods and physical survival as well as social identity, mestizo and Afro-descendent Colombians are sometimes seen as one more group to be resisted. This experience has caused some indigenous groups to increase their "within group" bonding social capital at the expense of bridging social capital with outside groups, and to confront human security threats with isolation or village-level social exclusivity as strategies to avoid place-based elimination (Zaragocin 2019).

The Kichwa groups in the Central Andes have adopted a different strategy, integrating more fully into mainstream Ecuadorian culture and successfully navigating within a capitalist economy at national and transnational levels. In particular, the Otavalo community in Imbabura and the Cañar in the southern-central highlands near Cuenca have used emigration abroad as a key strategy to build wealth and power, and to use the leverage this gives them to negotiate and selectively resist cultural assimilation (de la Torre and Striffler 2008; Stone-Cadena and Álvarez Velasco 2018; Stolle-McAllister 2019). At a national level, indigenous groups have shown an impressive capacity to mobilize when they perceive an existential threat—especially an economic threat to their livelihoods because of central government policies—and national mass protests during the uprising in 2000 led to the ouster of a president (Gerlach 2003). The indigenous uprising in October 2019 against austerity measures and the elimination of fuel subsidies resulted in eleven deaths and 1,192 arrests according to the ombuds office, and although a negotiated dialogue resulted in policy changes, the government sought to deflect attention from indigenous agency and legitimacy by claiming (with

---

[4] Interview 129QN 2008.

little evidence) that protesters were the pawns of foreign Colombian and Venezuelan provocateurs or of former president Correa's allies (Ramírez Gallegos 2020).

The Afro-descendent population is primarily concentrated in the on the northern coast in Esmeraldas, where supposedly a slave ship was shipwrecked on the way to Peru in the 1500s and the descendants of its occupants established a colony (Rapoport Center 2009). Despite being an important agricultural center for fishing, shrimping, and African palm production, and more recently as the site of a major oil refinery, Esmeraldas has been perpetually marginalized socially and politically. Because it was governed by opposition politicians, the province was subject to economic extraction but denied political and budgetary control over infrastructure and many of the needed social services. As a result, residents saw the natural resources of the province contribute to national wealth while their local well-being atrophied (Valdivia 2017). There is a long tradition of cross-border commerce and family ties, and the fishing villages near San Lorenzo and along the Colombian border are characterized by many Afro-descendent and mestizo families with mixed Colombian and Ecuadorian households. This has made it easier for Afro-Colombian migrants to integrate into Ecuadorian society and to reduce the level of racialized stigmatization and discrimination that they face (Méndez 2013).

Economic Activity

Trade and commerce are principal activities in Santo Domingo, Ibarra, and Tulcán, in part resulting from these cities' geographic location along major highways connecting Quito with the coast and with Colombia, respectively. The surrounding provinces are largely dominated by agriculture. Quito as the capital city has a large and diverse economy, with trade, construction, manufacturing, public service, and transportation some of the key sectors. Nueva Loja, more commonly known as Lago Agrio, is the largest city in the Amazon region, and it is dominated by the petroleum industry. It was dubbed with its informal name after Sour Lake, Texas, in the United States where Texaco oil company was headquartered. The reliance of the local economy on petroleum and on services designed for single men who work for oil companies or who are associated with Colombian armed actors or illicit trafficking organizations has gendered and human security effects, and it illustrates the ways that insecurity is sometimes fueled by economic incentives (Bayón et al. 2020).

The economy of Esmeraldas on the coast consists largely of fishing, lumber/agriculture (including African palm production), and tourism, and is quite poor compared to the other localities. In the wake of the 2016 Colombian peace agreement, the security situation has worsened in the border regions as splinter militias have crossed over and changed the informal norms of eschewing violence in Ecuador. Esmeraldas in particular has seen tourism and other economic activities suffer because of fear of these actors, such as the armed splinter group under the Ecuadorian dissident FARC commander "Guacho," which kidnapped and killed a team of journalists in 2018 and launched a car bomb attack on a police station in San Lorenzo on the coast in 2017.[5]

Table 4.1 summarizes some of the basic comparative information on the population, distribution of migrants generally and refugees specifically, and the unsatisfied basic needs index for the six cities and the provinces in which they are located.

In order to understand the relationship between governance networks and protection and the human security of Colombian migrants, the following sections compare the six subnational localities in Ecuador on the experience of violence and conflict, the political context as it intersects with network building and governance, and the relative strength and interactions between state and nonstate actors as a key factor in the variation of effectiveness of governance networks in the different localities. This subnational comparison leads to a more nuanced set of observations about the ways that governance networks emerge, act, and provide protection and effective governance (or not) in migrant-receiving areas. In particular, the chapter highlights the key importance of personal relationships and the revolving jobs of key leaders in both government and NGOs/IGOs, city size and geographic proximity as they relate to social distance and connectedness, the degree to which migrants who have experienced discrimination and violence directly may be more motivated to reach out and access nodes in the governance network as a strategy of resilience, and the degree of mutual interdependence and resource sharing that comes from state incapacity in some localities. Illustrating the dynamics laid out in the theoretical framework developed over the previous chapters, the evidence presented here from interviews,

---

[5] "Quién es alias 'Guacho,' señalado por el atentado con carro bomba en Ecuador," *El Universo* (January 29, 2018). Available at https://www.eluniverso.com/noticias/2018/01/29/nota/6591451/quien-es-alias-guacho-senalado-atentado-carro-bomba-ecuador. See also "Lenín Moreno confirma asesinato de tres periodistas ecuatorianos," *El Universo* (April 13, 2018). Available at https://www.eluniverso.com/noticias/2018/04/13/nota/6711781/probable-muerte-periodistas-diario-comercio.

Table 4.1 Characteristics of six migrant-receiving cities compared

	Quito, Pichincha	Esmeraldas	Lago Agrio, Sucumbíos	Ibarra, Imbabura	Santo Domingo	Tulcán, Carchi
Population of canton	2,239,131	189,504	91,744	181,175	411,000	86,500
Population of province	2,576,287	534,092	176,472	398,244	368,013	164,524
% province population growth, 2001–10	2.26	3.63	3.48	1.63	2.76	0.81
Unsatisfied Basic Needs Index, province, 2010	34%	78%	87%	54%	74%	57%
% of total refugees in province (2013)	26.8%	10.9%	23.7%	7.6%	3.6%	9.0%
Migrants as % of population, province (census)	2.3%	1.6%	6.1%	1.8%	1.8%	7.4%

Source: INEC/census 2010; UNHCR 2014.

surveys, network analysis, and secondary sources further supports the argument that nonstate actors, IGOs, and the state can provide greater access to rights, resources, and protection when they are more densely connected with diverse types of organizations. It also supports the argument that migrants who overcome the dilemma of the invisibility bargain to connect with key organizations in a well-connected governance network have better protection and more resilience than those who do not.

Security and Violence

Security, both in terms of perception and by concrete indicators like the homicide rate, varies significantly across the six provinces being studied. It is important here to recognize that human security is relative and requires the specification of a referent (who is to be protected), a threat, a protector, and the means of protection (Wibben 2016). Defining these categories is a socially constructed, political act. For this reason, different populations might have different perceptions and experiences of how secure they are, depending on whether powerful actors define them as the referent, the threat, or members of an indifferent category. Powerful actors like states have incentives to use the language of threat and security to describe migrant populations and to emphasize migrants' victimhood or their potential threatening characteristics through speech acts, policies, and promotion of specific narratives in the media and public discourse (Buzan et al. 1998; D'Appollonia 2012; Pugh 2017). One commonly employed narrative in Ecuador is that the border region is a dangerous place, so one would expect that human security would be lower in this region than in inland provinces. Politicians and pundits often claim that migrants bring insecurity with them, so a greater concentration of migrants in the border provinces might be one possible explanation for perceived insecurity here. However, the empirical evidence for this claim is unconvincing. In fact, a careful econometric study by Fernández and Pazzona (2019) found no significant correlation between the arrival of asylum seekers in the Ecuadorian border provinces and an increase in violent crime in these areas. This evidence indicates that much of the causal logic between migrant presence and violent outcomes is a function of perception and constructed narratives (Rivera 2013; Pugh and Moya 2020).

It is indeed true that the violence levels (homicide rate) in Sucumbíos province in the Amazon region and Esmeraldas province in the coastal region are higher than the average for Ecuador, but a careful look at the data over time shows that this is more likely to be a function of spillover activity from Colombian armed groups than from migrants themselves, and from shifting informal institutions and expectations between the Ecuadorian security forces and the illegal Colombian armed groups (Idler 2019; Jaskoski 2015). In Figure 4.3, the homicide rates for Esmeraldas, Sucumbíos, and Ecuador as a whole are charted from 1990 to 2016 (Ponton et al. 2016). There is a sharp spike in the murder rate of Sucumbíos in 2000–2002, followed by a steady decline over the next decade and a half.

If the violence were being driven by the flow and/or presence of migrants, it should have continued increasing over time, as the refugee flow continued steadily over most of this time period. Instead, as Maiah Jaskoski points out, the late 1990s through 2002 was a time of significant change in

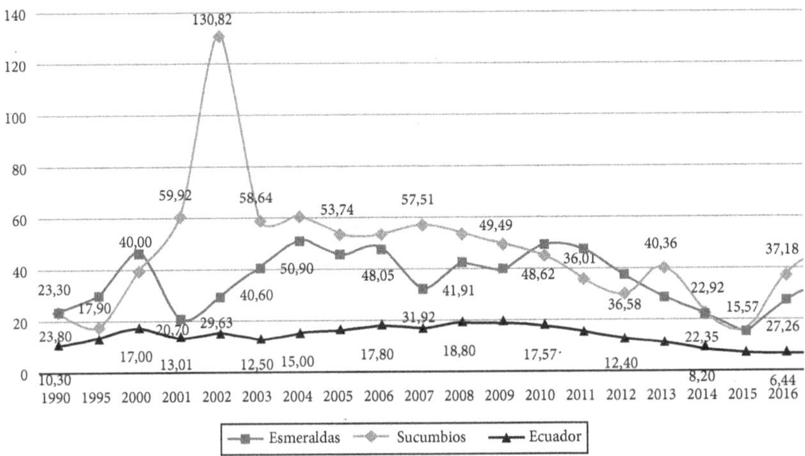

Figure 4.3 Murder rate per 100,000 in Esmeraldas, Sucumbíos, and Ecuador over time
Source: Ministry of the Interior (Ponton 2016).

the border region. Previously, FARC had established its dominance in the Ecuadorian border territory by attacking Ecuadorian military forces, which were overstretched and focused on defending their southern border against Peru and thus responded by withdrawing or avoiding confrontations with FARC. However, with the increased militarization and state capacity in the Colombian border area that came with Plan Colombia in 1999–2000, FARC had a much stronger incentive to preserve its access to Ecuador as a place to rest and resupply, so it developed a strategy of presence and exercising "practical authority" in Sucumbíos province, but not using violence or attacking state forces (Jaskoski 2015). This new strategy was reflected in informal understandings and explicit agreements between FARC commanders and Ecuadorian military officials in the border region (Idler 2019). Since FARC was the primary competitor to the Ecuadorian state, these informal institutions were successful in reducing violence levels beginning in the mid-2000s.

Esmeraldas, in contrast, had the presence of several different armed groups, including FARC, Ejército de Liberación Nacional, and various paramilitary groups, leading to a more complex security context (CODHES 2015; Moreno Parra 2019).[6] As a result, similar informal agreements did not produce results

---

[6] Interview 26CS 2017.

that were as predictable since no group had the level of hegemonic control to be able to enforce agreements. In both Esmeraldas and Sucumbíos, neither the presence or absence of migrants, nor the presence or absence of the Ecuadorian state, provides convincing explanations for the variation in violence over time. Rather, the nature of the connections and relationships between Ecuadorian state actors (i.e., military and police) and nonstate actors (i.e., FARC and other illegal armed actors crossing into Ecuadorian territory) seems to provide a more useful explanation. In this sense, the networked governance idea can be extended to include illegal armed actors, whose local presence, coercive capabilities, and ability to enforce a form or order while settling local disputes and even providing resources in the communities where they were present certainly influenced the human security experienced by both Ecuadorians and Colombian migrants living in these border communities.

The perception of migrant criminality and involvement in delinquency appears to be more a function of securitizing discourses and media narratives than of demonstrable fact. According to a study by the Citizen Security Observatory of Quito, Colombians represented approximately 5% of those arrested for crimes in Quito in 2009, at the peak of the migration inflow to Ecuador (Ponton 2013: 78). The human rights ombudsman of Ecuador issued a report around the same time demonstrating that the prison population included a number of Colombians that was roughly proportional with their share of the general population, in stark contrast to the media narratives that portrayed the vast majority of violent criminality in Ecuador as being the work of Colombian criminal gangs and delinquents.[7]

Perceptions of Insecurity

Lending credence to the argument that security is a socially constructed phenomenon, the comparison of Ecuadorians' and Colombian migrants' perceptions of the security of the neighborhood where they live shows that the perception of safety and security is not always directly tied to objective indicators of incidents of delinquency or violence. The Ecuadorian national victimization survey (INEC 2011) asked Ecuadorian respondents, "How would you rate the security of this neighborhood?" Figure 4.4 compares the responses of Ecuadorians in the six study provinces with the responses of

[7] Interview 143QS 2009.

migrants who were asked on the MNS, "Do you feel secure in the neighborhood where you live?" For both sets of responses, the multilevel scale was collapsed into a binary variable, secure or insecure.

This comparison of perceptions of security in the neighborhood where respondents live (showing differences by locality, and between Ecuadorians and Colombians) results in two key observations. First, the localities with the least dense governance networks, as discussed subsequently (Quito, Esmeraldas, Santo Domingo), are also the ones in which respondents reported the greatest level of perceived insecurity, compared to localities with denser and more diverse networks (Lago Agrio, Ibarra, Tulcán). In general, smaller towns and those closer to the border tended to have a better perception of neighborhood security than larger cities further away. The second observation is that a similar trend can be seen for both Colombian migrants and Ecuadorians surveyed in the national victimization survey. Although Ecuadorians tended to report much higher levels of insecurity than Colombians (perhaps because of Colombians' social desirability bias and desire to avoid complaining about their host country), the pattern was similar across the localities, with Ecuadorians living in the provinces of Pichincha (Quito) and Santo Domingo feeling the least secure, and those in Sucumbíos province (Lago Agrio) and Carchi province (Tulcán) feeling the most secure, just like their migrant counterparts. This suggests that while migrants and

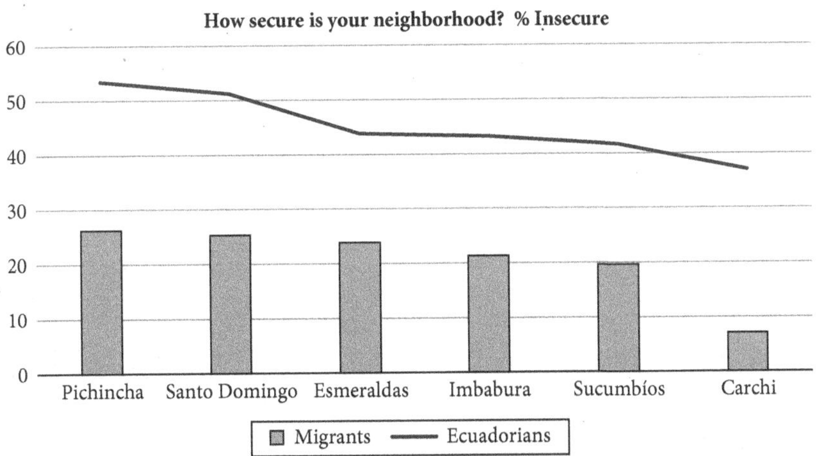

Figure 4.4 Perceived security of neighborhood: Ecuadorians and migrants, by province

Source: MNS 2016; INEC/EV 2011.

citizens certainly experience risks differently and the stakes for their own livelihood can differ significantly, the perceptions of security across the two populations seem to be similarly related to the characteristics of their locality, particularly the available protections in it and the social distance that allows or impedes access to these protections.

In order to deepen the comparative analysis of migrant perceptions of their own security across these localities, the MNS asked respondents what their greatest fear was living in Ecuador. Table 4.2 summarizes the top response in each city.

Interestingly, there is a fairly clear distinction in the fears expressed by migrants in the poorer border towns (Lago Agrio and Esmeraldas), where fear of the state denying rights trumped social integration worries versus those in the generally wealthier towns along the Pan-American Highway and commercial centers (Tulcán, Ibarra, Santo Domingo), where economic anxiety was paramount. In the border, then, migrants sometimes perceived the state to be the source of threat more than protection, while in inland towns, they feared that their inability to integrate into society would lead to a lack of economic resources. Indeed, according to interviews, migrants in these towns often had difficulties in finding a job, or reported abuses by employers who would exploit or refuse to pay them for work they had completed.

In order to confront and address the fears of migrants, institutions in several of these cities, especially Lago Agrio and Santo Domingo after 2015, built working groups and solutions networks to coordinate on urgent and vulnerable cases and provide effective solutions, essentially establishing parallel institutions (or sometimes cooperative channels) with the state. Violence, including gender-based violence, is a major problem in Santo Domingo,

Table 4.2 Greatest fear expressed by migrants in each city

City	Top Fear	(% respondents)
Esmeraldas	Discrimination/denial of rights	26
Lago Agrio	Being deported	31
Tulcán	Not having sufficient economic resources	38
Ibarra	Not having sufficient economic resources	18
Santo Domingo	Not having sufficient economic resources	24
Quito	Discrimination/denial of rights	17

Source: MNS 2016.

for example, where femicides are frequent. In the wake of the murder of a refugee woman that left a dozen orphaned children, a women's organization joined together with the municipal government, the human rights ombudsman, NGOs, and a group of women who lived in some of the poorest neighborhoods of the city to develop an early warning "violence observatory." According to one of the leaders, who also worked for the municipal government, this mechanism provided a useful and effective counterbalance to the indifference, ineptitude, and even hostility that sometimes impeded the protection provided by the state justice and law enforcement systems, especially toward poor and/or migrant women:

> So some ten Colombian refugee women joined as part of the observatory, too, and helped follow up on cases of violence, because the violence that refugee women receive is different from what we experience. For example, I will give you an example that is ugly, but it happened: a woman in one workshop told us that she went to visit her son, who was imprisoned in Bella Vista jail, and as she arrived a little bit late, she asked the guard to please let her in. She was worried that she might need to give him some money or something, I don't know, but the guard lowered his pants and said, "OK, come here, then I will let you in." He did that because she was Colombian. . . . You hear the accent and you immediately know that she is Colombian. . . So that is one thing, for example, where the violence observatory is key, because I told them that happened two years ago; if it had been last week, the observatory could mobilize to make sure that policeman was removed from his job, because that is the very least that should happen, no?[8]

This reflection illustrates intersectionality in practice, as discussed in chapter 2, in which the Colombian woman's nationality and gender expectations (and perhaps class) intersected to increase her vulnerability to abusive treatment by the state and to exclude her from protection, and to do so in a way that was violent and sexual, which would not be likely to occur for a man or an Ecuadorian visiting a family member in the jail. As she recounts the story, she apparently did not have access to any source of protection or relief at the time that the event occurred; only when she was telling the story to her trusted group of friends in the women's organization two years later did she have access to others (including the interviewee sharing this incident

---

[8] Interview 31DS 2015.

with me) with institutional connections and influence who were both trusted enough to have her share such a personal story and powerful or connected enough to do something about it. Localities with networks that combine different types of institutional actors in a well-coordinated network (often glued together by overlapping personal relationships) are better able to mobilize and offer this sort of protection for migrants and refugees who might be excluded from more traditional and formal channels.

Politics and Governance

The degree of political compatibility between the central and local governments helps to explain the effectiveness and coordination of connections between state agencies within the governance network. In municipalities and provincial governments controlled by opposition political parties, there was often a lack of political will to work together with ministries on complex problem-solving, and since migration, refugees, and open borders were issues promoted by President Correa's government in the early years of his administration, localities like Tulcán were somewhat resistant to accept refugee integration government programs.[9] In Esmeraldas, the combination of opposition control and racial difference reportedly contributed over time to frequent neglect and marginalization by the central government, with crumbling infrastructure as one indicator of this phenomenon. Figure 4.5 depicts a political mural for an opposition party, painted on a crumbling wall above a potholed street with open runoff ditches.

According to a 2012 interview with one IGO observer in this coastal city,

> The needs are many and the resources are few. In order to meet local needs, the government has to supplement what it has, and it cannot give adequate attention to the 189,000 Ecuadorians or give more than exists. And since there are political tensions between the different levels of government over revenues, and money does not arrive as it should, it is logical that they are not going to be able to give adequate attention to the needs of this population. So they begin to prioritize: who are the ones who will vote for me? Ecuadorians. Colombians don't have anything to offer. So they have to prioritize in this sense. . . . If I have good revenues, I can give better attention

---

[9] Interview 98IM 2014; Interview 18CS 2015; Interview 115QN 2012; Interview 116QN 2012.

Figure 4.5 Infrastructure and political opposition in Esmeraldas
Source: Photo by author.

to all of the populations. But can you imagine, the budget of the city of Esmeraldas is around $14 million per year right now, with 189,000 people and a mountain of needs. Do you think that they are going to give attention to the 12,000 Colombians who live here? Difficult.[10]

While *social* networks among migrants and Ecuadorians, especially Afro-descendants of both nationalities, were often stronger and more open in Esmeraldas than in Quito because of shared kinship, familial ties, and racial similarity,[11] these did not connect as well to *governance* networks because of barriers to institutional cooperation, the geographic spread of the city, and a siloed and even competitive approach to service provision (Valdivia 2017; Moreno Parra 2019).[12]

The pattern of cooperation or competition between the central government and local municipal and provincial governments has had an impact

[10] Interview 33EI 2013. See also "Aprobado nuevo presupuesto municipal," *La Hora* (December 24, 2012). Available at https://lahora.com.ec/noticia/1101442025/aprobado-nuevo-presupuesto-municipal.
[11] Interview 33EI 2013; Interview 119QN 2016.
[12] Interview 36EN 2013; Interview 50ES 2012.

Table 4.3 Political control of localities over time[1]

	2009 municipal	2009 provincial	2014 municipal	2014 provincial
Quito	Alianza PAIS	Alianza PAIS	SUMA-Vive	Alianza PAIS
Esmeraldas	MPD	MPD	AP	MPD
Tulcán	MSC	ID	MSC	MID
Lago Agrio	AP	PSP	PSP	PSP
Ibarra	AP	AP	Avanza	Avanza
Santo Domingo	AP	AP	SUMA-Vive	AP

[1] Political parties included in this table: Alianza PAIS (AP); Movimiento Popular Democrático (MPD); Movimiento Social Conservador del Carchi (MSC); Izquierda Democrática (ID); Partido Sociedad Patriótica 21 de Enero (PSP); Sociedad Unidad Más Acción (SUMA)-Vive; Partido Avanza; Movimiento Integración Democrática del Carchi (MID).

on the implementation of refugee and migrant protections at the local level, and receptiveness to national policy initiatives. This was particularly true during the administration of President Correa, when migration policy was somewhat more politicized as a partisan issue, with his Alianza PAIS (AP) party supporting (at least rhetorically) more progressive protections and policies under the label of "universal citizenship" (Pugh 2017; A. Correa 2016). While Correa's Alianza PAIS party consolidated its control at the local level in the 2009 local elections, by 2014, all but one of the six municipalities under study were controlled by opposition parties, as were all but two provinces (see Table 4.3 for the parties that controlled each locality after these two elections). This partisan competition sometimes resulted in less willingness for local governments to work closely with central government ministries to promote migrant protections, especially when doing so would be perceived by their constituents as coming at the expense of resources or services for local Ecuadorians.[13] As Correa confronted higher political costs for his migration policies and began to hollow out his "universal citizenship" rhetoric with more regressive practices—even while maintaining the welcoming

[13] In some cases, the partisan rivalry had deadly consequences at the level of local governance, such as in the town of Muisne in Esmeraldas province, where the Alianza PAIS mayor-elect, Walker Vera, was gunned down outside his home before he could take office, a crime for which the former mayor (whom he had accused of corruption) of the coalition (and later opposition) party Avanza was convicted and sentenced to prison along with three Colombian hitmen. See "Condenan" 2015 and "3 Sentenciados" 2015.

rhetoric—after 2012 (Pugh 2017), the partisan gap may have mattered less, since the central government was no longer pushing as hard for real implementation of migrant/refugee protection.

Partisan divides between the central and local governments were not the only barriers to constructive migration policies and protection; the individual political calculations and priorities of local politicians often set the agenda for how open the municipality was to cooperative relations on migration policies. For example, the mayor of Santo Domingo from 2009 to 2014 was a member of President Correa's Alianza PAIS party. Because she was not very interested in spending time or political capital on policies related to foreign migrants and refugees, the interinstitutional network of organizations that was forming in 2012, mostly with the participation of NGOs and IGOs, began to atrophy and eventually ceased to exist in active form in 2013. One participant reflected on the importance of state presence as part of a diverse governance network: "I think one of the reasons why the previous network dissolved is because we felt that the state was not going to do anything. At the end of the day, the one that defines public policy is not the Jesuit Refugee Service or others, it is the municipal government. So if the municipality doesn't create an agenda, doesn't invest money, who will? So I think perhaps that is why the network disappeared."[14]

After the 2014 municipal elections brought to power a mayor from a different party (although still an ally of President Correa), the municipal government became a strong central node in the migrant governance network. This seemed more a function of the personal interests and political agenda of the two mayors than any partisan or ideological distinction.[15] Personalistic politics mattered: a member of the mayor's staff, who had previously worked for a UNHCR partner NGO, was one of the driving forces behind re-establishing and organizing the interinstitutional human mobility network, which began to coordinate joint strategies and policy recommendations. Her existing relationships with former colleagues in NGOs and the UN system were an important resource that gave her the credibility and convening power to lead the network, according to several members.[16] Reflecting on her move from civil society into a position in the municipality, she said, "Once you are part of the state, you can contribute to the construction of public policy within

---

14 Interview 31DS 2015.
15 Interview 31DS 2015.
16 Interview 21DM 2015; Interview 27DN 2015.

this theme [of migration]—and obviously people feel included, because they sense there is municipal support.

The personal networks of this official and her colleagues in the newly established network in Santo Domingo were an important form of social capital that bridged the power of the state and these officials' technical knowledge and legitimacy with refugees (representing their combined "practical authority") that they brought from their former jobs in NGOs and IGOs: "I think the possibility of being able to work on these issues within the state, or the fact that some of us who have worked on these issues are now working in the state, that has been an advantage. We have here three people who previously worked in UNHCR and HIAS, another who worked in IOM . . . so we have people who come from these organizations who are now able to push [for a strong governance network on migration and human rights]."[17]

Nonstate Actors and Governance Networks

Given the role of social and political invisibility expectations discussed in chapter 2 in impeding migrants from building relationships with Ecuadorians and seeking out sources of support and protection in visible ways, the survey data in this chapter provide useful evidence to show the relationship between a migrant's experiences, attitudes, capabilities, and connectedness to the governance network. In particular, since the default option under the invisibility bargain is maintaining a low profile and withdrawing from social spaces in order to avoid negative social and political sanctions, migrants tend to reach out and seek help from institutions when they have experienced a negative event that spurs them to disrupt the status quo, and when they have the education and confidence to understand the possibilities of help that these institutions can offer. In order to test this argument, I calculated the average number of organizations that migrants reported receiving help from (disaggregating by state and nonstate institutions), as well as the average number of *types* of assistance that they received (i.e., help finding a job, legal/documentary assistance, money, emotional support, protection/security, etc.). I then ran ANOVA tests to measure the significance of any correlations between these measures of connectedness to the governance network and a range of personal experiences and attributes.

[17] Interview 31DS 2015.

Both the average number of organizations and the average number of types of assistance were negatively and highly significantly correlated with self-reported perceptions of security in the neighborhood where the respondent lived, as illustrated in Table 4.4. In other words, those who felt totally secure where they lived were connected to fewer organizations and received fewer types of assistance than those who felt safe most of the time, some of the time, or who felt unsafe. Given the fears of institutional sources of authority and the dominant coping strategy of invisibility and isolation, these results suggest that specific experiences of violent victimization or discrimination were more likely to motivate migrants to contact institutional sources of protection. Interestingly, feeling insecure was very significantly correlated with the number of *nonstate* institutions from which a respondent received help, but the number of *state* institutions was not correlated at all. This indicates that migrants were more likely to seek out the governance network when they felt unsafe, but to do so by approaching nonstate organizations as their entry point.

Both number of organizations and type of assistance were highly correlated with victimization as well, with migrants who had been the victim of violent crime since coming to Ecuador reporting a larger number of organizations and more types of assistance that they had received. Those who had been the victim of violent crime reported receiving an average of 2.38 forms of assistance from an average 1.72 organizations, compared to 1.82 forms of help from 1.47 organizations for those who had not been a victim. These are both highly significant correlations. Here the number of both state and nonstate institutions was significantly correlated with victimization, although nonstate organizations had a higher level of significance. This suggests that physical protection needs are fundamental enough that migrants do still seek out state assistance, despite their fears and distrust. This pattern

Table 4.4 Security compared to organizational connections

	# organizations		# types of assistance	
	Yes	No	Yes	No
Do you feel secure?	1.37***	1.74***	1.69***	2.32***
Have you been victim of violent crime?	1.72**	1.47**	2.38***	1.82***
Have you experienced discrimination?	1.63***	1.38***	2.17***	1.66***

Source: MNS 2016. Note: ***p<0.01, **p<0.05.

can be compared to the correlation between number of organizations and types of assistance and whether or not respondents had felt discriminated against since coming to Ecuador. Here again, those who had felt discriminated against sought out a larger average number of organizations and more types of assistance than those who had not felt discrimination, but in this case, only the number of *nonstate* organizations was significantly correlated with discrimination, not the number of state institutions. One interpretation is that, compared with experiencing violent crime, discrimination was not an existential enough threat to push migrants out of the shadows to claim state protection, and they simply bore the discrimination or sought social support from nonstate organizations.

In an interesting illustration of the importance of social proximity and community diversity for migrants' access to the governance network, the data suggest that Colombian migrants who lived in neighborhoods composed primarily of other Colombians received fewer types of help (1.64 for Colombian neighborhoods, 1.89 for mixed, and 2.13 for Ecuadorian neighborhoods), and from fewer *nonstate* organizations (1.01 for Colombian neighborhoods), than those who lived in mixed communities (1.09) or those composed primarily of Ecuadorians (1.28). The correlation between neighborhood composition and number of *state* institutions providing help was not significant. This suggests that being immersed with Ecuadorian neighbors, friends, and organizations expands the number and type of access points through which Colombians can find protection and assistance more than when one's network is primarily made of other migrants, and that this networked access works mostly through nonstate actors rather than state ones.

Access to the governance network, and to social ties that could facilitate assistance and protection, was greatly influenced by legal status; although the invisibility bargain applies to migrants of all types, the vulnerability, exclusion, and risks that they experienced were greater for those without full legal documentation. In the MNS, migrants whose presence is authorized with legal documentation (either refugee status, a different visa, or as an asylum seeker) received more types of help from more organizations than those without documentation. Their residence patterns reinforced their isolation; those with documentation were significantly more likely to live in neighborhoods with mostly Ecuadorians, while undocumented respondents were much more likely to live in neighborhoods with mostly Colombians. Expectations of the future were also different for the two groups, with undocumented respondents significantly more likely to expect that they would still be in Ecuador or return to Colombia within the next five years, while those with documentation were more likely to expect that they would resettle in a third country. Interestingly, in a counterintuitive finding, respondents with documentation were significantly more likely to report having experienced discrimination, being the victim of violent crime, and having less positive perceptions of Ecuadorians compared to undocumented respondents. This could perhaps be an indication of these migrants' greater exposure to society, combined with undocumented migrants' greater incentives for responses reflecting social desirability bias.

Education was a very important factor influencing the number of organizations with which migrants were connected. As illustrated in Figure 4.6, the higher the educational level, the more connected the respondent tended to be. This finding has important implications for policymakers and program designers developing interventions to increase the protection and access to the governance network for Colombian migrants in Ecuador: education, both formal and informal, makes it more likely that migrants know their rights and know how to pursue them.

In addition to Colombian migrant attitudes and experiences, it is also important to measure the impact of intergroup relationships, connectedness, and interaction on the attitudes and experiences of Ecuadorians. Given the limitations of available data, I compare Ecuadorians in border provinces versus those living in inland provinces as a rough proxy for those with more

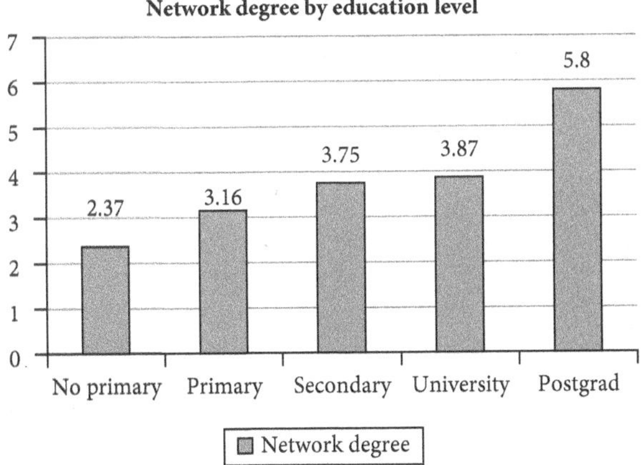

Figure 4.6 Education level compared with average number of organizational connections
Source: MNS 2016.

or less interaction and experience with Colombian migrants. Migrants and Ecuadorians have higher levels of interaction in the border provinces than in more inland localities, most of which have lower concentrations of migrants and less frequent migratory flows. In Zepeda and Carrion's (2015) national survey, Ecuadorian respondents who lived in the border zone differed from the respondents who lived elsewhere in the country in both their frequency of interaction and their attitudes toward migrants. Compared with 33% of Ecuadorians who lived elsewhere, 40% of border residents reported that they had one or more relationships with foreigners living in Ecuador. When asked their general opinion of foreigners living in Ecuador, 65% of respondents who lived in border provinces reported a "very good" perception, while only 49% of respondents living inland shared the same "very good" assessment. Forty-seven percent of border residents surveyed believed that there were too many foreigners living in Ecuador, compared with 58% of respondents living in inland provinces. The influence of border proximity (and by extension greater interaction and experience with migrants) seems to have a stronger effect on economic threat measures than on cultural threat or realistic group threat. While there was a nineteen-point difference in the level of strong agreement that foreigners contribute to the Ecuadorian economy between residents of the border region versus other localities (61% vs. 42%, respectively), there was only a four-point difference between border and inland residents in their strong agreement that foreigners generate insecurity, and no difference in their level of agreement that foreigners weaken the traditions and customs of Ecuador (Zepeda and Carrion 2015). These findings provide additional evidence that the social networks that connect migrants and Ecuadorians and promote better intergroup relations work in both directions—on Ecuadorians as well as Colombians.

Institutional Governance Networks Compared
across Localities

Scaling up from the individual networks through which migrants received help, I also used their responses to construct a visualization of the organizational networks in each locality, assuming that when two organizations shared the same beneficiaries, this could serve as a proxy indicator of a coordination tie between those two organizations, and that the number of shared beneficiaries could serve as a proxy for the strength of that tie. The MNS asked migrant respondents to list in open-form blanks any organizations or institutions from which they had received help since coming to Ecuador. The square nodes in the sociograms in Figures 4.7–4.12 represent these organizations, which could be local or national state agencies, international organizations, NGOs, or informal groups like Ecuadorian or Colombian friends. The edges (lines) connecting two nodes represent that the two organizations helped the same migrant, which is the measure of institutional linkage. The thickness of the edge connecting two organizations reflects the strength of the tie, in the form of the number of migrant beneficiaries whom they have in common. The different localities vary in the number of organizations actively reported to be part of the governance network by the migrants they serve; the density of the linkages that connect these organizations with each other; the extent to which these networks are distributed versus revolving around a few central actors; and the diversity of the types of organizations that are active in the network—whether state, nonstate, IGOs, or informal groups. Figures 4.7–4.12 provide graphical representations of the migration governance network structure in the six study cities, and Table 4.5 summarizes some of the key indicators of human security for each city. The variation in these governance network structures will then be analyzed throughout the following section.

Controlled Comparisons: Host-Migrant Relations and Outcomes for Human Security and Peace

Building on the process analysis in the previous section, which showed *how* governance networks can link migrants with access to resources, rights, mutual understanding with Ecuadorians, and physical protection at an individual level, systematic data comparing different cities suggest that there may be a relationship between the density and diversity of the governance network and the degree of migrant human security produced at the city level. Lago Agrio, the smallest of the cities and one of the three that lies on the border with Colombia, has the densest network, with a diverse mixture of state agencies, international organizations, NGOs, and informal groups tightly linked with each other. In this city, most of these organizations are also geographically close, within walking distance of each other in the main downtown area. The interinstitutional migration coordinating body (*mesa de movilidad*) brings together many of these organizations on a weekly or

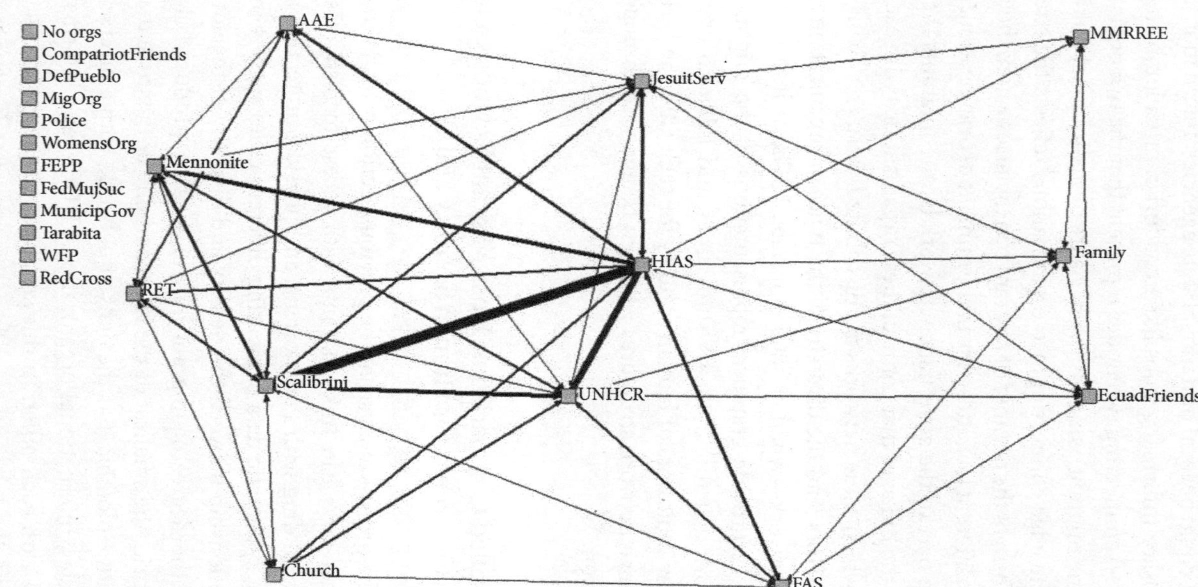

Figure 4.7   Quito governance network structure

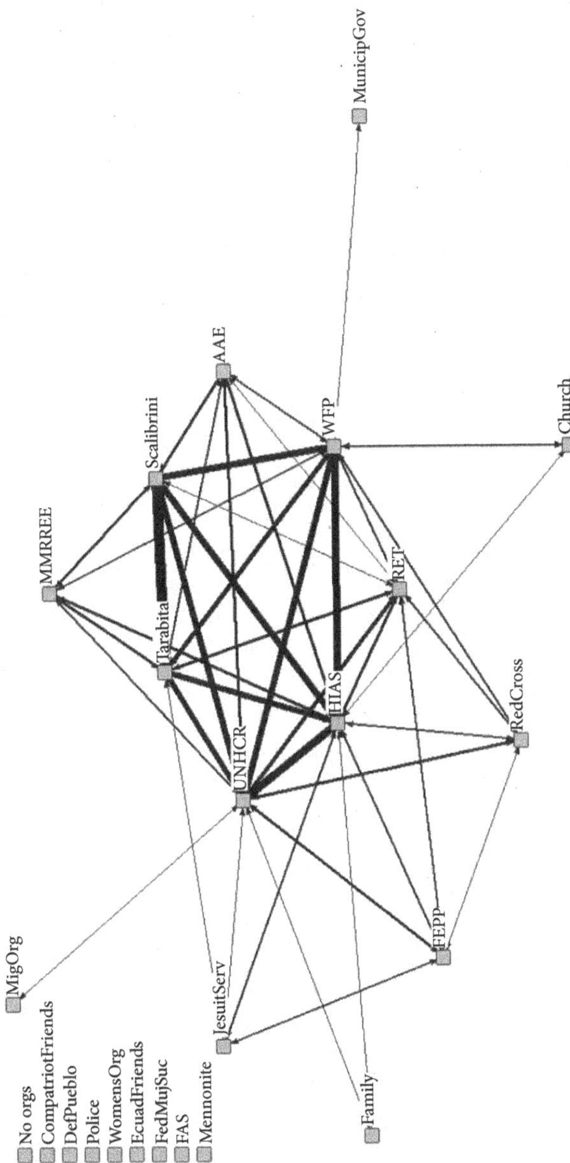

Figure 4.8 Lago Agrio governance network structure

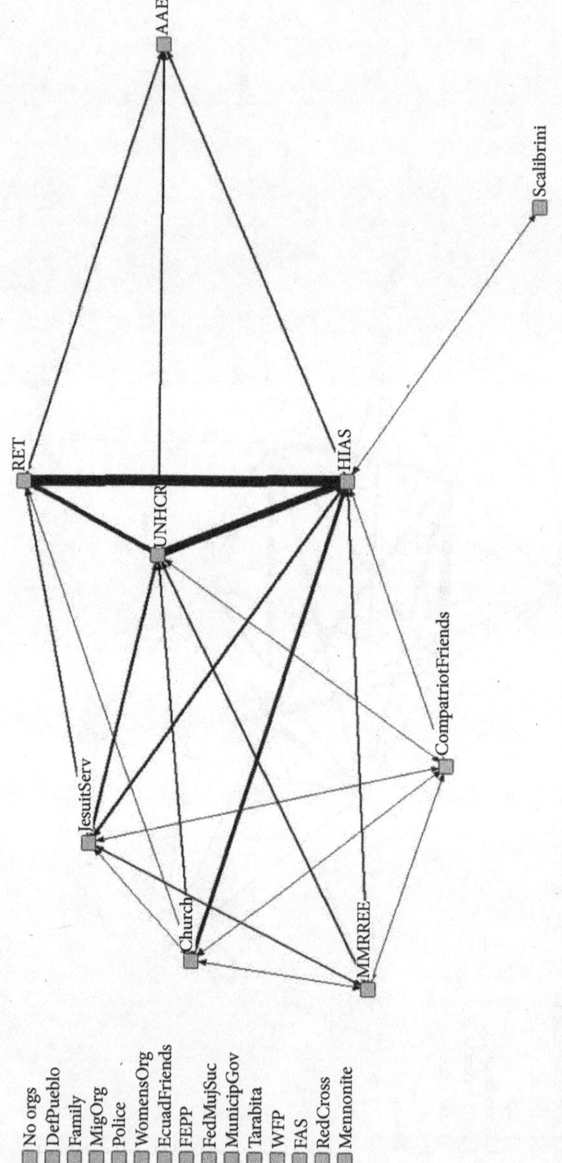

Figure 4.9 Esmeraldas governance network structure

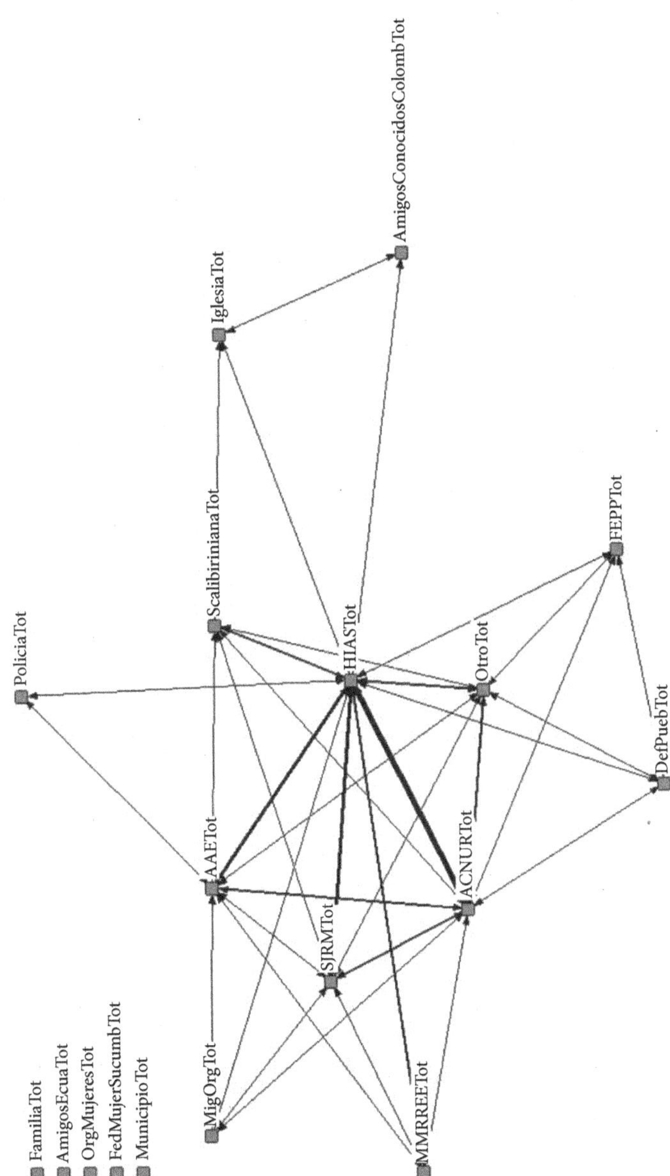

Figure 4.10 Santo Domingo governance network structure

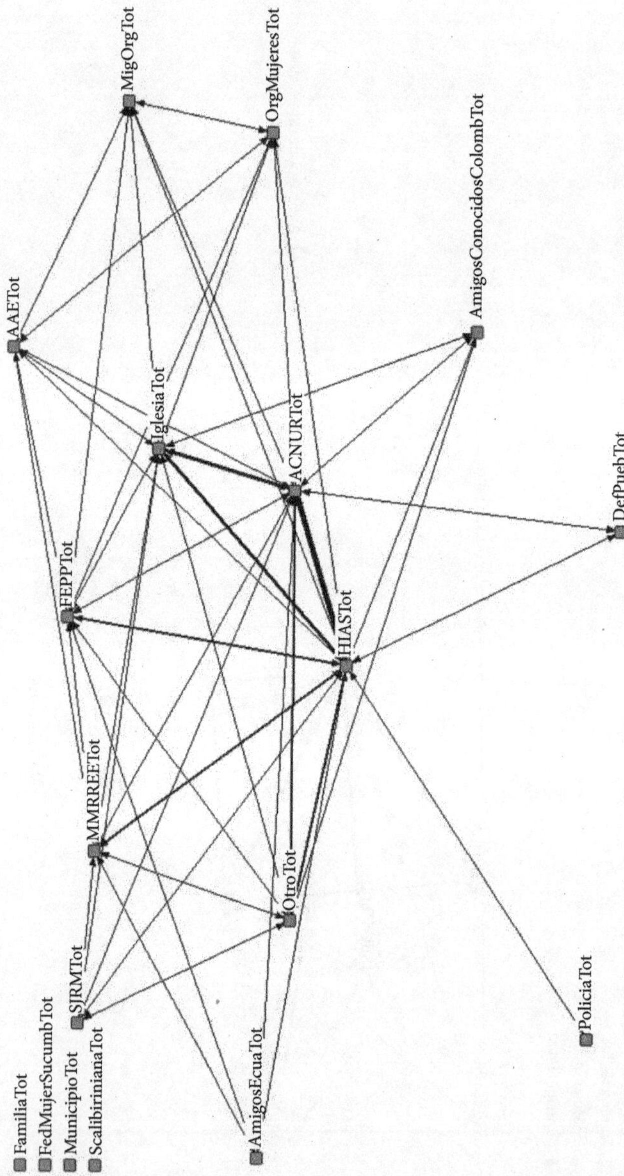

Figure 4.11　Ibarra governance network structure

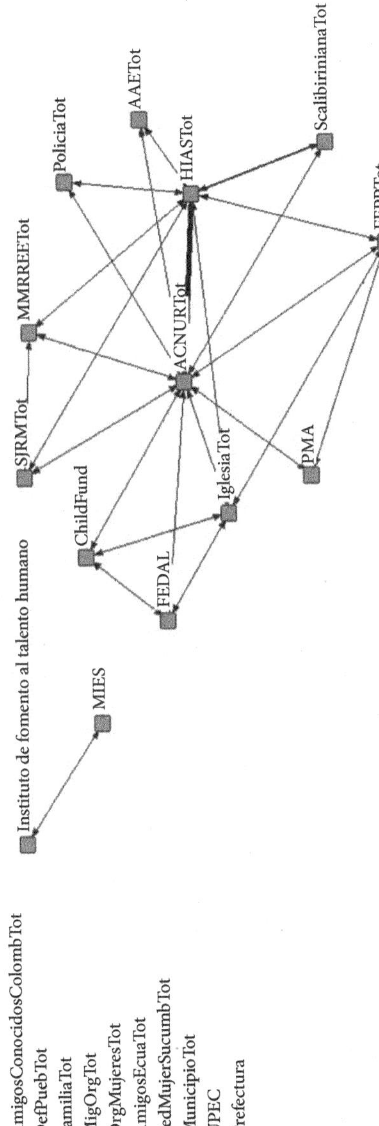

Figure 4.12 Tulcán/Carchi governance network structure

monthly basis to meet and define common goals and strategies, and to coordinate on specific cases. Quito, Ibarra, and to a lesser extent Santo Domingo all have larger, but less dense networks. Compared to the other two, Quito's network is less diverse and more poorly integrated in its linkages between state and nonstate actors. Esmeraldas in particular, and to some extent Santo Domingo, represents a governance network that is not very dense, and one that is centered mostly around the UNHCR and its implementing partners, such as the Hebrew Immigrant Aid Society (HIAS).[18] Tulcán shows a more fragmented network, and with greater presence of state institutions.

Conventional approaches to international development assistance, peacebuilding, and migration would predict that locations that had greater economic development and more institutional state presence would likely be characterized by higher levels of human security and peace experienced by migrants. The preceding comparison suggests that this explanation is not persuasive in understanding how migrants in these cities of Ecuador access protection and improve their livelihood. Quito is by far the wealthiest city and the one with the lowest levels of unsatisfied basic needs, according to Table 4.1 and Table 4.5. As the capital city, it certainly has the highest concentration of state agencies and institutions of any of the cities being compared. Lago Agrio, on the other hand, has the highest level of economic deprivation, with 87% of the population suffering from unsatisfied basic needs. Historically, it has been relatively neglected with a weak state presence, especially any agencies other than security forces. However, migrants in Quito reported experiencing the highest level of discrimination of any of the cities, at 83%, whereas migrants in Lago Agrio experienced the lowest level, at 60%. Likewise, migrants in Lago Agrio had the most favorable perceptions of Ecuadorians, with 68% having a generally positive view, compared with only 38% of migrants in Quito who had a positive view of Ecuadorians.

Both of these indicators suggest that social conflict among migrants and the host population is more intense in Quito than in Lago Agrio, and that migrants in the border town are more satisfied with their social environment than in the capital city. In addition to visual differences detected when comparing the sociograms for Quito and Lago Agrio, the comparison in network degree, or average number of institutional connections reported by migrants in the two locations, also provides useful insights. Migrants in Quito reported the lowest average number of connections to the governance

---

[18] Interview 36EN 2013; Interview 31DS 2015.

Table 4.5 Average human security outcomes and connectivity for migrants, by city

		Quito	Esmeraldas	Lago Agrio	Ibarra	Santo Domingo
Rights	Discrimination	83%	71%	60%	76%	73%
Resources	Migrants earning < $2/day	45%	61%	70%	46%	34%
Recognition	Positive view of Ecuadorian people	38%	64%	68%	65%	54%
Protection	Violence victim	37%	35%	24%	41%	40%
Context: overall 2012 homicide rate for city	Homicides per 100,000	4.3	27.3	37.3	9.4	18.9
Network degree	Avg. # institutional aid connections	1.46	2.06	2.35	1.99	2.07

Source: MNS 2016; homicide data from National Police of Ecuador.

network (1.46 average ties), while migrants in Lago Agrio reported the highest number (2.35 average ties). Lago Agrio, as a smaller city with a tradition of Colombians crossing across the border and with binational social and family networks creating a strong social fabric, has a governance network with better-coordinated and more diverse types of access points that are available to Colombians and Ecuadorians seeking to improve their security, livelihoods, and peaceful coexistence.

As an additional piece of evidence that access to governance networks is an important factor in the economic as well as the personal security of migrants, one can compare the economic development of the provinces where the six localities are located with the network connectedness of migrant respondents. Tables 4.1 and 4.5 show that Quito, Ibarra, and Tulcán are located in provinces with lower unsatisfied basic needs (i.e., they are richer), while Lago Agrio, Esmeraldas, and Santo Domingo are in poorer provinces. Likewise, migrants in Quito, Ibarra, and Tulcán had fewer ties to migrant-serving organizations than those in the three poorer provinces. This illustrates the degree to which social capital serves a real economic livelihood function for migrants.

Conclusion

This chapter has introduced the empirical context and key subnational variations among the six provinces in the northern border region of Ecuador where the study examined the experience of Colombian migrants. It then laid out evidence from the survey data to examine the ways that migrants use access to governance networks to improve their livelihoods, ability to realize rights, and achieve protection, and to lower the barriers that violation of the invisibility bargain's expectations might raise. To summarize the evidence presented in the preceding pages, migrants who are more vulnerable tend to seek out more sources and more types of institutional help, especially from nongovernmental organizations. Those who are more visibly/audibly different, however, are more likely to use social isolation and invisibility as a coping and survival mechanism to avoid backlash under the invisibility bargain (even though such isolation likely increases their vulnerability and deprives them of access to rights and resources that may help them). Those localities in which migrant-serving organizations are more densely networked, and in which there are good working relations among a diverse range of organizational types (state, nonstate, and IGO actors) seem to be associated with better human security outcomes than those localities where there are sparse networks oriented around a few organizations. This phenomenon is quite independent of the economic development level of the locality in question.

In the next chapter, I introduce the three major sets of institutional actors that shape the migration governance network at a national level: the state, the United Nations system, and the Catholic Church. I explain the involvement of these actors in influencing the governance and experience of migrants in Ecuador and trace the evolution of their involvement and relationship with each other over time. Highlighting differences between state and nonstate actors, this chapter provides a nuanced and dynamic institutional analysis that uncovers the inner workings of the Ecuadorian governance network and how institutional and relational factors enhance or degrade migrant human security.

5

Evolution of the Central Actors in the Governance Network

The State, the UN, and the Church

The three most influential institutions in Ecuador dealing with migration and especially refugee protection at a national level are the Ecuadorian state (particularly the Ministry of Foreign Relations and the police), the United Nations system (particularly the UNHCR), and the Catholic Church, including a number of faith-based Catholic NGOs like the Jesuit Refugee Service, Fondo Ecuatoriano Popularum Progressio (FEPP), and Catholic Relief Services.[1] This chapter introduces and compares these three sets of institutions and their role in providing protection and shaping the governance of migration in Ecuador. I argue that differences in mission, capacity, and geographic presence historically led to an inversion of "practical authority" in which, outside of the two major cities of Ecuador, nonstate actors often had greater legitimacy, trust, and effectiveness than the state in providing services that Ecuadorians and migrants needed to improve their lives. This inversion was challenged during the era of Rafael Correa, who sought to increase the role of the state, both its level of social control and its primacy as the strategist and provider of public goods. Tracing the ways in which authority is shared, divided, and contested among state, nonstate, and international organizations with distinct types of legitimacy over time illuminates the contours of sovereignty as an empirical practice, and the "micro-manifestations of sovereignty"[2] that show how human security is constructed in practice. This chapter shows that nonstate actors and

---

[1] As described in the previous chapter of subnational comparisons, illicit armed actors such as FARC and criminal bands, as well as the indigenous movement, are also very important and influential actors that shape the possibilities and experience of migration within particular territories— illicit armed actors most notably in the immediate northern border provinces of Esmeraldas and Sucumbíos, and the indigenous movement most strongly in Imbabura province and the Amazon (including the border regions of the Amazon).

[2] I am grateful to Margaret Keck for suggesting this term to describe what I was thinking about.

The Invisibility Bargain. Jeffrey D. Pugh, Oxford University Press (2021). © Oxford University Press.
DOI: 10.1093/oso/9780197538692.003.0005

international organizations performing state-like security functions some-times challenge the authority of the state, but that often the state willingly cooperates or cedes such functions, borrowing the "practical authority" of the nonstate actor to shore up the legitimacy of its own actions, or to navigate tricky political incentives that complicate acting alone.

The United Nations High Commission on Refugees entered Ecuador in 2000 at the invitation of the government to help figure out a solution to the "Colombian problem" and to bring technical expertise from other parts of the world in dealing with refugee flows to help support the Ecuadorian state, which was overwhelmed and lacking in capacity to deal with the sudden spike in Colombians seeking asylum. In these early years, state functions of refugee registration, asylum claim interviews and investigations, and recommendations on eligibility for asylum were all performed either by UNHCR directly, by NGOs that were UNHCR implementing partners, or even by state officials in the Ministry of Foreign Relations that were being paid through an NGO contract using UNHCR funds.[3] Because of this "state-like" role exercising significant autonomy and authority, UNHCR was seen by many refugees as virtually synonymous with the state (Rivera et al. 2007), and like the police and courts, suffered from a level of suspicion and distrust especially from those Colombians who knew people who had been denied refugee status.[4] As the Ecuadorian government increased its capacity to manage the refugee process, especially after the Correa government invested more political capital and economic resources in the issue, most of these functions were transferred to the state, and UNHCR played more of an advo-cacy and technical assistance role.

One can think of the relationships among the state, UN, and the church as distinct (and sometimes competing) poles of authority that may operate together or separately in order to influence the behaviors of people as well as their beliefs about what they should do. Each authority pole may coop-erate with the others if it believes this will allow it to achieve its institutional goals and mission through complementary division of labor, pooling re-sources, building a stronger coalition of allies, or for some other reason. It may also cooperate, or at least use language to appear cooperative, in order to reinforce acceptance of its proper institutional role according to legal hier-archies. In particular, international organization agencies like UNDP or the

---

[3] Interviews 141QS 2017 and 145QS 2018 with two former Ecuadorian government officials.
[4] Interviews 126QN 2010; 102QM 2009; 41EN 2013.

World Food Program operate in Ecuador at the invitation of the Ecuadorian government, so they consider it important to emphasize their subordinate/supporting role, and that they are not competing with the authority of the state to change the behavior of people in opposition to state goals. Alternatively, the UNHCR derives its mandate from an international treaty, and the church from a shared belief in God, so these organizations may be less hesitant to offer a competing interpretation of shared norms, or to push for action that is different from what the state is calling for, since their presence does not depend as totally on the state's programmatic guidance.[5]

As the state began to develop greater capacity and stronger controls under President Correa, one notable change was its increased tendency to stifle dissenting or competing NGO voices by revoking the ministerial agreements that recognized and registered their organizations as nonprofit organizations (*fundaciones*) in Ecuador (Lalander and Ospina 2012; Cherrez 2012). It did this in several high-profile cases with environmental and indigenous NGOs (Lewis 2016; Picq 2016). This illustrates that greater capacity and authority for the state may sometimes lead to a more aggressive assertion of state institutional predominance, whereas weaker state presence may lead to its greater acceptance or even encouragement of complementary nonstate institutional sources of "practical authority" in issue areas like migration. Thinking of these three sets of institutions as distinct poles of authority that negotiate the way governance happens will help to structure the analysis in this chapter.

Emergence of Institutional Authority via Primary Actors of the Governance Network

The legacy of regionalism in Ecuador's early years of political development led to Ecuador's politics often being torn between the competing population centers of Quito in the Sierra and Guayaquil on the coast. A strong cohesive national identity and effective national governmental institutions suffered from the greater salience of city/regional identities and political loyalties defined by clientelistic patronage networks and regional caudillos and power brokers, often based on hacienda owners' spheres of influence (Hurtado 1977). As a result, most of the state institutions at the national level are concentrated in Quito, and historically, the provinces outside the major

---

[5] Interview 91QI 2008.

population centers were left to fend for themselves. A relative absence of the state in many of the other provinces left a void that was filled by various non-state and informal institutions.[6] In the northern border region, the military was the primary state institution with a visible presence, but under a national security mission, it was focused primarily on controlling the flow of illicit goods and illegal armed actors through checkpoints and patrols (Jaskoski 2015).[7]

Catholic missions planted by the Salesians, the Carmelites, and other orders were often the primary providers of educational and health services, and churches provided an organizing social institution for smaller communities (Navas et al. 2004). In indigenous areas of the northern Sierra and the Amazonian jungle, consensus-based communal governance, local control over public goods like water, and institutions of reciprocal support that had been in place since before the influx of the Incas provided the "practical authority" to ensure mutual protection and to organize politically when necessary to pressure local and national governments, according to several indigenous community leaders.[8] For example, in order to accomplish community road repairs, build a neighborhood soccer court, or help a particular family build a shelter for their animals, indigenous leaders would call a *minga*, or community workday, in which everyone would come and help accomplish the collective goal, then celebrate with a collective meal afterward. Community members were bound by reciprocal expectations to attend each other's *mingas*, and would face social isolation if they did not, as an indigenous leader in Imbabura province explained.[9]

Beginning in the 1960s with the influence of Vatican II and liberation theology, Catholic missionaries in the Amazon and the Sierra began helping indigenous communities organize, sought to increase literacy and educational levels in these communities, and evangelized (Becker 2019).[10] The efforts of the church as well as these indigenous federations led the way for a politically active, well-organized civil society in Ecuador that had a major influence on social policies and services, as well as on political leadership in Ecuador, particularly from the 1990s on (Gerlach 2003; Martinez Novo 2004).

---

[6] Interviews 81QI 2010; 164QN 2007.
[7] Interview 26CS 2017.
[8] Interviews 165QN 2012; 70IN 2007; 71IN 2012.
[9] Interview 70IN 2007.
[10] Interview 165 QN 2012.

International organizations were a much more distant source of political authority that affected the lives of Ecuadorians primarily through conditional loans from the IMF and World Bank that incentivized governments to reduce social spending and pursue privatization schemes. IGOs also supported NGOs and direct provision of microcredit or other projects through development assistance from UNDP and others. The United Nations system operated to coordinate Ecuador's foreign policy goals with those of other countries in the world, and provide a forum for negotiating agreements at the international level, but prior to 2000, their role as a subnational political actor in Ecuador was fairly limited, and consisted mostly of technical assistance and coordination of development aid.

These three clusters of institutions—the state, the Catholic Church, and the United Nations system—represent the three primary actors in the national Ecuadorian governance network. All three have sometimes blurred the line between state and nonstate authority in the provision of services and security in Ecuadorian territory. After summarizing the institutional dynamics of each cluster, the chapter will trace the ways in which they interact with each other and reproduce formal and informal authority to influence who is protected, how, and in what ways. Comparisons of the institutions' levels of trust, missions/mandates, and capacity help to illuminate why and how they employ various forms of Keck and Sikkink's (1998) transnational political strategies to advance their institutional goals with respect to the reception of migrants and refugees in Ecuador. The chapter will also briefly examine two additional sets of actors whose impact on migration experiences, participation, and security is also significant, but mostly concentrated in specific geographic territories: illicit violent actors (especially in Sucumbíos and Esmeraldas on the border) and indigenous groups (especially in Imbabura province and the Amazon jungle). In understanding the governance networks that provide (or impede) access to protection in these specific localities, it is important to understand these groups, even though their influence on migration and refugee policy and experiences is not as consistent at a national level as the three clusters discussed before.

Ecuadorian State

In the period of 2000–2006, the state had a relatively light presence in the border provinces, where many Colombian migrants were concentrated, consisting mostly of military patrols and checkpoints, and poorly funded local governments. The only place that asylum seekers could apply for refugee status was in Quito at the Foreign Ministry, which created enormous problems for Colombians crossing the border. The Rumichaca bridge between Ipiales and Tulcán was five to six hours away from Quito by bus along the Pan-American Highway under the best of circumstances, not counting the additional challenges of those crossing at a more remote part of the border in the Amazon or coastal regions. Many Colombians arriving in Ecuador after fleeing violence had no knowledge of the asylum process, little understanding of their own rights, few institutional connections to orient them, and little money to travel to Quito, much less support themselves there while waiting for the status determination process to play out. This could take from three months to over a year, in which time they were legally prohibited from working (Schussler 2009).

Because of the weak institutional presence of the state in the border regions where many forced migrants lived, gaps in service provision for refugees increased after the year 2000. These gaps, combined with the dramatically escalating flow of Colombians (an increase of 8,400% in the number of recognized refugees from 2000 to 2007),[11] highlighted the need for alternative actors that could address political as well as humanitarian needs, and which had enough authority and legitimacy to interact on a high level with the state. In particular, the determination of which migrants would be recognized with refugee status, and under Ecuador's obligations in the 1951 Refugee Convention provided with protection, was the responsibility of the state and one that held thousands of people's lives in the balance, but the Ecuadorian state's institutions were overwhelmed and incapable of dealing effectively with the scale of the influx during this initial phase (Rovayo and Colem 2007; Poe and Isaacson 2009).

As the state responded by issuing asylum seekers refugee status using the overwhelmed processes that they developed in the face of the spike, intelligence reports warned that some of the Colombians who had been issued refugee status actually included agents and members of FARC and other illegal armed groups, making the security sector suspicious of the refugee population.[12] The state under President Lucio Gutierrez responded to these

---

[11] "Situación del refugio en el Ecuador," Conference presentation given by the Refugee Office of the Directorate of Human Rights, Social and Environmental Affairs, Ministry of Foreign Relations, Quito, Ecuador, May 29, 2007.

[12] Interview 145QS 2017.

reports by imposing a visa requirement for entering Colombians as well as a police record, a move that was supported by some local politicians, including Carchi prefect René Yandún Pozo.[13] Both of these restrictions implied bureaucratic processes in Colombia that were difficult for asylum seekers to complete when they were fleeing for their lives, and the policy change was criticized by human rights organizations (González 2008).[14] As a result of this change, the number of asylum claims dropped dramatically after 2004 compared to 2003, although thousands of Colombians continued coming into Ecuador in search of safety.

Between 2007 and 2012, the geographic presence of the state in refugee-receiving parts of the border expanded, and the Foreign Ministry opened field offices to register asylum seekers and conduct interviews in Tulcán, Ibarra, Esmeraldas, and Lago Agrio. The transition from the previous state development institution, the Unit for Northern Border Region Development, to Plan Ecuador under President Correa also brought about greater state cooperation and attention to integrating development and security strategies in these communities, with at least some increase in state spending. According to the Ecuadorian military, the Ecuadorian side of the border received a much greater investment of state control and infrastructure than previously, and greater than the border zone on the Colombian side.[15] Indeed, public sector investment in the border zone increased more than fourfold between 2008 and 2014, dropping somewhat after this as oil prices plummeted (see Figure 5.1).

In terms of national security investment, Ecuador had deployed an estimated ten thousand ground forces in the border region by the early 2010s to monitor and control the security impact of the Colombian conflict (Ponton 2016: 51), especially after the breakdown of trust with Colombia's military and government following the Angostura bombing in 2008. Despite the decimation of FARC leadership and the dramatic reduction in FARC membership under Colombian president Alvaro Uribe's hardline policies, and the signing of a peace agreement with FARC in 2016, security threats remained prevalent throughout the border region on the Colombian side, where the Ecuadorian defense ministry

[13] Interview 145QS 2017. See also "El prefecto," *El Universo* (September 4, 2004). Online at https://www.eluniverso.com/2004/09/04/0001/8/D7FB67BDC4A9458CB140DA365A839BD5.html.

[14] Interview 110QN 2007.

[15] Interview 26CS 2017.

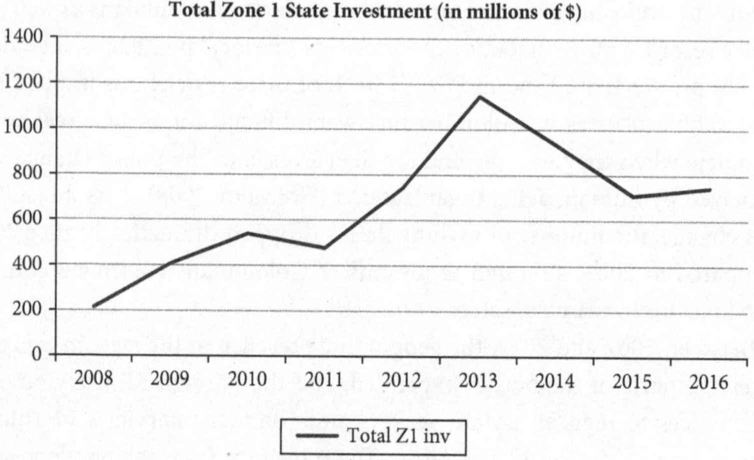

Figure 5.1 State investment in Zone 1 (northern border region)
Source: Ponton 2016: 80.

estimated that there were still active dissident guerrilla remnant groups, among other illegal armed actors (Ponton 2016: 49). The signing of the peace agreement in 2016 seemed actually to multiply the threats in the northern border region due to a fragmentation and proliferation of illegal actors in the power vacuum left by FARC (Ponton 2016; Idler 2019; Pugh et al. 2020).

This mirrored a national trend under Correa of geographically dispersed government presence and focusing significantly larger portions of the national budget on social spending for the poor and infrastructure in provinces that had often been neglected in previous administrations, funded largely through windfall oil profits and increased taxation. Correa's "Citizen's Revolution" resulted in a dramatic expansion of the state across the board. According to John Polga-Hecimovich (2020), the number of civil servants in Ecuador more than doubled between 2003 and 2011, from 230,185 to 510,430, while public sector salaries more than tripled between 2006 and 2014. To underline the importance of scale (and the potential that such a large bureaucratic apparatus provided to Correa for controlling political narratives and mobilizing significant numbers of people for public performative affirmation of his populist program), these half million well-paid civil servants represented more than 5% of the entire working-age population of Ecuador at the time of the 2010 census.

UN System/UNHCR

In 2000, the UNHCR set up an office in Quito to help strengthen the government's capacity to deal with the sudden escalation of Colombian asylum seekers. It soon became clear, however, that a more systematic response was needed. Accordingly, the government of Lucio Gutiérrez in 2003 asked UN secretary-general Kofi Annan to help do something about the "Colombian problem," which the state viewed largely through the lens of a national security challenge. After Annan visited Ecuador, the UN sent an interagency assessment team at the invitation of the government to evaluate the situation on the northern border with Colombia and to provide recommendations. Following this assessment, UN agencies, including UNHCR, UNDP, and others, expanded their assistance to the government and the scope of projects in the country, including scaling up local integration initiatives in the border zones.[16]

In 2006, UNHCR commissioned a comprehensive study of refugee populations throughout the country and found that many Colombians in need of protection had not accessed the asylum system and were living in isolated communities along the border (Bilsborrow 2006). In order to develop and leverage its comparative advantage of geographic presence and capacity in the far-flung regions where many forced migrants actually lived, UNHCR adopted a decentralized operational structure. UNHCR created field offices in Lago Agrio (Sucumbíos province) and Ibarra (Imbabura province), with later expansions creating a permanent field presence in the cities of Cuenca (Azuay province), Santo Domingo (Santo Domingo province), and Esmeraldas (Esmeraldas province).

UNHCR decentralized earlier than the state; after establishing offices in the UN national headquarters building in Quito in 2000, it began carrying out mobile registration clinics over the subsequent years, often in partnership with existing NGOs and the church, which had a presence in the border provinces. UNHCR had established field offices in Lago Agrio in 2000 and Ibarra (Ortega 2007) in October 2001 (the state opened refugee offices in these cities in 2008), and by 2012 had seven field offices/presences throughout the country. Figure 5.2 illustrates the growth in decentralized geographic presence through UNHCR field offices over time.

---

[16] United Nations, "Interagency Assessment of Ecuador's Northern Border Region: Summary," United Nations presentation document, Quito, Ecuador, September 2004.

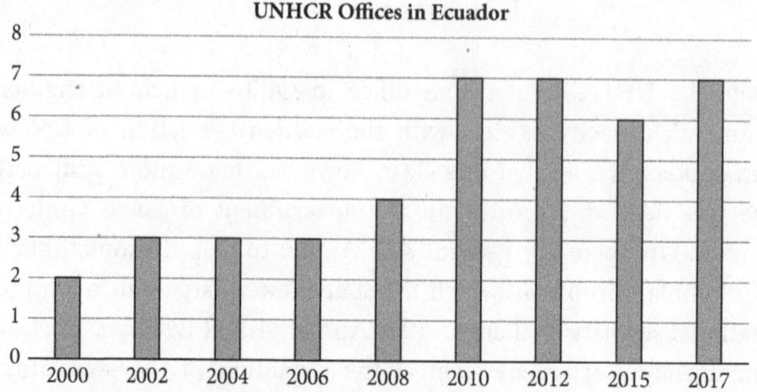

Figure 5.2 UNHCR offices and personnel in Ecuador over time
Source: Compiled by author from UNHCR annual reports.

The strategy of geographic decentralization was necessary in part because Colombian forced migrants often had friends, relatives, or other contacts already living in Ecuador with whom they could initially stay, and very few were interested in staying in temporary camps. This preference also stemmed from the fact that the flow from Colombia tended to be steady rather than one massive wave, and from the stigma and distrust of temporary shelters and camps, which Colombians feared might increase their visibility and expose them to infiltrating agents of the Colombian illegal armed groups.[17] UNHCR did initially set up tents in camps when it first arrived in Ecuador, following the practice adapted from other regions, according to a human rights ombudsman and former NGO activist with deep experience in migration. However, UNHCR soon learned that this strategy did not work in Ecuador because, as I have mentioned, Colombians often distrusted high-visibility camps and shelters that could be identified by insurgent agents and because Colombians often had friends or relatives in Ecuador who could help them find a place to stay temporarily (Poe and Isaacson 2009). In response to this learning process, UNHCR eventually adapted to a community-based approach in refugee-receiving areas and geographic decentralization of refugee attention offices.[18]

In addition to its geographical expansion, UNHCR also underwent a significant increase in budgetary scope and personnel. Figure 5.3 shows the

[17] Interview 56IN 2007.
[18] Interview 143QS 2009.

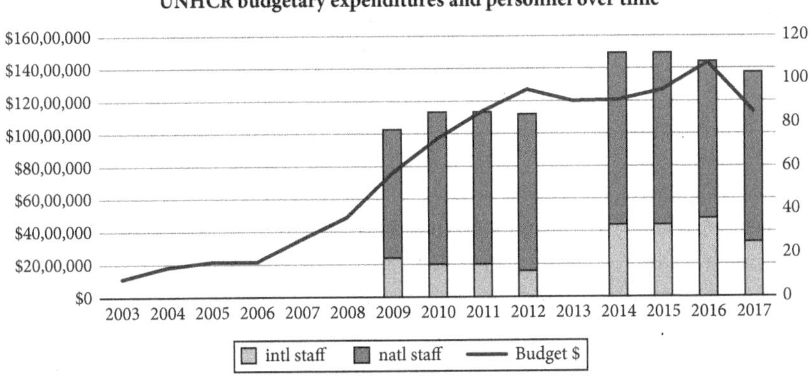

Figure 5.3 UNHCR's expenditures and personnel in Ecuador, 2003–2017
Source: Compiled by author from UNHCR annual reports.

increase in UNHCR expenditures in Ecuador in response to continued flows of Colombian refugees and state incapacity. The budget increased more than tenfold, from just over $1 million in 2003 to more than $12 million in 2012 before plateauing during the "regression" phase in which the state took more of the lead. It is worth observing that Ecuadorian nationals make up the vast majority of the UNHCR payroll, which increases local capacity, as these staff members may in the future move into government or national NGO roles, which did take place, according to my interviews.

In the early years of its operations after establishing offices in Ecuador, UNHCR focused most of its assistance, services, and programs on officially recognized refugees or asylum seekers who were applying for this status. Over time, the organization realized through observation and reports from partner agencies and beneficiaries that a large portion of the "population of interest," or those who were in refugee-like situations of fleeing violence and seeking refuge in Ecuador, did not have the economic capacity or the knowledge to seek refugee status, and thus were being excluded from services.[19] Accordingly, the agency began to expand the proportion of the "population of interest" that it was reaching.[20]

This still did not address, however, the fact that UNHCR's limited mandate, to protect and assist those seeking refuge in countries outside of their

[19] Interview 81QI 2010; see also Brown 2009.
[20] Interview 164QN 2007.

place of origin, provides assistance and often tangible economic benefits to the refugee population to the exclusion of the host population, in whose midst refugees live. As a result, program evaluations, observation, and dialogue with partners and refugees in 2007 brought to the attention of UNHCR workers in Ecuador that their programs were sometimes exacerbating tensions between refugees and their Ecuadorian neighbors, who were also poor and sometimes resented what they perceived to be special treatment given to refugees.[21]

For example, a food ration program that was carried out together with the World Food Program in 2007 in the northern border region of Ecuador highlighted the problems with excluding nonrecognized refugees, which are the most vulnerable group with the most need, and also created resentment on the part of the local Ecuadorian population who were excluded from its benefits.[22] According to a program evaluation, part of the problem was that the feeding program raised expectations and then suffered from persistent underfunding, which resulted in benefits not being delivered as promised (WFP 2008). The fact that nonrefugees and Ecuadorians were initially excluded also increased resentment. The problem of creating raised expectations without sufficient political will or coordination to ensure efficient follow-through has been a persistent challenge for UNHCR, the state, and other organizations working with migrant populations in Ecuador.[23]

Catholic Church

The Catholic Church has been intricately linked to the power structure of Ecuadorian society since the country's inception, and it has had a major role in education and the provision of social services, especially to rural, poor, and indigenous populations. Of the 92% of the population who claim a religious belief, more than 80% identify as Catholic, although a growing evangelical Protestant movement has expanded the number of non-Catholics over the past two decades.[24] During the early years of Ecuador's history as an independent country, the Catholic Church, and not the state, was responsible for education and social service functions. Especially under the rule of

---

[21] Interview 82QI 2009.
[22] Interview 82QI 2009.
[23] Interview 126QN 2009; see also Servicio Jesuita 2009.
[24] INEC 2012.

Conservative dictator Gabriel García Moreno beginning in 1860, the linkages between Catholicism as the official religion and the state were strongly enforced, with citizenship being associated with adherence to the Catholic faith. The separation of church and state, a policy reform championed by the Liberal Party, did not legally occur until 1902. This move, which was targeted toward reducing the influence and power of the church-allied Conservative Party, is generally credited to President Eloy Alfaro, who also legalized divorce and established civil marriage (Skidmore et al. 2009: 184–85).

In another manifestation of the linkage between Catholic missions and state power, the Ecuadorian state signed a contract with a Carmelite mission in 1929 establishing the Apostolic Prefecture of Sucumbíos in the Amazon border region in order to strengthen the Ecuadorian de facto presence in this peripheral zone where the state was absent, defend against Colombian and Peruvian territorial claims, and "civilize" the indigenous groups there by establishing infrastructure, health and education centers, towns, and so on. As one history of the region put it, "Religious missions were always considered to be the lifeguards of Ecuadorian possession in the Amazon, proponents of the defense of borders and creators of civilization and progress" (Garces 2009: 27).

Despite the end of state-sponsored Catholicism, the church remained a pillar of authority, power, and institutional legitimacy in Ecuador. It was a force legitimizing the status quo, and its paternalistic management of vast land holdings prior to the twentieth century maintained the continuity of the hacienda plantation system, in which indigenous peasants were tied to the land through systems of dependency and peonage, with their labor being appropriated and exploited by wealthy landowners. In a 1977 book, Osvaldo Hurtado (who later became president of Ecuador) reflected on the role of the church in perpetuating existing economic, social, and political hierarchies:

The values of the Church transmitted through the educational system and through the pulpit favored the preservation and smooth functioning of the hacienda system. The more or less explicit affirmation that present economic structures, social hierarchies, and authority relationships were unchangeable because they reflected God's will was a notion that rendered rebellion an act necessarily contrary to divine order. . . . The existence of rich and poor was normal and the circumstance of poverty was viewed as a godsend that assured eternal salvation in the "other life," at which time one could expect to be rewarded for his suffering on earth. Faced with a condition of misery, the only appropriate response was one of resignation, patience, and reliance on charity. (1977: 58)

The Catholic Church, despite being one of the most important powerful institutions that was concerned with the lives of the poor in rural Ecuador, often dispensed charity in a way that encouraged dependence and obedience, rather than rights, collective mobilization, or self-development.

This practice began to change during the mid-twentieth century, as increasing numbers of clergy began to contest the status quo hacienda system and the church's role in maintaining and legitimizing it at the expense of the self-sufficiency of the poor. Influenced by the liberation theology movement that swept across Latin America beginning in the 1960s, which emphasized social justice and empowerment of the poor, the church provided a crucial space for development, political organizing, and advocacy for marginalized populations, as shown by the important role of religious groups in the formation of indigenous political organizations discussed earlier (Cleary 2009; Gutierrez 1988). Likewise, the church was one of the earliest actors providing social services to foreigners coming into Ecuador, and it served as UNHCR's in-country representative from 1976 until 2000, when UNHCR opened its own offices in Ecuador. Prior to 1976, the only agency promoting humanitarian assistance for refugees in Ecuador was the Red Cross (Navas et al. 2004). In the case of Colombians prior to the early 2000s, the church played an important role in rural border provinces with few state services available to either citizens or foreigners. According to the former director of the Jesuit Refugee Service (JRS), Jesuits and other missionaries and priests in rural areas incorporated the care of forced migrants in search of help into their existing social services "in a very domestic way" (meaning providing help in an ad hoc, personalized manner, as opposed to developing institutionalized structures to channel assistance systematically).[25] This later changed as the increasing scope of migration required greater coordination among service providers and among regions, but the church remained at the forefront of this effort.

The church was the institution that had had the longest and broadest geographic presence in rural areas of the border zone. Pastoral Migratoria was the church's migration agency, and it had a presence in every province of Ecuador. The FEPP, a Catholic NGO inspired by the principles of Vatican II

---

[25] Interview 166QN 2009.

and focused especially on economic development and entrepreneurship, was an established social institution for over forty years in Ecuador, and more than twenty-five years in most of the border provinces. Iglesia San Miguel de Sucumbíos (ISAMIS), a church in the Amazonian province of Sucumbíos, had been a pillar of community life and social protection for migrants and Ecuadorians alike since 1970, and before that as a Carmelite mission since 1928. Scalibrini, an international Catholic congregation that has a particular focus on migration and refugees, became an important part of the migrant welfare and assistance social infrastructure. Catholic Relief Services, an international Catholic NGO, was very active throughout Ecuador, though it kept a bit lower public profile. Jesuit Refugee and Migrant Service was one of the most visible Catholic organizations working specifically on issues of migration and refugees, and it was recognized by the Ecuadorian state as the chair (and primary spokesperson) of the civil society steering committee on refugees and human mobility.[26]

Through its charitable works and educational institutions, the church continues to fill important gaps in the services provided by the state. Furthermore, this represents one of the most trusted institutions in Ecuador, with at least 70% of surveyed respondents in the 2007 national-level Latinobarometer poll expressing "a lot" or "some" trust in the church, compared to 8% of respondents expressing similar amounts of trust for political parties, 24% for newspapers, 24% for private enterprises, and 41% for the government.[27] The history of humanitarian assistance offered to immigrants and refugees coming into Ecuador and the degree of trust that Ecuadorians have in the church underscore the key role of the church as a social and political actor complementing, and sometimes replacing, government programs.

Evolution of the Three Institutions, 2000–2017

From the year 2000, when the large-scale flow of Colombians into Ecuador began, to 2017, when Rafael Correa stepped down from the presidency, the country experienced three distinct phases in the institutional

---

[26] Interview 126QN 2009.

[27] Latinobarómetro 2007. This public opinion survey was administered in Ecuador between September and October 2007 to a representative national sample of twelve hundred respondents, with a margin of error of approximately 3%. This is not only a one-time "snapshot" picture, since the Latinobarometer is administered annually, and previous years' results for trust in the church have been reasonably consistent with this figure, generally measuring at least a 70% confidence level.

Figure 5.4 Three phases

governance network relating to migration: (1) Absence (2000–2006), characterized by state neglect and national security orientation, in which the Catholic Church and the UNHCR were the predominant protective institutions in the governance network, (2) Coordination (2007–11), characterized by engaged partnership, in which the UNHCR was the predominant actor in partnership with NGO implementing partners and the state, which was actively trying to build its capacity and become an internationally recognized progressive state for migration and integration, and (3) Regression (2012–17), characterized by the decline and hollowing out of certain protections and institutional structures, in which the state took primary control of migration policy and institutions. In reaction to political pressure, it increased restrictions for refugees, reduced drastically the number of refugees it accepted, shifted to the language of "human mobility" rather than refugees (which allowed it to base its practices on executive decrees rather than international treaty obligations), promoted the use of Mercosur visas rather than asylum claims (Duoos 2015), and cut staff and budget for refugee and immigration government agencies even as UNHCR and nonstate actors also scaled down.[28] These three phases, illustrated in Figure 5.4, provide a temporal framework for analyzing the shifts over time.[29]

Largely because of the historical weakness of the Ecuadorian state beyond the cities, much of the institutional infrastructure for receiving and

[28] In the years following Correa's exit, the cross-border effects of the demobilization of FARC combined with the new agenda of the Moreno presidency and the influx of Venezuelans to once again raise the profile of migration, but with more focus on security.

[29] It is worth noting that a number of other studies of NGOs, international organizations, and the Ecuadorian state have echoed this temporal categorization, particularly highlighting 2007 as a critical juncture dividing "before Correa" from "during/after Correa"; in a sign of the historic significance of his Citizen's Revolution in reshaping Ecuadorian politics, scholars have pointed to shifting power dynamics and greater state control and weakening of civil society and organized social movements as Correa consolidated his power, across sectors from the environment and indigenous movements to migration and economic development (Lewis 2013; Alvarez et al. 2017; Chiriboga 2014; Sanchez and Pachano 2020).

integrating migrants has been developed by nonstate institutional actors. The Catholic Church represents one of the institutions with the longest history of assistance, advocacy, and attention for migrant populations in Ecuador, and the Episcopal Committee of the Catholic Church was the authorized representative of the UN for serving the refugee community prior to 2000, and continued as UNHCR's primary implementing partner thereafter (Navas et al. 2004).

After establishing offices in Quito, then placing additional field offices in Lago Agrio and Ibarra, UNHCR worked in close partnership with the state and with the church. During this period of 2000–2007, a growing number of other NGOs and IGOs also became active in providing protection and promoting the rights and development of migrants in Ecuador, many of them working in some capacity with UNHCR and/or the state through its Unit for Development in the Northern Border (UDENOR). NGO partners in Santo Domingo, Cuenca, and San Lorenzo (Esmeraldas province) registered refugee applicants on behalf of UNHCR and sent the files to the Refugee Office of the Ministry of Foreign Relations in Quito for status determination.[30]

In January 2007, UNHCR and the Catholic Church ended their partnership, and UNHCR replaced the church with the Hebrew Immigrant Aid Society (HIAS) as its major implementing partner in Ecuador. According to one study, this occurred because of differences over the conduct of the joint refugee-integration project. One of the points of conflict was reportedly the restriction of assistance to refugees by UNHCR (especially from 2000 to 2004) as opposed to the broader and more inclusive conceptualization of migrants in need of protection advocated by the church, a long-standing tension between the two institutions.[31] The church also claimed that UNHCR selected its NGO implementing partners technocratically without adequate consideration of strengthening existing institutions both of the state and civil society in Ecuador (and especially the church itself). It argued that UNHCR's selection of international NGOs like the HIAS and the Italian Cooperazione Internacionale excluded domestic institutions and failed to strengthen Ecuadorian civil society. A statement released by the Episcopal Conference of Ecuador claimed that

---

[30] Most of these partners, like Caritas in Santo Domingo and Pastoral Migratoria in San Lorenzo, Esmeraldas, were associated with the Catholic Church during this period.

[31] Interview 166 QN 2009; see also de la Torre 2009.

UNHCR, during the past years, has imposed itself by "making contact" with non-governmental organizations so that they will become implementing agencies of its programs in the countries, without strengthening existing national structures, and excluding the participation of civil society and the church in the decisions with the Ecuadorian Government. Therefore, the Episcopal Conference of Ecuador . . . will no longer carry out its humanitarian assistance, registration, case and eligibility analysis for asylum seekers and refugees through the framework of the institutional agreement with UNHCR, effective January 1, 2007.[32]

Some critical state officials claimed that UNHCR replaced the church with the international NGO HIAS and a network of partner NGOs in a clientelistic move to increase its control over implementation by its "clients" and its ability to use financial resources as a patron to drive the agenda in favor of refugees, per its mandate.[33] In other words, this argument claimed that the church was more capable of demanding and exercising greater "associational autonomy" than international and local NGOs that depended on UNHCR funding and thus faced a greater power differential, and so UNHCR's preference for these latter types of partners could be interpreted as shoring up a clientelistic structure of dependent aid provision. During much of the Coordination phase beginning in 2007, the church and UNHCR carried on operations in large part independently from each other, before JRS and several other Catholic organizations once again began collaborating with UNHCR some years later, although not as the primary implementing partner as before. Through these changes in partnership status, the organizations associated with the church and the secular/international implementing NGOs contracted by UNHCR formed the two major sets of nonstate institutions providing human security in migrant-receiving communities of Ecuador. These two groups continued to work in similar geographic areas, often collaborating on ad hoc joint projects such as advocacy for a reform of Refugee Decree 3301 with a new Human Mobility Law, or on longer-term partnerships through independent Catholic organizations like Catholic Relief Services or ISAMIS. In order to get a sense of the variation in UNHCR partnerships over time, Figure 5.5 illustrates the number and relative distribution of state, NGO, and

---

[32] Quoted in "UN Places Refugees at Risk by Preferring NGOs to the Church in Ecuador," *Aciprensa* (January 2, 2007), http://www.aciprensa.com/noticia.php?n=15281.
[33] Interview 145QS 2017.

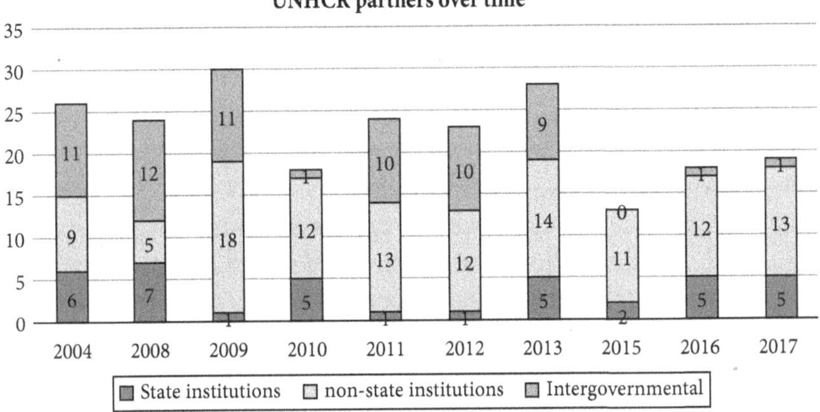

Figure 5.5 UNHCR partner types over time
Source: Compiled by author from UNHCR annual reports.

IGO partners specifically named in UNHCR annual reports between 2004 and 2017.

During approximately this same period, Rafael Correa's election to the Ecuadorian presidency fundamentally transformed the political context for migrant-serving interventions in general, and the work of UNHCR in particular. After campaigning on a platform of greater development and more open assistance for migrants and refugees, and opposing the restrictive visas proposed by his opponent, Alvaro Noboa, Correa assumed office in 2007 and began promoting this agenda and reinforcing norms of greater inclusion and human rights. With the development of Plan Ecuador, Correa reinforced a more permissive political climate for the development of institutions to protect human security and build peace in migrant-receiving communities. UNHCR leveraged its close working relationship with the government to translate this into more concrete commitments to implement the international agreements that previous regimes had signed but not taken very seriously in practice.

At the same time, Rafael Correa's commitment to increase the size and capacity of the state led to many of the functions previously carried out by UNHCR, the church, and other nonstate actors being transferred to the state. The registration, interviews, and investigations that the UNHCR and its NGO partners had previously carried out leading up to the state eligibility commission's decisions on refugee status determination were absorbed completely by the Ministry of Foreign Relations' refugee office. From 2005 to at least 2009 (some estimates said later), the personnel in the ministry's Refugee Office were largely hired and paid for by UNHCR through a contract with an Ecuadorian NGO.[34] As the state developed its own in-house capacity, especially with the investment and training of the mobile brigade initiative known as Enhanced Registration (discussed in greater depth in chapter 7), the state conducted the entire status determination process itself, with UNHCR providing technical support and assistance for asylum seekers and refugees during and after the process. Because of concerns that many asylum seekers were denied because of their lack of preparation or understanding of the status determination process, NGOs like Fundación Fabian Ponce and Asylum Access began offering them free legal advice and accompaniment, which was later funded by UNHCR. In 2017, this function was also transferred to the state, with a declaration from the public defender's office that it would provide free legal counsel for any asylum seeker in preparation for the refugee status determination process,[35] although the realization in practice of this commitment was uneven (Losier 2020).

The next four sections compare the three institutional authority poles along four dimensions—trust/legitimacy, mission, capacity, and transnational linkages—that influence their ability to exercise practical authority within the governance network, and help to understand the reasons for which they do so, and their strategic choices about which institutions to cooperate with (or not).

Trust and Legitimacy

Trust is a key component of legitimacy and of the "practical authority" that any institution exercises with specific constituencies and contexts. According to Mitchell and Hancock (2018), legitimacy—of which trust forms an important part—is a contested good, with competing actors vying for the "right" to exercise power and authority and be seen by the population as deserving to do so. Legitimacy is also not binary, and especially in areas of weak governance, it increases or decreases in degree, and assessing the ability of different institutions to influence people's decisions and compliance is an important

---

[34] Interview 145QS 2017.
[35] Interview 93QI 2017.

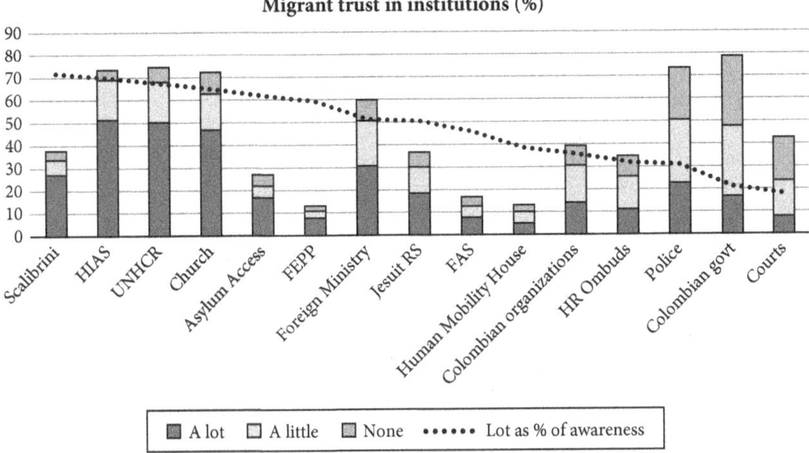

Figure 5.6 Migrants' levels of trust in various institutions
Source: MNS 2016.

part of measuring one form of power. The degree of legitimacy enjoyed by different actors—and who perceives them to have this legitimacy—is often both a function of and a contributor to their ability to provide the security, protection, and peace that their constituents desire (Hancock and Mitchell 2018). Since trust is more intuitively understandable than legitimacy, and in order to be consistent with similar standard questions asked in the Latinobarometer and LAPOP polls, I asked respondents about their level of trust[36] in institutions as a proxy for the legitimacy enjoyed by these organizations. When asked in my MNS about the level of trust (a lot, a little, or none) that they had in various organizations, Colombian migrants in Ecuador tended to trust nonstate actors, including international organizations, more than they did state institutions. In fact, Figure 5.6 shows that, in general, the more aware migrants were (i.e., they did not say "don't know," and provided an opinion about their level of trust in it) of a nonstate organization like UNHCR or the church, the more likely it was that they would report having a lot of trust in it. In contrast, the more aware they were of a *state* institution, such as the police, the courts, or the human rights ombudsman, the more likely they were to report little or no trust in it.

---

[36] I used the Spanish word *confianza*, which can be translated either as trust or confidence in the organization.

Table 5.1 Trust by migrants as percentage of overall awareness of specific institutions, by city

	Quito	Lago Agrio	Esmeraldas	Ibarra	Santo Domingo	Tulcán
Foreign Ministry	47.5	41.1	32.5	73.2	63.2	29.9
Police	15.5	24.1	30.0	27.9	32.9	46.4
UNHCR	64.8	61.8	56.0	79.8	75.9	54.1
Church	65.6	53.8	44.2	66.2	62.7	80.0

Source: MNS 2016.

When comparing trust levels in the specific institutions across localities, a more complex picture emerges, as illustrated in Table 5.1. Although UNHCR has higher levels of trust than the state in all cases (the foreign ministry and the police are reported here as proxies since they are the most visible state agencies for migrants), and the church is more trusted than the state in all cases except Ibarra and a near tie in Santo Domingo, the degree of difference varies, as does the relative position of the church and the UNHCR.

Trust is not a static resource. Changes in policies, demonstrated effectiveness of track record, the personal reputations of key actors, and changing population dynamics have all influenced the changing levels of confidence that migrants have in various institutions over time. Table 5.2 shows the change in the level of those reporting a lot of trust in a series of different organizations (as a percentage of those who report knowing about the institution at all), comparing the responses to the 2009–10 Migrant Organization Survey (MOS) with those for the same question on the 2013 MNS, both reflecting answers in Quito only.

It is important to consider changes in migrants' trust in key organizations in the context of overall societal trust in these organizations. Some of the changes are specific to migrant and refugee perceptions, while others may reflect broader trends in society that include both Ecuadorian and Colombian inhabitants. In Figure 5.7, the broad dynamics of Ecuadorians' trust in key institutions over time is reflected by the percentage of Latinobarometer respondents reporting that they have a lot or some trust in the following three institutions: the church, the police, and the judiciary (courts). The clearest trend is that, after a decade of gradual decline, Ecuadorians' trust

Table 5.2 Trust by migrants in Quito as percentage of overall awareness, change 2009 to 2013

Organization	2009 %	2013 %	Change
UNHCR	44.7	64.8	+20.1
Asylum Access	62.5	75.6	+13.1
HIAS	55.4	64.3	+8.9
Police	13.4	15.5	+2.1
Jesuit Refugee Service	49.8	51.1	+1.3
Ministry of Foreign Relations Refugee Office	46.8	47.5	+0.7
Courts	14.7	8.9	−5.8
Church	75.8	65.6	−10.2
Human rights ombuds	45.2	21.8	−23.4
Migrant organizations	67.7	39.0	−28.7

Source: MOS 2010; MNS 2016.

in state institutions, and especially the police, increased dramatically beginning in 2007, the year Rafael Correa took office. This is important evidence that the shift from the Absence period to the Coordination period depended not only on building state capacity and infrastructure, and better

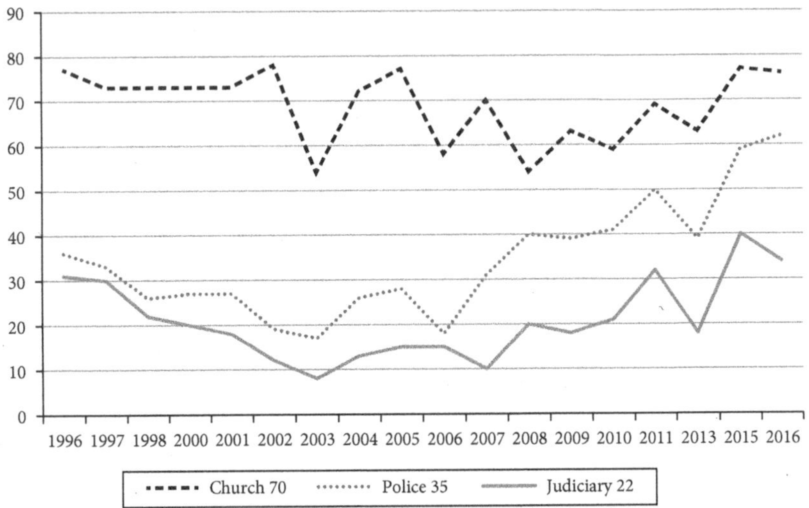

Figure 5.7 Trust in three key institutions over time
Source: Latinobarometer 1996–2016.

Table 5.3 Change in trust over time for Ecuadorians and migrants

	Ecuadorians			Migrants		
	2009	2013	Change	2009	2013	Change
Church	27	52	+25	24	44	+20
Police	7	17	+10	10	13	+3
Judiciary	2	8	+6	3	4	+1

Source: Ecuadorian data from Latinobarometer 2009, 2013; Migrant data from MOS 2010; MNS 2016.

coordination with trusted nonstate organizations with moral authority, but also on increasing levels of trust that lead to greater "functional legitimacy" of the state (Hancock and Mitchell 2018).

When comparing change during the same years that are available (2009 and 2013) for the perceptions of both Ecuadorians and Colombians, there was a similar increase in the level of trust in the church for both groups, indicating that both groups perceived an increased legitimacy and effectiveness of this nonstate institution. While both Ecuadorians and Colombian migrants had much less trust in governmental agencies than in the church, the *change* in these levels differed by population. The increase in trust in the two state institutions that is clear for Ecuadorian respondents between 2009 and 2013 is negligible for Colombian migrant respondents (illustrated in Table 5.3), suggesting that any perceived improvements in the legitimacy or effectiveness of the police and the courts seemed primarily to be favoring Ecuadorians, not Colombians.

The state, in a bid to leverage the legitimacy of international and nonstate actors like NGOs, the UN, and the church, often convened forums, deliberative committees, and other spaces to consult with these institutions and allow them to channel public feedback and input, supposedly to inform decision-making with a broader range of perspectives. While many nonstate actors felt a need to participate in such spaces as a way to influence policy, there was a growing frustration that these processes often seemed designed to legitimize a predetermined outcome more than capture and integrate competing perspectives from civil society.[37] Some civil society leaders criticized the negotiations over the Human Mobility Law, saying that lawmakers would

---

[37] Interview 141QS 2017.

sometimes create their own NGOs and civil society coalitions, invite only these groups to hearings, and then proclaim the support of "civil society" for their resulting legislative proposals.[38] In other words, politicians were sometimes reproducing patron-client networks by appealing to or co-opting groups within society to offer support for their policies in exchange for particular benefits, and other times by creating the illusion of broader support by inventing civil society organizations, with members receiving more material rewards in exchange for performative support. In this way, attempts by the state to co-opt the "practical authority" of nonstate actors through the appearance of consultation and partnership with a clientelistic logic inventing and showcasing "their" supporters may in practice have increased the legitimacy of the policy processes in the public eye, even if insider civil society leaders grew disillusioned with the possibilities of such processes for allowing genuine shared governance opportunities.

Focus of Mission

One of the key distinguishing factors that drives differences among the three types of institutions is the focus of their mission and the primary constituencies and activities that are included in their mandate. As mentioned in previous chapters, the state in a democratic country like Ecuador is primarily accountable to Ecuadorian citizen voters. Ecuador is a unitary presidential system with a unicameral legislature (National Assembly) controlled by the president's party, which was weakened by the constitutional reforms of 2008 that further empowered the executive as the populist voice of the people against the "partiocracy" (de la Torre 2017). The president sets the foreign policy agenda and exercises significant control over the migration and security policies of ministries.

President Correa centralized power in the presidency and positioned Ecuador as an influential member of the international community through membership and leadership in ALBA along with Hugo Chavez's Venezuela, Evo Morales's Bolivia, and other members of the so-called Pink Wave, and through high-profile policy that was innovative and confrontational to the hegemony of US and European interests in Latin America (Montufar 2013). Internationally, this included the discontinuation of the lease for the US

---

[38] Interview 22DM 2015.

military base on the coast of Manta, Ecuador, (Ikeda 2018) and the expulsion of USAID from the country. Ecuador was also a leading proponent of South American solidarity institutions that specifically excluded the United States, de-emphasizing the Organization of American States, for example, in favor of the Union of South American Countries (UNASUR), which was headquartered north of Quito.

These measures combined with the domestic adoption of the principles of "Good Living" and "universal citizenship" and nature having juridical rights within the Ecuadorian constitution, and the Yasuni proposal to leave oil unexploited in the biodiverse Amazonian rainforest in exchange for payments and resource transfers from international donors in the Global North, to earn Correa a reputation for progressive, technocratic innovation. On the other hand, his charismatic and populist governing approach framed all of these advances in personalistic terms, the gift of a leader ushering in a new era for "the people" against enemies who would block progress.

At times, those who did not align with Correa's narrative of what progress looked like were dismissed, infantilized as naive or pawns of nefarious interests, or were actively persecuted for critical speech or protest (Picq 2016; Martinez Novo 2014, 2018). The large infrastructure of civil servants working for the state as well as party activists and allies throughout the country were frequently mobilized for performative acclamation in the streets and plazas to legitimize proposals and projects and solidify their support for Correa's personal leadership in a newly updated type of relationship that Carlos de la Torre (2020) calls "technopopulism." The "permanent campaign mode" of the Correa presidency (Conaghan and de la Torre 2008), combined with the heavy investment in infrastructure and social spending (financed by oil profits and borrowing, especially from China), led to unprecedented and sustained levels of high approval ratings for the first seven years of the presidency followed by growing dissatisfaction and protests as oil prices decreased, some progressive policies were reversed or hollowed, corruption increased, and repression of dissent became more authoritarian (Sánchez and Pachano 2020). Grace Jaramillo (2020) has argued that Correa's foreign policy reflected a paradox that combined discursive sovereignty—in his rhetoric of protection of rights, environment, and Latin American autonomy against intrusive powers in the Global North and their militarized allies—with practical dependency, especially on extractive industry investment and foreign debt, which reinforced capitalist structures of exploitation (see also Riofrancos 2020).

The military has historically exercised quite a bit of institutional autonomy in Ecuador, occasionally becoming what Raul Madrid calls a "veto player" in checking presidential imperatives that threaten the institutional cohesion of the armed forces and the national security establishment (Madrid 2012; Martz 1987). The military's decision to prioritize its own institutional stability over protecting Presidents Jamil Mahuad in 2000 and Lucio Gutierrez in 2005 from massive street protests led to the ouster of these two presidents (Gerlach 2003; Lalander and Ospina Peralta 2012). In contrast, the military intervened on behalf of President Correa in September 2010,[39] defending him against a protest by the police over wage and benefit changes that trapped the president in a hospital room and that some labeled as an attempted coup. This event reinforced the president's understanding of his dependence on security forces, to whom he owed his presidency's survival (Becker 2016). For these reasons, although the president is the primary political power in the Ecuadorian system, he is constrained in designing and implementing national security-related policies by military and security agencies with their own institutional memories, cultures, and understanding of the national interest (Jaskoski 2012; Martz 1987; Hurtado 1977).

This disjuncture has sometimes led to progressive presidential rhetoric regarding migration and refugee reception that is hollow when it is implemented by a bureaucratic and security apparatus that has distinct interests and a more skeptical view of open borders (Pugh 2017; Correa 2016). According to a former high-level official, the state security sector was always suspicious that the president's open-borders policies and widespread hiring of human rights NGO workers for state jobs would result in lax refugee policies that could weaken national security. The official observed, "The security sector after 2009 never stopped scrutinizing the phenomenon closely, the refugee problem here in Ecuador. It wasn't something they said directly, but they certainly watched and acted. In other words, they were not going to contradict the official language openly, but through the daily practices of the police and intelligence agencies, they continued being the same."[40]

Eventually, this resistance through implementation practices by "street-level bureaucrats" (Lipsky 1980) that differed from the formal policies influenced the norms and expectations of the state to the extent that they

---

[39] The military and police also vigorously defended the state and the president—including with violent repression—against the October 2019 indigenous protests (Ramirez Gallegos 2020).

[40] Interview 145QS 2017.

changed official policy. Correa, who depended on personal popularity and being able to marginalize opponents as part of the enemy, could hardly confront directly the entire military and security establishment to defend his "open borders" program, and his populist style and weak intermediary institutions gave him the flexibility to hollow out his migration policies while maintaining the rhetorical form. Especially after 2009–11, the president faced increasing internal pressure to link crime and migration policies, and to address them by adopting more restrictive refugee policies, which he did with Decree 1182 in 2012.[41] This led to the Regression phase, in which the state asserted its dominance in setting refugee policy and used this dominance to weaken competing nonstate sources of authority and accountability. During this period, the state signed an agreement in 2013 with Mercosur, in which both Ecuador and Colombia were observer members, to reduce visa requirements for each other's citizens. Afterward, the Ecuadorian government accompanied its more restrictive asylum process with the active encouragement that forced migrants from Colombia apply instead for a Mercosur visa. Given that it was a faster process and free for Colombians and did not carry the stigma of refugee status, many Colombians did so (Gómez Martín and Malo 2020). However, one underlying problem was that this visa only lasted two years before needing to be renewed, and it did not carry the international protections of refugee status against non-refoulment (requiring instead proof of steady employment to be renewed), so it was a way the state could recapture control over when and if to define Colombians as forced migrants needing protection versus immigrants who were not making a valued contribution and should thus be denied renewal (Duoos 2015).[42]

As evidence that these state efforts did indeed result in increasingly restrictive narratives, and that both official and societal narratives marginalized the language of refugees and the institutional influence of UNHCR, in previous work I conducted discourse analysis of 437 of President Correa's speeches from 2007 to 2015 (Pugh 2017) and more than eight hundred newspaper articles related to migration in *El Comercio*, *El Universo*, and *Diario Extra* from 2012 to 2018 (Pugh and Moya 2020).[43] Figure 5.8 shows that Correa's use of

---

[41] Interview 145QS 2017.

[42] Interview 124QN 2015.

[43] Analysis was conducted using automatic word searches of the speech and newspaper article databases in QDA Miner and WordStat software. See the respective articles for more methodological detail.

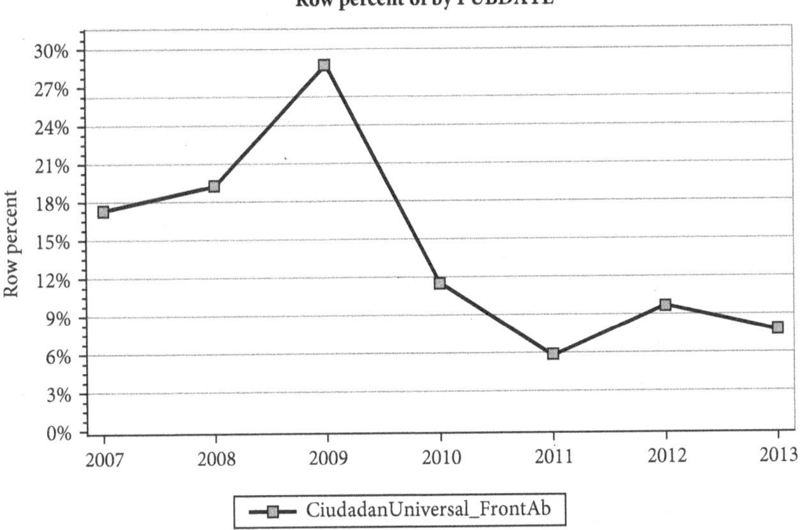

Figure 5.8 "Universal citizenship" Correa speech mentions per year (% of total mentions)

Source: Pugh 2017.

the terms "universal citizenship" and "open borders" in his speeches declined drastically over time (illustrating the transition from the Coordination to the Regression phase), and Figures 5.9 and 5.10 show that mentions of "UNHCR and "refugee" in the news media declined significantly during the Regression phase from 2012 to 2018, while "migration" (Figure 5.11) fluctuates, but does not follow a descending pattern.

The multiple levels of government in Ecuador discredit the myth of a unitary state, instead revealing a plethora of competing and overlapping interests. The difference between the goals and political incentives of the central government and local municipal or provincial government officials can be quite significant. This difference can influence the ways in which various state actors cooperate (or not) with the UN, the church, or other NGOs in protecting refugee rights and in deciding whose priorities and well-being to prioritize with beneficial policies. For example, municipal and provincial governments in Esmeraldas and Tulcán were controlled by opposition political parties, and as a result, municipal officials and the local offices of ministries frequently did not cooperate closely, or even meet to coordinate joint strategies. The prefect of Carchi, General René Yandún Pozo (later elected

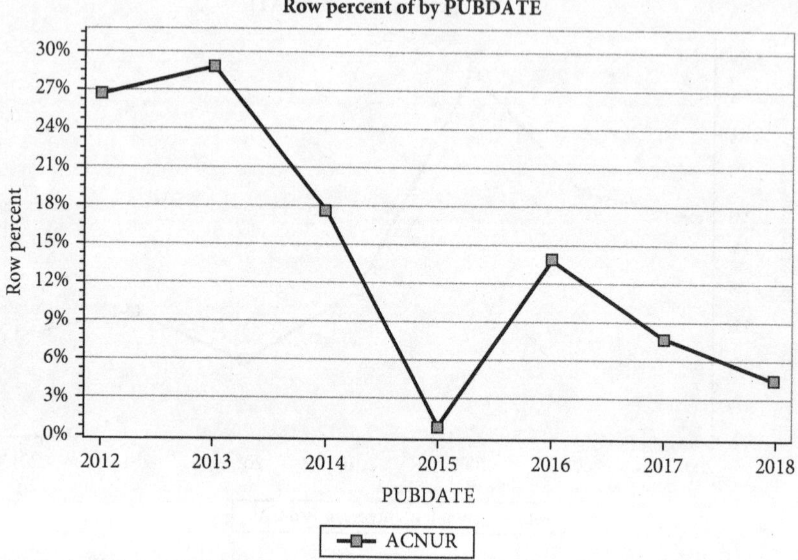

Figure 5.9 "UNHCR" newspaper mentions per year (% of total mentions)
Source: Pugh and Moya 2020.

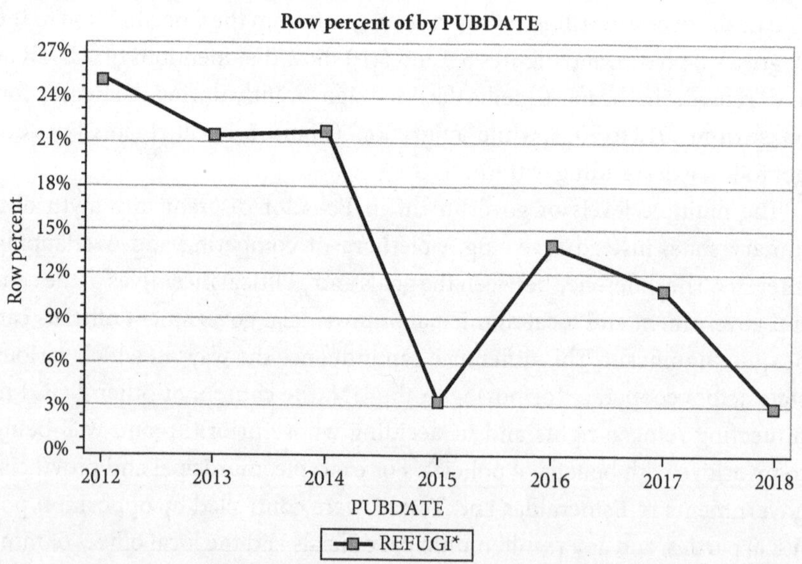

Figure 5.10 "Refugee" news mentions per year (% of total mentions)
Source: Pugh and Moya 2020.

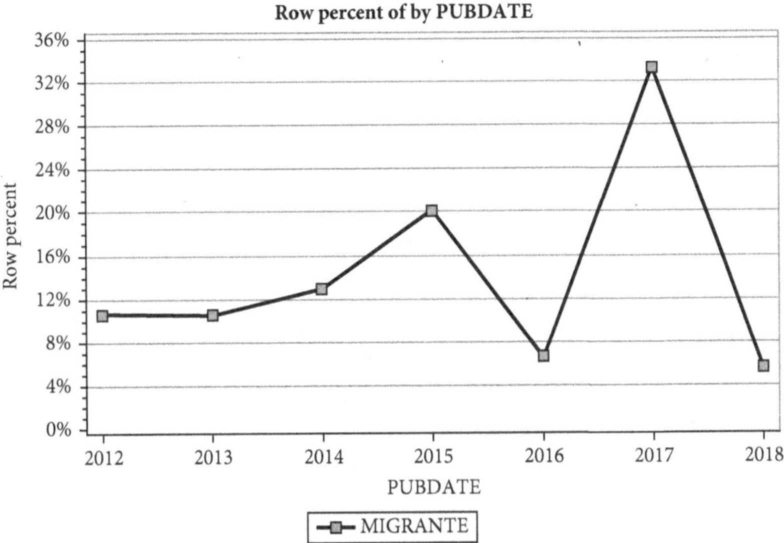

Figure 5.11 "Migrant" news mentions per year (% of total mentions)
Source: Pugh and Moya 2020.

to the National Assembly), openly blamed President Correa for rescinding the police record requirement for asylum seekers and accused him of preventing the Ecuadorian military in the border region from exercising adequate controls, alleging complicity with FARC's goals as repayment for campaign support (Vaca 2018). Both Yandún and Esmeraldas prefect Lucía Sosa supported a Border Development Law in the National Assembly, only to see it vetoed by Correa.[44]

UN offices in Esmeraldas sometimes found that they could play a helpful role in convening meetings and institutional spaces, using the credibility of their institution to get officials in the same room together to talk.[45] Another IGO official in Tulcán, however, observed that this type of convening activity could be politically risky, depending on the political sensitivity of the specific government officials, as some resented this type of activity as an outside organization trampling on the sovereign prerogative of the state. As a result, the IGO official in Tulcán said, "We try to keep ourselves out of the

---

[44] "Lucía Sosa: 'Demandamos que se apruebe la Ley de Desarrollo Fronterizo,'" *El Universo* (April 15, 2018), https://www.eluniverso.com/noticias/2018/04/15/nota/6714108/lucia-sosa-demandamos-que-se-apruebe-ley-desarrollo-fronterizo.

[45] Interview 33EI 2013; Interview 34EI 2013.

fight among government agencies . . . this is about respecting what the government decides to be valid locally. We can't involve ourselves in political matters because as an agency of the United Nations, an ethical principle of the UN is impartiality."[46] In contrast, the municipal governments of Lago Agrio, Ibarra, and Santo Domingo were controlled by the president's Alianza PAIS party, and, accordingly, the technical cooperation with central ministries on migrant-related policies was stronger.[47]

The UN system represents a range of specialized agencies of the international organization that operate in Ecuador, with more than one hundred full-time personnel in the country as of 2016 (UNHCR 2016).[48] As a mandate-driven organization, UNHCR derives its legitimacy to act in the interest of protecting refugees in Ecuador from the country's signature of the 1951 Refugee Convention and the 1967 protocol, as well as the 1984 Cartagena Declaration. Other agencies, such as the UNDP, sign a memorandum of cooperation each year with the Ecuadorian government, which defines the scope of the government's invitation for UNDP's work. This allows UNDP to sometimes have a closer working relationship with the government and greater access to decision-makers, which can be useful for some types of coordination. On the other hand, UNHCR's autonomy and reliance on an international instrument for its permission to operate give it a layer of political insulation that allow it to sometimes push back against government policies that it sees as unhelpful for refugee protection in ways that UNDP might not be in a position to do.[49]

The degree of programmatic autonomy and sustainability prioritized by different agencies also influences their relationship with the state. According to an official of the World Food Program, for example, that agency avoids the project-cycle framing of two- to four-year interventions that characterize many of the initiatives sponsored by other international development agencies (Pugh 2016a), attempting instead to cooperate with local governments to integrate an inclusive development framework that benefits both constituents and refugees into long-term sustainable policies.[50] This is easier, of course, for an agency like WFP that works on concrete beneficial policies that are more attractive to local politicians who want to be seen

---

[46] Interview 7CI 2015.
[47] Interview 4CI 2015; Interview 53II 2014.
[48] Interview 89QI 2017.
[49] Interview 91QI 2008.
[50] Interview 1CI 2015; Interview 7CI 2015; Interview 2CI 2015.

as responsible for bringing economic investment and food aid that benefits their Ecuadorian constituents as well as Colombians. In the border town of Tulcán, municipal politicians were often less interested in talking explicitly about refugee issues or working closely with UNHCR, since these were perceived to imply costly obligations to foreigners more than economic benefits to Ecuadorians.[51]

UN agencies are compartmentalized in issue-specific agencies, and in individual country teams, in ways that make it difficult to coordinate joint strategies that are more integrated and take into account complex transnational realities, and so learning and adaptation have sometimes been slower than would be ideal.[52] However, strategies like the PNP-ZF project have attempted to overcome this silo effect by convening joint technical working groups to address complex border issues.[53] This coordination across agencies with different missions, despite numerous challenges, has resulted in some important successes, such as the binational Track II dialogue group sponsored by UNDP, the Carter Center, and the OAS that helped to rebuild relations between Ecuador and Colombia when diplomatic relations were severed after the 2008 Colombian bombing of the FARC camp at Angostura in Ecuadorian territory (Carter Center 2011).[54]

The Catholic Church's view of its own mission in Ecuador has remained relatively consistent through the time period of interest, when forced migrants were entering the country in large numbers. Drawing inspiration from the scriptural call to provide clothing for the poor, food for the hungry, and refuge for the stranger, the church and its associated organizations sought to provide protection for forced migrants, particularly those with the greatest economic or security vulnerabilities (Cleary 2009). Unlike UNHCR, the church was less concerned about the specific legal status of economic migrants versus refugees than about the needs of those in their communities who asked for help. Through networks of village-level churches in the border region, as well as local and national offices of the church's migration social service agency Pastoral Migratoria, the church was able to draw on its widespread geographic presence and local trust to mobilize protection resources and services. It amplified these efforts further by partnering with national and international Catholic organizations that specialized in

---

[51] Interview 18CI 2015; Interview 4CI 2015; Interview 98IM 2014.
[52] Interview 89QI 2017.
[53] Interview 91QI 2008.
[54] Interview 92QI 2009; Interview 18CS 2015; Interview 137QS 2017; Interview 121 QN 2016.

migration/refugee issues and local development, including FEPP, Catholic Relief Services, JRS, Caritas, and Scalibrini, among others. JRS, for example, identified aspects of its organizational identity and mission to justify serving migrants in isolated parts of the country. The initiation of its refugee work in Lago Agrio in the Amazon region "has much to do with the Ignacian spirit of JRS's work, because the Jesuit Service goes where others are not; so obviously if we had started here in Quito, it would have meant ignoring the reality of what was happening at that time in the border region, and especially in the Amazon border zone," explained JRS's former executive director.[55]

The Catholic Church's view of its mission in Latin America had earlier experienced a significant institutional shift in the 1960s and 1970s as liberation theology and the Vatican II council inspired a generation of priests in local communities to promote the empowerment and social organization of peasant communities against poverty and injustice (Gutierrez 1988). In doing so, these priests recognized the church's role in justifying the status quo, and they sometimes pushed the more conservative national authorities to advocate for policies that would favor the poor and promote bottom-up self-organization (Cleary 2010). During the influx of forced migrants in Ecuador, these debates over the mission of the church continued to be contested. For example, ISAMIS is the major church in Lago Agrio, and it was run under the leadership of Monseñor Gonzalo López, head of a Carmelite order that was a steadfast ally of Colombian refugees, and the institutional home of many protection and social/economic justice programs over forty years, including Radio Sucumbíos, which facilitated communication with far-flung rural villages in the jungle, and the Federation of Women of Sucumbíos, a powerful incubator of female leaders in the region (Garces 2009).

In October 2010, the Vatican in conjunction with the church hierarchy in Quito replaced the Carmelites with an order known as the Heralds, who were much more conservative and focused on evangelism rather than social work or justice work. They adopted a more hierarchical and clerical approach than the more horizontal style of the Carmelites, which had included significant lay leadership and frequent community assemblies (Angostura 2011). As a result, many of the church's programs for refugees were shuttered, and the social fabric of the community was torn as the congregation split between those loyal to the Carmelites and those who welcomed the new Heralds (San Roman 2011; Luis 1994; Gallego 2014; Angostura 2011; Macipe

---

[55] Interview 166QN 2009.

2013).[56] Xavier Creach, director of the UNHCR office in Lago Agrio, commented, "I don't know if that was the Vatican's motive, but it is certain that the Catholic Church has not played the same role in defense of the population after the arrival of the new congregation" (quoted in Macipe 2013).

In an illustration of the adaptive and informal nature of the governance network, however, several of the Carmelite nuns and priests who had run ISAMIS founded an NGO called Fundación Tarabita. With the personal relationships they had built over the years and partnerships with UNHCR and other organizations, they continued in parallel form many of the faith-based migration programs that they had previously run from ISAMIS through the new NGO (Macipe 2013).[57] Through these moments of institutional evolution and adaptation, the church, like the UN system in Ecuador and the state, shifted its programmatic strategies toward the protection of forced migration in response to both internal changes in its own view of its mission and external dynamics in its relationship with other institutions with sometimes competing missions.

Capacity: Security and Rights Provision by *Minga*

One of the primary factors motivating the linkages and relationships of mutual dependence among the state, the UN system, the church, and other private nonstate actors is the resource constraints that limit the provision of public goods like security, social welfare, and dispute resolution. Ecuador has a long tradition of relatively inefficient tax collection, and prior to the mid-2000s, social services were a very small component of government spending, with many such programs being provided by the church and NGOs, and social infrastructure being financed by private companies (especially oil companies) or provided communally through community workdays, or *mingas*, in more rural areas (Garces 2009).

Military officials identify border protection from Colombian armed groups and combating FARC presence/criminal activity within Ecuador as their top national security priority (Jaskoski 2012).[58] Accordingly, one would expect that this would be a priority area for state-led expenditures

---

[56] Interview 150SN 2013.
[57] Interview 153SN 2013.
[58] Interview 26CS 2017.

and institutional presence. However, even core security functions have relied on shared resources through networked governance, rather than simply reflecting the political decision-making of a unitary state directed by the elected civilian leadership. Maiah Jaskoski's excellent study of military services responding to private clients highlights the way in which such linkages occur: "Army brigade and battalion commanders in northern Ecuador have sold their security services to private oil companies, as well as to US military representatives, wealthy landowners, and subnational government officials. These local arrangements have shaped the extent to which army units carry out different missions, as well as who benefits from that work" (2012: 85).

The central government often underfunded local military units, providing as little as 20% of operational budgetary needs beyond salaries and food in some cases, and requiring local commanders to raise the rest through entrepreneurial partnerships, providing security to private clients in exchange for in-kind support like fuel, vehicles, base improvements, and so on. While this resulted in locally negotiated cost-sharing arrangements in which companies, private landowners, local government agencies, or international organizations/NGOs would contribute part of the needed resources to offer protection and investigate potential threats, these services were not really public, prioritizing instead the interests of the paying client over those of the broader community in the territory being served (Jaskoski 2012). The greater the diversity of types of organizations participating in this type of cost-sharing network, the more likely it is that a larger cross-section of community interests will be taken into account. In contrast, a single wealthy client might significantly divert the security services being offered to tasks that contributed little to the overall well-being or protection of the local residents—both Ecuadorian and Colombian.

In some cases, like the military's suppression of indigenous protest against extractive industries' negative environmental effects, this prioritization of the private client's interests actually worsened the human security of the majority of the community's inhabitants, who suffered repressive violence, detainment, and negative environmental and health effects (Lewis 2016; Martin 2011; Riofrancos 2020). The growth of private security companies during the 1990s and 2000s is an indication of this privatization of security provision by nonstate actors in urban areas as well, which extended greater protections for those who could pay for it.[59] Between 1990 and 1995, the number of private

---

[59] Interview 136QS 2015.

security firms registered with the Superintendent of Companies, the government oversight body, increased from 54 to 163. This number grew to 390 in 2000, and by 2007, 855 companies were registered, representing an increase of 525% in a little more than a decade.[60] By 2012, the number was 984, and 1,008 by 2014.[61] This slower expansion mirrored the broader trend under Correa toward more state-dominated services at the expense of the private sector and civil society. In a further reversal, the number of private security companies had actually declined to 789 by 2017.[62]

The use of networked governance as a cost-sharing innovation in the face of limited resources was not limited only to security provision by military and security units within the state; it was also mentioned as a key part of the reason for cooperation among UN agencies, NGOs, the church, and local state agencies on migration and refugee protection issues. According to an official of an international organization in Tulcán, "The strategies and the alliances that we have achieved, more than a vision of working as a joint team together, have been a *minga* putting together what almost all of us lack, which is resources. So, while some of us contribute one thing, we have to ask such-and-such ministry for another thing, and we have to bother them, so it requires our presence to attend the meetings they convene there in order to try to formalize the arrangement."[63] This comment emphasizes the reciprocal expectations that underlie cooperation in many of the governance networks in Ecuador. Not only is a direct exchange or joint contribution of material resources often expected, but organizations see attending meetings and investing time in institutional spaces convened by each other's leaders as necessary in order to influence programs, agendas, and budgets, and to get reciprocal commitments from the other institutions to help with their priorities.

The balance of power among the different types of institutions is influenced by fluctuations in their relative budgetary capacity as well as the popular perception of the quality of their human resources. In particular, the state during the 1990s and early 2000s suffered from underfunding and relative disadvantages in attracting bright, energetic talent to work on social

---

[60] "Las firmas de seguridad privada crecieron como la Espuma," *El Comercio* (January 18, 2009).

[61] "En 6 años se crearon 135 compañías de seguridad," *El Telégrafo* (February 24, 2014), https://www.eltelegrafo.com.ec/noticias/judicial/12/en-6-anos-se-crearon-135-companias-de-seguridad.

[62] "Ecuador cuenta con 789 compañías de seguridad privada registradas," *El Tiempo* (August 1, 2017), https://www.eltiempo.com.ec/noticias/ecuador/4/ecuador-cuenta-con-789-companias-de-seguridad-privada-registradas.

[63] Interview 1CI 2015.

problems, compared with the NGO or UN/IGO sectors. Dual events in 2007 began to change this calculus. President Correa launched a significant expansion of state spending on social programs, which increased from around 4% of GDP in 2006 to over 11% in 2016, as shown in Figure 5.12.

In addition, the recession in the United States and Europe resulted in a constriction of much UN and international NGO donor funding as well as weaker transnational political support or attention. This had an impact across the NGO field in Ecuador, including in the environmental sector, where Ecuador's NGOs had been major actors in the field. According to Tammy Lewis, "The shift in social structure—the simultaneous strengthening of the state and weakening of international influence—debilitated national *ecodependent* NGOs . . . there was a brain drain from the NGOs into the state as government agencies grew and poached staff from the leading environmental organizations" (2016: 171).

Cooperation, transnational partnerships and funding also began to flow directly to the state, which now had the capacity and political leverage to implement projects and demand that cooperation flow through official channels. As the economic crisis in the Global North reduced the amount of transnational funding donors could offer, Lewis argues, "Transnational actors [could] no longer run the show. Structural changes led to the declining influence of foreigners on both Ecuador's political economy and its environmentalism. Many of the INGOs formerly had influence with NGOs and the

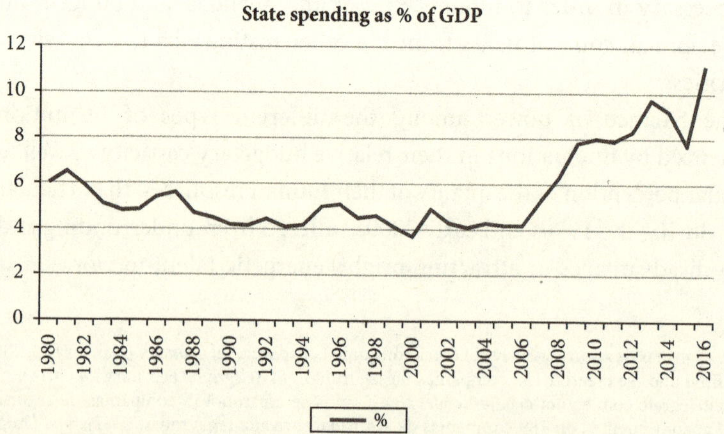

Figure 5.12 State social spending as % of GDP over time
Source: Ponton 2016.

state via their roles in transferring resources from the Global North to the Global South. With their funds limited by the slowed global economy, [their] influence also became limited" (2016: 174).

The migration sector differed from the environmental sector because mass migration was a more recent phenomenon, and thus the organizations working on the issue were more recent and less established, with their institutional growth period being 2000–11, rather than the 1990s and early 2000s. However, Correa's period of statebuilding resulted in a similar shift in the balance of power from NGOs and IGOs to the state. A former internal security official said that this shift at first populated government ministries working on migration with former human rights NGO workers, raising the profile of refugee issues and providing political will for rights protection, even while capacity and training lagged.[64] According to an analyst in Quito, migration represented the one area (in contrast to economic development, democracy promotion, environmental protection, etc.) where Correa seemed content to allow IGOs and NGOs to maintain a prominent role in service provision and even agenda-setting, perhaps because this could provide political cover for services that were seen as primarily benefitting nonvoting foreign citizens rather than Ecuadorians.[65] In the context of scarce resources, the state, the UN system, the church, and other nonstate actors developed new ways of cooperating and competing as part of a governance network to meet capacity needs for migration protection while attempting to manage the shifting balance of power and political interests.

Transnational Linkages, Resources, and Credibility

Institutions in all three of the institutional poles have leveraged their linkages with other transnational actors and access to resources that cross borders in order to increase their own ability to accomplish their mission goals with respect to the reception of Colombian forced migrants in Ecuador. The four categories of transnational politics proposed by Keck and Sikkink (1999) offer a useful way to analyze the effects of these networks and resources on the institutional activities of the state, UN system, and the church/NGOs in domestic political space.

---

[64] Interview 145QS 2017.
[65] Interview 124QN 2015.

Information Politics

Information politics was among the most powerful tools wielded by the UN and NGOs in Ecuador. One of the most important factors driving state policy changes like Enhanced Registration was systematic data collected by UNHCR in its 2006 study/census of refugees in the northern border region (Bilsborrow 2006). For the first time, the state and UNHCR had access to more reliable information about where refugees were living, and they discovered that many forced migrants had not accessed the refugee recognition system because of fear, lack of knowledge of rights/laws, or lack of financial resources to travel to Quito to initiate the asylum process and survive while it was in process. This became a key argument for the mobile brigades and compressed timeline developed in Enhanced Registration in 2009–10. The role of Ecuadorian institutions, often in consultation with and funded by UNHCR and IOM, was especially important as a component of information politics that shaped refugee policy. Several studies by FLACSO (Rivera et al. 2007; Ortega y Ospina 2012; Santacruz 2013) provided rigorous social scientific evidence about the experience of Colombian refugees in Ecuador, including analysis of their expectations of the future, which largely did not include returning to Colombia soon. This information reinforced the need for UNHCR and the state to develop policies and programs for local integration rather than planned repatriation, and for both institutions to try to develop stronger international cooperative links to increase the availability of third-country resettlement, including policies adopted within the frameworks of the 2004 Mexico Action Plan and the 2014 Brazil Declaration and Plan of Action.[66] The provincial government of Imbabura played an important role in gathering systematic data to provide a mapping of the local government agencies, NGOs, and UN offices in the Zone 1 border region. This information about the availability and distribution (and gaps) of the state and nonstate institutional presence helped to drive policy-planning strategies by local governments and other actors in the governance network of the northern border region (Oviedo et al. 2013).[67]

Leverage Politics

The primary transnational relationships that the Ecuadorian state drew on to enhance its resources and political goals were its alliances. Prior to 2007,

---

[66] Interview 93QI 2017.
[67] Interview 75IS 2014; Interview 53II 2014.

this included a strong relationship with the United States, whose funding through USAID and military cooperation through its naval base at Manta strengthened the national security and development goals of the Ecuadorian state, according to the US ambassador at the time.[68] Once Correa came to power, he defined his political interests through an antihegemonic discourse, in contrast to the United States and its primary ally in the region, Colombia (Ikeda 2018). Instead, Correa became a key member of the ALBA alliance, joining Venezuela, Bolivia, Cuba, Nicaragua, and others to mobilize greater institutionalization and regional solidarity within Latin America, seeking to weaken what they perceived to be US-dominated institutions like the World Bank, OAS, and the Inter-American Human Rights Commission, in favor of UNASUR and a new Bank of the South. Correa ejected USAID from Ecuador in 2014, and shifted his economic partnerships to China rather than the World Bank. This new set of transnational alliances empowered different domestic political constituencies (i.e., state bureaucrats over the private sector, mining and hydroelectric industries over environmentalists and indigenous social movements). Correa's appeal to and leadership of a broader international audience made his brand of populism different from previous manifestations in Ecuador, such as that of President Velasco Ibarra earlier in the twentieth century (Montufar 2013). Correa defined *el pueblo* whose interests and moral boundaries he claimed to articulate and whose voice he claimed to channel in terms that surpassed the boundaries of the Ecuadorian territory, just as the enemies he sought to defend against were not just corrupt Ecuadorian politicians, but US hegemony, predatory capitalism and privatization, and international institutions like the World Bank and IMF.

The promotion of innovative concepts like universal citizenship as a government policy, Enhanced Registration as a way to increase access to rights for refugees, an international funding scheme in exchange for *not* exploiting oil in Yasuni, or guaranteeing nature juridically defensible rights in the constitution, paid international political dividends for Correa in terms of recognition and attention as an ideas leader (Falconí 2010; Martin 2011). Ecuador is a small country with little geopolitical strategic advantage, but the fact that it was acting as a policy laboratory for such interesting progressive ideas gave Correa an outsized platform from which to position himself as a leader in

---

[68] Interview 167QS 2007.

Latin America, and the natural person to inherit Chavez's influence in the region, even without Chavez's oil-funded pocketbook.

In addition to transnational linkages that provided Correa with leverage, these linkages sometimes were used to apply pressure on him for policy changes. For example, many countries in the Americas became concerned that Ecuador's open borders policy was being exploited to make Ecuador a transit country that could be used by undocumented migrants from Cuba, Haiti, and China to enter other countries like Costa Rica, the United States, or Brazil. In 2015 and 2016, these countries put diplomatic pressure on Correa to place more entry restrictions, and shortly thereafter, visas began to be required for Cuban and Chinese migrants, and visa fees were increased (Correa 2016). A 2016 protest by some six hundred Cubans in Parque Arbolito in Quito requesting humanitarian transit to Mexico to enter the United States was met with violent repression, a mass detention, and deportation of 121 people without adequate due process (Correa 2020; Picq 2016). This seemed to be a selective action by nationality, in part in response to international pressure about Cuban transit migration.

At times, the UN system and the church leveraged their own international legitimacy and political capital to mobilize positive recognition of the state's efforts when they saw these as contributing to the protection of migrants and refugees—as in the case of the 2008 constitution, Enhanced Registration, and the 2017 Organic Human Mobility Law.

Accountability Politics

UNHCR, the church, and other nonstate actors often used the statements of public officials and the laws and international agreements signed by the state to hold the government accountable and advocate for better implementation in practice of the rights and protections contained in formal state institutions. In the decade of the 2000s, UNHCR's presence (with voice but not vote) on the Eligibility Commission, composed of representatives of the Foreign Ministry and Interior Ministry who made refugee status determination decisions, allowed UNHCR to announce its recommendations publicly. A UNHCR representative reviewed all status determination recommendations issued by the Ministry of Foreign Relations based on interviews with the asylum seekers and provided comments and her own independent recommendation—including sometimes negotiating or trying to convince the officials to change their recommendation—before the case went before the Eligibility Commission for a final decision at its monthly meeting.[69] Given UNHCR's reputation for technical expertise and international credibility, the state often publicized the (high) percentage rate at which its own eligibility decisions matched the recommendations of UNHCR as a way of boosting popular perceptions of its own performance quality. This allowed the state to borrow some of UNHCR's practical authority in this issue area.

On the other hand, when political tensions began pushing the state toward more restrictive policies that prioritized security in the Regression phase after 2012, the UNHCR was disinvited from participating in the Eligibility Commission, so it no longer carried out any independent recommendation about eligibility. In this case, the state was attempting to distance itself from an unwelcome source of accountability, emphasizing the sovereign prerogative of the state to make status determination decisions. By this point, it could highlight that the state had much greater capacity and experience to carry out the investigation process itself, and that it therefore no longer needed the technical assistance of UNHCR. In similar efforts to weaken the accountability politics of nonstate actors, in 2013 the state stopped making public the difference between the number of asylum seekers and the number of officially recognized refugees, with the official acceptance rate statistics from that year remaining as the most updated figures on the Ministry of Foreign Affairs public web page six years later (Losier 2020). NGO activists consulted at the time estimated the rate to be much lower.[70]

When asked directly by the author about the acceptance rate, officials of the Foreign Ministry would sometimes provide ambiguous answers, responding instead with the ratio of those requesting asylum to those deemed *admissible* to begin the status determination process (but not those who were ultimately granted refugee status at the end of that process). A UNHCR audit reported that the state stopped sharing the acceptance rate and other statistics not only with the public, but also with UNHCR, from 2013 to 2015, in part because the state itself was uncertain of the exact number due to flaws in the usage of its registration software, ProGres (UN OIOS 2017). In an example of the parallel governance functions of nonstate actors within the governance network, UNHCR responded to the lack of official state data by launching its own baseline survey and an independent reform of its own ProGres system, separate from the state, after which it supported the state's efforts to reform

---

[69] Interview 111QN 2018.
[70] Interview 5CI 2015; Interview 141QS 2017.

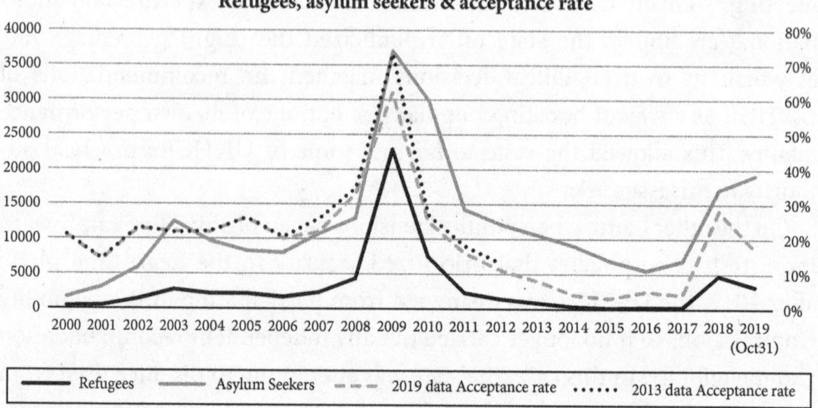

Figure 5.13 Refugees, asylum seekers, and acceptance rate in Ecuador, 2000–2018

Source: Ministerio de Relaciones Exteriores, "Estadísticas de refugiados (histórico)," updated November 5, 2019; Ministerio de Relaciones Exteriores, "Estadísticas peticionarios desagregado por año, sexo y grupo etario," updated November 5, 2019.

its software system as well (UN OIOS 2017). An official of an international organization who was asked in 2017 about the acceptance rate confirmed that the state by then knew this information, but that the state policy was not to make it public. In order to avoid shining an awkward light on the state and applying too much negative pressure when it was perceived to be trying to implement constructive policies to improve its backlog and its ability to improve the status determination process, the IGO had decided to comply with the request not to make the status determination rate public.[71]

Only in November 2019, more than two years after Lenin Moreno replaced Rafael Correa in the presidency, did the Foreign Ministry finally publish the number of refugees and asylum seekers for the full time period from 2000 to 2019, making it possible to calculate the acceptance rate for the full time period. As shown in Figure 5.13, the period between 2014 and 2017 did indeed feature an acceptance rate below 5%, suggesting that the state's evasion of transparency about this rate during the Regression phase of Correa's presidency was an intentional act to avoid accountability to civil society and international actors that could undermine the "universal citizenship" rhetoric still being maintained by the regime. Interestingly, the newly published 2019

---

[71] Interview 93QI 2017.

numbers for the period preceding 2013 differed somewhat from the original statistics that had been published previously on the Foreign Ministry's website, suggesting that the reform of the software system may have revealed gaps and mistakes, and that there may be a reason to be somewhat skeptical of the state's statistics. The new, revised 2019 numbers generally reflected slightly lower numbers of asylum seekers and slightly higher numbers of refugees beginning in 2005, with the resulting acceptance rate being slightly higher for the years 2005–12 in the 2019 data release.

Correa's use of universal citizenship discourses to position himself as a regional leader also opened up an opportunity for coalitions of domestic political actors, NGOs, and international organizations to hold him accountable for the consistent implementation of these principles (Correa 2016). In my previous work analyzing Correa's 437 public speeches over eight years, I showed that although his discourse referred to universal citizenship, he was primarily concerned with (and his political incentives responded most strongly to) the protection of Ecuadorian emigrants living abroad, in Europe and the United States. Indeed, of his mentions of "migration," 60% referred to Ecuadorian emigrants abroad, and only 27% referred to refugees or immigrants in Ecuador (Pugh 2017). By emphasizing reciprocity arguments, however, domestic actors who favored extending such rights to Colombians in Ecuador could press him for policies that would welcome foreigners without discrimination in the interest of maintaining consistency.

For example, the law clinic at Universidad San Francisco de Quito and Fundación Asylum Access used a successful lawsuit before the Ecuadorian Constitutional Court to defeat some of the most egregious restrictive elements of President Correa's Decree 1182 in 2012 (Ubidia Vazquez 2015; Palma Lozana 2017). As a result of the court's finding that these elements (including the requirement that asylum seekers must make their refugee claim within fifteen days of entering Ecuadorian territory and the elimination of the Cartagena Declaration criteria in favor of the more restrictive 1951 Convention criteria for refugee status determination) were unconstitutional, the state was being held accountable for providing greater protection to refugees. Likewise, the abandonment of the restrictive and unreasonable police record requirement for asylum seekers was produced in large part by a network of nonstate actors contesting this part of migration governance. The Constitutional Court ruled that this requirement was unconstitutional, in response to a lawsuit filed by a coalition that included the human rights NGO INREDH, the Jesuit Refugee Service, the Colombian migrant organization

Figure 5.14 Mural image of Colombian-Ecuadorian solidarity, Esmeraldas, Ecuador
Source: Photo by the author.

ASEREX, and the Ecuadorian migrant association Asociación Rumiñaui 9 de enero.[72]

Symbolic Politics

Symbolic politics refers to the way that images and discourses are used to frame and shape the emotions and meaning attached to issues and policies, tying domestic political debates to narratives that resonate with international audiences. In many of the anti-xenophobia campaigns launched by the UN and a coalition of nonstate actors, a key component was to emphasize the cultural, historical, and geographic similarities between Ecuador and Colombia, highlighting the theme of fraternal solidarity. Figure 5.14 shows an example of this type of imagery, with a street mural in Esmeraldas painted by students in a campaign by HIAS/NRC/UNHCR depicting an Ecuadorian and a Colombian, dressed similarly in their respective national colors, shaking hands while playing soccer with the Andean mountains connecting both countries in the background.

[72] Sentencia No. 035-17-SIN-CC, Caso No. 0006-09-IN, Corte Constitucional del Ecuador (December 13, 2017).

A leader of a Colombian association in Quito reported that one of the most powerful strategies that his group used was to humanize refugees by telling their personal stories in talks with Ecuadorian groups, to increase empathy and the perception that those seeking shelter through no fault of their own could just as easily be Ecuadorians.[73] A coalition of eighty NGOs, UN agencies, state institutions, and faith-based organizations (two-thirds nonstate actors, and one-third state institutions) promoted a campaign in 2011 called "Coexist in Solidarity." This campaign reinforced the imagery of similarity between Ecuador and Colombia, and the idea that migrants and refugees contributed to, rather than took from, receiving communities. Through binational cultural fairs, publicity materials, and media spots, Colombian-Ecuadorian business plan competitions, and other programs, this campaign reframed narratives, from the "refugee problem" and securitization to humanitarian and economic opportunity (Crawley et al. 2016; D'Appollonia 2012). The state also deployed symbols and narratives of universal citizenship, open borders, and human security to position itself as an innovator of political concepts and policies (Pugh 2017). These discourses provided an organizing frame for the debate on specific policies like the 2017 Human Mobility Law, as well as for campaigns by nonstate actors to reframe the popular conception of migrants and refugees in Ecuadorian society.

Conclusion

The three institutional authority poles discussed in this chapter—the state, the UN system, and the church—form the central core of the governance network for refugee and migration policy at the national level in Ecuador. Their dynamic interaction with each other, through cooperation and competition, can be understood as a function of differences in trust, mission, capacity, and transnational linkages, as analyzed in this chapter. These factors have evolved over time, so the patterns of the governance network and the resulting outcomes for the human security of Colombians and their Ecuadorian host communities have shifted accordingly. Table 5.4 summarizes some of the most important migrant governance outcomes in Ecuador, identifying the key actors involved in proposing or pushing for them as well as the actors responsible for their implementation. The institutional analysis of this chapter

---

[73] Interview 102QM 2009.

Table 5.4 Origin and impact of policies and programs

Policy/ program	Years	Origin/ proposer	Implementer	Impact
Plan Ecuador	2007–	Correa/ government	Government	Adopted a development/ security framework for northern border based on human security/ rights rather than military control and neoliberal market solutions
Constitution	2007–	Government/ Constituent Assembly	Government	Codified universal citizenship and *buen vivir* as guiding principles; prohibited discrimination by immigration status; ensured refugees had same basic rights as Ecuadorians
Enhanced Registration	2009–10	UNHCR	UNHCR/ Foreign ministry/ NGOs	Doubled registered refugees; generated some backlash
Interagency Peace/Dev Program in NB	2006–10	UNDP/ UNHCR	UNDP/ UNHCR, USAID, NGOs, Plan Ecuador	Coordinated international aid with conflict-sensitive framework, encouraged local/national planning/ dialogue spaces

Table 5.4 *Continued*

Policy/ program	Years	Origin/ proposer	Implementer	Impact
Organic Human Mobility Law	2007– (passed 2017)	NGOs/UNHCR	National Assembly	Updated migration legislation in a permanent law, combining refugee, immigrant, emigrant mobility in one integrated framework relevant to new empirical context and constitution
Public Defender refugee representation	2017–	UNHCR/ AAE/ public defenders	Government/ judiciary	150 cases in first three months; uneven implementation in long term

serves as a foundation, illustrating many of the ways that the key actors developed and evolved the networked governance that shaped the experience of refugees and migrants in Ecuador. The next two chapters apply the lens of the invisibility bargain to explain how the informal expectations of migrant valued contributions and social invisibility (chapter 6) and political invisibility (chapter 7) influence the negotiation of migration identity and policy, as well as the participation strategies of forced migrants from Colombia through governance networks in Ecuador and the resulting outcomes for migrant human security.

6

Valued Contribution and Social Invisibility in Ecuador

In Ecuador and the Global South, there is often a significant difference between the rights and protections guaranteed by law and their implementation in the everyday lives of migrants—especially those who are racially differentiated from the dominant population—and other minority groups (Losier 2020). In many parts of Latin America, for example, a state project of mestizaje has projected a homogenizing national identity that denies the existence of domestic racial discrimination (Dulitzky 2005) and excludes indigenous and black minorities from decision-making spaces and full belonging in society (Telles 2014). This pattern has been replicated in migrant-receiving communities across Latin America, as foreigners become the new "out-group," confronting the same gap between formal rights and de facto exclusion (Kushner 2012; Foote and Goebel 2014). The unwritten set of expectations and racial hierarchies that accompanies the formal citizenship regime in such contexts shapes the opportunities and challenges for migrants attempting to gain access to rights and protections.

As discussed in chapter 2, migrants whose visible characteristics and practices violate norms that the host society deems to be acceptable or who engage in overt political claim-making on the state often risk sparking a nativist backlash. Many choose instead to change or minimize these identity differences or withdraw from public spaces altogether, seeking refuge in invisibility by reducing their interactions with others. Given intersecting social hierarchies of race, gender, class, and nationality, these identity-shaping strategies have different stakes for migrants depending on the subgroups to which they belong. The examination in this chapter of the ways that social (in)visibility, markers of difference, and social hierarchies in Ecuador make integration of Colombians easier or more difficult is critical to understanding how nonstate actors help migrants access protection from discrimination, rights violations, and violence.

The Invisibility Bargain. Jeffrey D. Pugh, Oxford University Press (2021). © Oxford University Press.
DOI: 10.1093/oso/9780197538692.003.0006

Colombian Migrants and the Invisibility Bargain in Ecuador

Colombians for most of the past two decades have been the largest and most visible migrant group in Ecuador, as described in the introductory chapter. Because Colombian migrants are associated with the conflict in their home country, they commonly confront fear and assumptions of criminality in Ecuador, where people do not always distinguish between Colombian perpetrators and victims in their perceptions.[1]

Over the past decades, the Ecuadorian state has also employed a boundary-blurring strategy that extends autonomous group rights to indigenous and Afro-descendent populations and a boundary-shifting strategy to redefine individuals in these groups as rights-bearing members of the community of value. The Correa government extended these efforts to the new migrant population as well, although for all three groups discrimination and exclusion remain rampant (Martínez Novo 2014). In fact, underlying assumptions of whiteness and mestizaje seem to define Ecuador's community of value, which lead to Ecuadorian populations of color being invisible and to Afro-descendent Colombian migrants in particular finding it difficult to integrate, as they are exposed to intersecting and multiplying structures of marginalization because of nationality, race, gender, and often class (Romo Perez 2019, 2020). Even with formal protections in the constitution and in law, the practical implementation of migration policy and societal behavior both reflect a contingent acceptance of Colombians, especially those whose "otherness" is magnified by race or class differences (which influence the perceived "valued contribution" that migrants make to the host society), more than the formal promises of universal citizenship (Balyk and Pugh 2013).

The data from my MNS and interviews, and from other surveys, illustrate how Colombians are expected to contribute economically to Ecuadorian society, while remaining socially and politically invisible to avoid negative social sanctions and backlash. As the surveys in particular show, Ecuadorians' perception of foreigners' economic contribution is relatively positive, with 73% of respondents in a national survey carried out by FLACSO believing that immigrants contribute economically to Ecuadorian society (Zepeda and Carrion 2015).[2]

---

[1] Interview 102QM 2009.

[2] This finding should be put into context, however, as in this same survey, two-thirds of respondents also believed that foreign migrants took jobs from Ecuadorians, and 85% believed

Both Ecuadorians and Colombians face difficult economic conditions, with many working in the informal sector for low and unstable wages, but the scope of the problem is much worse for Colombians. Eighty percent of surveyed migrants who worked full time reported that they earned less than Ecuador's legal minimum wage (MNS 2016). In comparison, 43% of full-time Ecuadorian workers earn less than minimum wage (Marinakis 2014). Partly because of the scarcity of formal employment, the violence that precludes the option of returning home, and the fact that Colombia's minimum wage is much lower than Ecuador's, many Colombian migrants work hard for lower wages, representing an attractive labor source for Ecuadorian employers.[3] Other Colombians are entrepreneurs who start their own small businesses, which may create additional jobs for Ecuadorians (Negocios 2005).[4] All of these factors contribute to the relatively positive perception of Colombians' contribution to the Ecuadorian economy, fulfilling the "valued contribution" expectation of the invisibility bargain.

In Ecuador, the host population's implicit tolerance sometimes turns toward a more active attempt to control or remove Colombian migrants when they are perceived to violate social invisibility. According to one NGO leader, such violations might take the form of speaking loudly with foreign accents or, for women, dressing in "provocative" ways that some Ecuadorian women fear will lure away their men (Camacho Zambrano 2005; Dancygier et al. 2019).[5] In part because there is a higher percentage of Afro-Colombians than there is of Afro-Ecuadorians (21% vs. 7%), race is a marker of difference that can identify Colombians and mark them for exclusion. By contrast, there is a larger proportion of indigenous Ecuadorians than indigenous Colombians,[6] which means that indigeneity has not usually been a major marker of difference influencing the host society's reception of Colombian

that Ecuadorian emigrants living in Europe and other places abroad contributed economically to their host country. The twelve-point difference in perceptions about the economic contribution of Ecuadorian emigrants abroad vs. foreign migrants in Ecuador seems to indicate an in-group bias, rather than a universal attitude toward migration in general.

[3] Interview 67IN 2014; Interview 60IN 2014. Ecuador had one of the highest minimum wages in Latin America at $366 per month in 2016, while Colombia had one of the lowest, at $222 per month, a mere 63% of the Ecuadorian wage (Así 2015). This may influence migrants' expectations and tolerance for wages under the legal limit in Ecuador.

[4] Interview 61IN 2014.

[5] Interview 110QN 2007.

[6] The exact size of Ecuador's indigenous population is contested. Census data on self-reported indigenous identity show that twice as many Ecuadorians are indigenous as Colombians (7% vs. 3.5%); however, other estimates claim that indigenous people represent much higher proportions of the Ecuadorian population, perhaps 25%–35%. See Chisaguano 2006; Becker 2016; and ECLAC 2014.

migrants.[7] Racialized and indigenous identities, of course, are already laden with meanings in Ecuador, including permissions or prohibitions to act in particular ways (Cervone 1999). The same behavior that would be ignored or excused for a mestizo Ecuadorian, for example, might result in social rejection or trigger persecution if done by a Colombian, even more if the person is Afro-Colombian. In communities in which racially distinct foreigners quickly diversify a previously homogenous society, migrants' visibility is likely to be heightened and the pressure for them to assimilate intensified.[8]

As shown in the subsequent sections of this chapter and the next, Colombian migrants quickly learn the invisibility bargain's spoken and unspoken rules, adapting their coping strategies and forms of political bargaining to this reality. The same coping strategy may take on different meanings, however, depending on the context, personal characteristics, and social capital of those carrying it out. The ways in which the social invisibility expectation is navigated across multiple forms of difference are discussed in the next section, which traces the connections among race, class, gender, and accent to analyze their role in shaping migrant acceptance and integration in the host society.

Constructing Markers of Difference in Ecuador

In Ecuador, social hierarchies are reproduced in everyday practices, and racial relations in particular are characterized by an internalized set of rules that privilege those in power by helping them find employment and housing, move freely, participate politically, and exist in public space without their visible differences inhibiting success (Cervone 1999). The recent phenomenon of large-scale immigration into Ecuador adds additional marginalized social categories to the existing categories of indigeneity and race and complicates the negotiation of ethnic identity and political agency by minority groups. Such negotiations, of course, have long and deep historical roots (de la Torre 2006). Ecuador's colonial legacy and history of haciendas relegated indigenous and Afro-descendent populations to manual labor in rural areas. The large cities, in contrast, became spaces that concentrated political and economic elites who constructed an exclusive community of

[7] Interview 129QN 2008.
[8] Interview 61IN 2014.

value that implicitly linked whiteness and mestizaje with political power and legitimacy. Combined with a state project of mestizaje and "whitening" of Afro-descendent populations to promote a homogenous and "civilizing" national imaginary, the state relied on labor segregation and the occlusion of subaltern bodies that did not conform to this dominant narrative (de la Torre 2002). This remains true today for Afro-descendent and indigenous Colombian migrants, who experience marginalization along and across lines of race, class, and nationality when they come to Ecuador, having already experienced different forms of exclusion and discrimination in Colombia (Wade 1993).

Given these intersecting forms of difference and the stigmatization of Colombians in Ecuador, how does one tease out the relative importance of these factors in their experiences of belonging and exclusion? In other words, if the invisibility bargain demands "social invisibility," which markers of difference provoke the strongest reaction by Ecuadorians against Colombians? Compared to other social categories, migrants are the target of particular distrust in Ecuador. Ecuadorian Latinobarometer respondents (2007), for example, reported lower levels of trust toward foreigners than toward indigenous people, Ecuadorian nationals, or poor people. When trying to tease out the weighting of different forms of difference *within* the migrant population, however, economic class takes on more importance. Latinobarometer respondents were asked how many foreign migrants of the same race as the country's dominant group should be let into Ecuador, how many of a different race, and how many from a poorer country. Although most respondents believed that few or no migrants should be allowed to enter, these exclusionary attitudes were most acute toward migrants from poorer countries (Latinobarometer 2007), confirming the invisibility bargain's expectation of economic contribution.

Ecuadorians surveyed by Zepeda and Carrion (2015) also distinguished among migrants of different nationalities, reporting more positive views of US, European, and Chinese migrants than of Latin American migrants, and especially Colombians, of whom Ecuadorians had the most negative perceptions. Colombians are often stigmatized as being associated with crime and conflict while US, European, and Chinese migrants are associated with investment or tourism. Although Colombians are more similar to Ecuadorians by phenotype, language, geographic proximity, and religion than these other groups, negative stereotypes associated with their nationality seem to be more salient in producing social exclusion. The next two sections attempt to tease apart the ways in which accent and race interact with gender and class to shape the possibilities for social inclusion or marginalization of Colombian migrants in Ecuador.

Nationality Marked by Accent and Style of Speech

Language and accent are key markers of difference that set migrants apart in many countries, although there is a debate about whether the presence of a different accent or language, or the values and social meaning given to it, increases prejudice and discrimination (Munro 2003; Hopkins 2015). In my MNS, 73% of migrant respondents in Ecuador reported that they had felt discriminated against while living in Ecuador. When asked on what basis they had been discriminated against, accent was second only to "being Colombian" as the most often mentioned reason for discrimination.[9] Indeed, at least some of the stigmatized response seemed to be amplified toward Colombians specifically, compared to baseline discrimination of migrants in general. In a 2020 study of migrants from six population groups living in Quito, my colleagues and I found that Colombians reported that they had experienced discrimination in much higher numbers than five other migrant groups living in the city—Venezuelans, Cubans, Haitians, Chinese, and returned Ecuadorian emigrants. Some 62% of Colombian respondents in that survey reported experiencing discrimination, compared to an overall average of 43% across all six groups (Pugh et al. 2020; Jimenez and Pugh 2020).[10]

Such experiences are also deeply gendered. Compared to Ecuadorian responses to migrants from other places such as the United States, Europe, or China (Zepeda and Carrion 2015), sexualized stereotypes of women and perceptions of threatening male criminality provide nationality-specific emotional baggage that becomes attached to Colombian accents (Romo Perez 2020). A Colombian woman in Esmeraldas, for example, reported in a 2013 interview that when she was out to dinner with friends and dressed in business attire, a man at the restaurant heard her accent and asked how much she charged per hour, implying that she was a prostitute. Notably, this

---

[9] Of course, being Colombian is a *form* of difference, whereas accent and style of speech are *markers* that make this difference obvious to others.

[10] This survey had an overall sample size of 720, with 120 participants from each population.

woman was a college-educated consultant working for an international organization. As this example shows, negative nationality and sexualized stereotypes can be activated by accent markers that cut across class lines.

Although these stereotypes apply across classes, their consequences for migrants' livelihoods are more severe for poorer migrants, who have access to fewer resources in the face of discrimination, or for women, who are more likely than men to face discrimination manifested through sexual assault or harassment (Santacruz and Vallejo 2012). These sorts of responses to different accents frequently lead Colombians to stay at home, to communicate mostly with other Colombians, or to remain silent in public, especially in close proximity to police and other state agents (Korovkin 2008). According to one female Colombian asylum seeker in a 2013 interview in Quito,

> I stopped selling empanadas in the streets because I am afraid. The migration police would often come by, and if they hear a Colombian accent, they would ask to see our documents. The photocopy of my asylum-seeker document that I carry serves very little use. They often claim that these documents are fake and detain Colombians anyway. When I go out, I try to keep my mouth shut.[11]

Echoing Engbersen and Broeders's (2009) discussion of the interactions between state attempts to identify and categorize migrants and migrant efforts to avoid identification, this social silence strategy results from fears of the state and of host society discrimination. These strategies, however, also further isolate migrants from potentially useful social networks and organizational allies, making it more difficult for Colombian migrants to access the rights, resources, and protection they need to live in dignity in Ecuador.

Disentangling Race, Class, and Gender

Race has always been a prominent marker of difference in Ecuador, as indicated by the historical experience of indigenous and Afro-descendent minority groups (de la Torre 2002, 2006). Both groups have been the target of economic and social exclusion, but indigenous groups have been more successful in organizing a viable political movement (Pugh 2008) by engaging

---

[11] Interview 109QM 2013.

in boundary-shifting work to redefine Ecuadorian national identity as "plurinational." Whereas the indigenous origins of most Ecuadorians have been incorporated into the national ideology of mestizaje, Afro-descendants have not been what Jean Muteba Rahier calls an ingredient in "the ideological biologies of national identity" (2012, 1). Instead, they have been excluded from the national fold and are frequent targets of fear and negative stereotypes (Beck et al. 2011; Wade 1993). At the same time that Afro-Ecuadorians have been hidden by and in national identity discourses, however, they have also organized around informal, nonstate organizations, regional identities, and kinship networks to gain access to resources and local political spaces (Whitten 1965; Handelsman 2019).

Since there is a high level of baseline racism toward Afro-descendants in Ecuadorian society, it can be tricky to tease apart a generalized racial prejudice from that which is specific to Afro-Colombian migrants. To disaggregate Ecuadorians' views of each group, the Race and Immigration Survey (RIS 2008) asked respondents to select from a group of fourteen words the images they most associated with Afro-Colombians, Colombians in general, and Afro-Ecuadorians. Table 6.1 summarizes the percentage of respondents selecting each word by identity group. These results provide evidence on how negative and positive images are applied to groups separated from the dominant Ecuadorian mestizo population by differences in race, nationality, or both.

Survey participants associated all three groups with a stereotyped view of criminality, with "thief" being the second most common image linked to each one (although the percentage mentioning this image for Colombians of all races was higher than for Afro-Ecuadorians). Colombians also confront other images such as "victims," "poor," "prostitutes," and "uneducated," in addition to more positive perceptions like "hardworking" and "friendly." Afro-Ecuadorians are not associated with criminality to the same extent as Colombians, with positive characteristics like "collaborative" and "honest" mentioned more frequently than for Colombians (suggesting greater nationality in-group trust). The results for Afro-Colombians, however, show how racial, national, and class differences reinforce each other, with negative characteristics being mentioned more often than for the other two groups. For example, "uneducated" is mentioned twice as often for Afro-Colombians as it is for either Colombians in general or Afro-Ecuadorians. Poverty and class, in contrast, seem to be linked more strongly to race than to nationality, with 60% of respondents associating "poor" with Afro-Ecuadorians,

Table 6.1 Images associated with Colombian migrants by Ecuadorians in Quito

	Colombians in general	Afro-Colombians	Afro-Ecuadorians
Refugees	59	52	14
Thieves (−)	50	50	45
Hardworking (+)	43	32	44
Friendly (+)	41	25	44
Victims (−)	40	37	18
Poor (−)	34	47	59
Prostitutes (−)	33	20	9
Neighbors (+)	25	23	16
Collaborative (+)	13	11	24
Uneducated (−)	12	24	12
Beautiful (+)	11	4	6
Leaders (+)	5	3	3
Ugly (−)	4	6	10
Honest (+)	3	8	17

Note: Figure are percentage of respondents selecting each word.
Source: RIS 2008.

more than Afro-Colombians or Colombians in general. These subtle variations in the behavioral and class perceptions of different groups suggest that simple positive/negative dichotomies are too crude to understand the social evaluations of outgroups, which may be influenced by whether the negative traits are perceived to result from the person's external circumstances or choices.

In this survey sexual stereotypes were triggered by national difference more than by racial difference, with "prostitute" associated most often with Colombians in general, less often with Afro-Colombians, and least often with Afro-Ecuadorians.[12] "Beautiful" was mentioned more often for Colombians than Afro-Ecuadorians but least often for Afro-Colombian, suggesting that race and nationality can have compounding effects on gender-based stereotypes. Given the similar language and race of most Ecuadorians and

---

[12] The secondary literature shows that blackness is often associated with debased sexuality in Ecuador (Rahier 2012). The survey evidence, however, seems to indicate that sexual stereotypes regarding Colombians may be even stronger.

Colombians, one Quito NGO leader who was asked in a 2007 interview how people distinguish between the two groups replied, somewhat tongue-in-cheek, "Colombians are perceived to be sexier."[13] Her description of both male and female sexualization reinforces the survey evidence that sexual stereotypes are more strongly associated with Colombian nationality than with race.

Evidence from both the interviews and the MNS extends and deepens the analysis derived from the RIS image association question to show the intersections of race, class, gender, and nationality. In the MNS, a higher percentage of white Colombian migrant respondents (81%) reported having experienced discrimination in Ecuador than any other migrant group (compared to 72% of Afro-descendent and mestizo respondents and 67% of indigenous respondents). This difference in perception may point to the important role of expectations and *relative* deprivation (Gurr 1970). Respondents likely compared the forms of privilege and discrimination they experienced in Colombia with those they now experienced in Ecuador. Because markers of difference take on new meanings in different contexts, there is a possible negativity bias: whiteness was a source of privilege in Colombia, but the racial privilege of whiteness is overridden in Ecuador by discrimination based on nationality. Blackness, by contrast, resulted in discrimination in both Colombia and Ecuador, so there was less surprise among Afro-Colombians that they experienced discrimination in Ecuador, which they may attribute more to nationality than to skin color. This common experience of social exclusion in Ecuador can help activate a shared Colombian identity and foster intragroup solidarity between mestizo/white and Afro-Colombians in the host country that may have been missing in their country of origin. A white, highly educated Colombian woman working in a Quito university echoed this national solidarity logic: "When you have a reason like discrimination, you have a reason to come together. I know with my own experience I have felt that."[14]

While common experiences of discrimination may strengthen a shared Colombian identity that is more salient than their racial subgroup to migrants' identities, the intensity of the invisibility bargain and its stakes for survival and security are not the same across differences of race, class, and

---

[13] Interview 110QN 2007. It is also possible that this response could reflect the exclusion of blackness from the dominant social construction of "Colombian" in the same way that "American" or "British" is often used as a coded proxy for "white."

[14] Interview 124QN 2015.

gender (Santacruz and Vallejo 2012). An Afro-Colombian woman in a 2015 focus group in Quito, for example, recalled the experience of going with a white Colombian friend to inquire about an apartment listed for rent. The landlord asked who would be the tenant. When they said both would live there, he said he would rent to the white Colombian woman, but not the black woman.[15]

In the same focus group, two university-educated Colombian women shared their personal testimonies. One was a white researcher who had migrated to Ecuador on an economic visa and later naturalized as a citizen; the other was an Afro-Colombian social worker who had fled death threats and was living in Ecuador as a refugee. Both women described incidents of discrimination and xenophobic comments triggered by people hearing their accents, as well as sexualized comments about prostitution that responded to gendered stereotypes of Colombians. The Afro-Colombian woman, however, responded to her compatriot's story by saying that the consequences of their experiences were very different because her precarity as a refugee meant that housing or job discrimination could put her life at risk if she had to return to Colombia or was "outed" in public to armed actors who might threaten her.[16] Her race added an additional visible target that increased the likelihood that social discrimination would lead to such consequences. Xenophobic comments, then, represented a greater threat to her livelihood and survival than to the other woman (and the white participant agreed). In this case, race, and potentially class differences, raised the stakes of harm. The two Colombian women's common educational level may have influenced the likelihood that they would offer resistance and understand that their formal rights were violated, but the Afro-Colombian refugee, marked with greater difference, confronted steeper social sanctions with higher personal human security costs.

Likewise, a study of Colombian and Ecuadorian women, black and mestiza, in a Quito prison found that police tended to stereotype black women as more aggressive, and thus to treat them more harshly, and to assume that Colombian women were sexually promiscuous, and thus to propose favors and special privileges in exchange for sexual reciprocity. Intersections of class, age, and sexual orientation also affected the degree of leniency or harshness that these prisoners experienced from police (Romo Pérez 2019). Some

[15] Interview 106QM 2015.
[16] Interview 105QM 2015.

reported trying to lie about their nationality as a survival tactic, or to emphasize one part of their identity (i.e., being a lesbian to avoid sexual advances or their education to signal not being naive) as a way of coping with the greater vulnerabilities presented by other parts of their identity, like being young, or Colombian, or poor (Romo Perez 2020).

Race, class, nationality, and gender, then, represent both forms of difference and systems of power that mutually constitute each other (Herrera et al. 2005) and influence whose bodies belong in the "community of value." As detailed in the next section, migrants who are expected to remain socially invisible often adapt to these power relations in the conception and presentation of their own identities. Their strategies to survive, thrive, and participate politically seek to avoid a violation of the invisibility bargain that might result in a nativist backlash against them.

Coping Strategies under the Invisibility Bargain

This research identified three key strategies that Colombian migrants often employ to overcome the negative effects of the social invisibility expectation: (1) reducing social distance by developing meaningful relationships with Ecuadorians, (2) minimizing differences by trying to become more like Ecuadorians or by avoiding Ecuadorians altogether, and (3) forming coalitions and networks with Ecuadorian NGOs and returned emigrant allies whose positionality is advantageous in opening space for participation. Together, the strategies expose a paradox: greater interaction between host and migrant populations can improve intergroup relations but is also difficult to achieve since the invisibility bargain itself produces self-censorship and isolation from the host society by those with visible differences. This dilemma is central to understanding both migrants' apparent avoidance of visible political organizing in favor of informal strategies and the persistence of anti-immigrant prejudice in many host societies.

Reducing Social Distance

Migrants whose differences are stigmatized by Ecuadorians face challenges in developing meaningful relationships with their citizen peers. This phenomenon can be understood through the concept of social distance, which refers to the ascribed differences that separate groups within society and regulate at what level of intimacy their cross-group interactions can occur and still be socially accepted (Bogardus 1925). The difference between intimate space, personal space, social space, and public space, and which groups are invited to interact in each space, influence social hierarchies and the negotiation of membership within society (Hall 1990).

A rich literature on contact theory has found that anti-immigrant attitudes are often moderated at the individual level when members of the host society develop friendships and other close relationships with migrants in personal and social space (McLaren 2003; Bohman 2015). Frequent, meaningful, and equal-status interaction can remind a person of the humanity and individuality of members of the other group, making it more difficult to maintain stereotyped images or discriminatory behavior and increasing the likelihood of constructive migrant integration (Berry 2005). A meta-analysis of over five hundred studies on contact theory by Pettigrew and Tropp (2008) provides further evidence for this finding, with a reduction of anxiety about intergroup interaction and an increase in empathy and perspective-taking being the most important mediating mechanisms through which interaction leads to less prejudice. It is much easier to maintain negative stereotypes of the out-group when one has few or no in-depth personal intergroup interactions (Pettigrew 1998).

The evidence from Ecuador shows that the frequency and quality of interaction between Ecuadorians and Colombians seem to influence their attitudes toward one another. In the RIS 2008 survey, 59% of Ecuadorian respondents who did not know a Colombian personally supported a policy of deporting all Colombian migrants to their country of origin, while only 27% of those who reported knowing a Colombian personally supported deportation. If we treat support of deportation as a proxy for hostile attitudes toward migrants more generally, this finding implies that social boundary crossing by migrants or Ecuadorians is an important factor in shaping migrants' reception.

Likewise, MNS migrant respondents were asked how frequently they interacted with Ecuadorians and what their general perception was of Ecuadorian people. Migrants reporting daily interaction with Ecuadorians had nearly double the level of positive perceptions of the native population compared to those who interacted less frequently. The results for quality—where the surveyed Colombian migrants in Quito most often interacted with Ecuadorians—were similar. Those who had no interaction with Ecuadorians reported more negative perceptions (71%) than those having interacted in public spaces (50%) or in personal and social spaces (16%) (MOS 2010).[17] This phenomenon works in both directions. Zepeda and Carrion (2015) asked Ecuadorian respondents about their general opinion of foreigners living in Ecuador, and also whether they had any relations with foreigners living in Ecuador. Of those who reporting having some relation with a foreigner, 67% had a good or very good opinion, 8.5% had a bad or very bad opinion, and 25% had a neutral (neither good nor bad) opinion of foreigners in general. In contrast, of those who had no relation with any foreigners, only 47% had good or very good perception, 18% had a bad or very bad opinion, and 30.5% had a neutral opinion. This shows that contact affects the attitudes and prejudices of both migrants and members of the host population.

Migrants' ability to form social ties to the host community is affected by various markers of difference. The combined stigma of being both Colombian and a minority race, for instance, can cause difficulties establishing harmonious relations with Ecuadorians (Korovkin 2008). Migrant respondents' racial identities correlated with their frequency of interaction with Ecuadorians in the MNS. Mestizo migrants, who are most similar to the majority Ecuadorian population, interacted more frequently with Ecuadorians than did Afro-descendent, white, or indigenous migrants.[18] White, mestizo, and to a lesser extent indigenous migrants also reported accessing more types of assistance from a larger number of organizations than did Afro-descendent migrants (MNS 2016).

From the perspective of the Ecuadorian host community, racial group identity can also intersect with nationality to limit intergroup trust and social interaction. When Ecuadorian Latinobarometer (2007) respondents were asked how much trust they had in foreigners, Afro-Ecuadorian and indigenous respondents reported less trust in migrants than did other racial groups.[19] This observation highlights the challenges that indigenous and

---

[17] Personal and social spaces included family, school/university, work, sports, and organizations, whereas public spaces included the street, neighborhood, and market.

[18] Eighty-five percent of mestizo migrants interacted daily with Ecuadorians, compared to 72% of Afro-descendent migrants, 73% of white migrants, and 63% of indigenous migrants; on the other side of the coin, only 5% of mestizo migrants *never* interacted with Ecuadorians, compared with 13% of Afro-descendants, 21% of whites, and 31% of indigenous migrants (MNS 2016).

[19] Among the 2007 Latinobarometer respondents, black (52%) and indigenous (48%) Ecuadorians were more likely than any other racial group to express "no trust" toward foreigners (compared to an average of 37% across all racial groups). This suspicion may stem in part from a legacy of conquest by mestizo outsiders and a social structure that relies on community cohesion, family relationships, and protection of in-group norms and traditions.

Afro-Colombians confront when trying to establish social ties on the basis of a shared racial identity with indigenous and Afro-Ecuadorians, since intergroup distrust toward other nationalities seems even stronger for these racial subgroups than for Ecuadorians in general.

The degree to which Afro-Colombians form closer social ties through racial affinity with Afro-Ecuadorians, rather than through co-nationality with mestizo Colombians, varies somewhat by region. In large cities like Quito, Colombians of all races often confront similar patterns of social exclusion that may lead them to interact more with each other than with Ecuadorians (Santacruz and Vallejo 2012). In the coastal border province of Esmeraldas, in contrast, fluidity across the border with Colombia, a history of cross-border family ties, and a larger Afro-Ecuadorian population lead to a greater likelihood that Afro-Colombians will form social ties with black Ecuadorians (CODHES 2015; Pugh et al. 2017). In San Lorenzo on the northern border of the coastal province, one Afro-Colombian refugee reflected, "San Lorenzo is a town of good people. The majority here are black like us and so they know how difficult it is for us to get ahead anywhere. Once we tried going to Ibarra because they say there is more work there, but we did not feel happy. Because of that, we preferred to return here because here we are all equal" (quoted in Méndez 2013: 79). In this region, Afro-Colombians may seek to reduce anti-Colombian bias toward themselves by "blending in" more with black Ecuadorians in this region, an option that is less available in other provinces. According to an NGO worker who has mediated conflicts with Colombians in both Quito and Esmeraldas,

> We noted a cultural clash related to the ways in which people coexist here in Quito more than in Esmeraldas because there the cultures are a bit more similar. Refugees who arrive in Esmeraldas are also looking for a society that is more similar to themselves, and there are a lot of Afro people there, so that helps them to become somewhat more invisible, and that is a strategy that they use to be able to better integrate themselves into society.[20]

The identity groups that become most salient in different contexts, thus, influence migrants' ability to form social ties (Greer 2013), which are key resources used to build coalitions to help migrants participate politically without violating the invisibility bargain (de Graauw 2016).

---

[20] Interview 119QN 2016.

Minimizing Difference

Many Colombians living in Ecuador try to balance maintaining their own identities with assimilating into their host society. To minimize difference from the host society, they employ two main strategies: reducing the visible/audible markers that distinguish them from Ecuadorians and reducing their level of contact and interaction with Ecuadorians altogether. Demonstrating the first of these strategies, many Colombians who successfully integrate into Ecuadorian society make a conscious effort to "unlearn" their accent, speak more softly and slowly, and use diminutive forms of speech to fit in better with Ecuadorians. According to one NGO worker in Quito,

> There are certain survival tools that allow some Colombians to blend in better, doing things the way Ecuadorians do them, and they tend to have an easier time than those who do not have these tools. Those who can do it, and feel comfortable doing it, will tend to have an easier time finding a job, getting housing, and building constructive relationships with Ecuadorians.[21]

As many Colombian migrants in Ecuador have discovered, their success in accessing rights, protection, and resources often depends on becoming less visible (and audible) as Colombian.

The second strategy that many Colombians use to minimize the differences between themselves and those around them is to avoid contact with Ecuadorians in favor of interacting primarily with other Colombian migrants. Given the difficulty of hiding differences marked by phenotype, this strategy of isolation was chosen more often by racial minority migrants. Afro-Colombians were less likely than mestizo Colombians, for instance, to live in neighborhoods with mostly Ecuadorian neighbors and nearly three times more likely to live in neighborhoods with mostly Colombian neighbors (MNS 2016). While some Colombian interviewees in a 2013 focus group in Quito pursued this strategy because of fear or distrust of Ecuadorians, others claimed that it was more the result of rejection from the Ecuadorian public sphere that they had experienced, which left other Colombians as the only social network available to them.

---

[21] Interview 132QN 2013.

This isolation strategy seemed less effective in giving migrants access to protection than did the strategy of minimizing differences. Avoiding public and social space allowed migrants to hide differences from the host population, but it also removed them from potential spaces where they could negotiate access to rights, protection, and resources and develop personal relationships with Ecuadorians to mitigate the prejudice underlying the invisibility bargain's social sanctions. As a result, Colombian migrants choosing isolation may be less resilient against attacks or discriminatory behavior because they lack a support network that stretches into the host society. Under the invisibility bargain, meaningful intergroup relationships are key protective resources for migrants, but they are also difficult to achieve.

Informal Bargaining through Allies and Intermediaries

To build coalitions with potential allies in the Ecuadorian host society, some migrants have employed a more sophisticated strategy that emphasizes the similarity between the experiences of Ecuadorian emigrants to Europe and Colombian immigrants in Ecuador. The fact that Ecuador, a major migrant-sending country, simultaneously became a major migrant-*receiving* country (especially of forced migrants) after 2000 allows migrants and their allies to deploy the argument that Ecuadorians should protect the rights of Colombians in their country just as they would like to have rights guaranteed for their relatives living abroad (Herrera et al. 2005). Thus, policy entrepreneurs in Ecuador propose a boundary-*blurring* strategy to strengthen norms recognizing migrant rights everywhere and legitimize migrants' political participation in countries of both origin and residence. This coalition builds on common identities and experiences of "human mobility" and invokes President Correa's rhetoric of "universal citizenship," in which every person has a right to migrate and should therefore have access to basic rights (Pugh 2017).[22]

NGOs and migrants in Ecuador have intentionally created migrant coalitions that advocate for the shared interests of immigrants, refugees, and returned Ecuadorian emigrants. Luis Jiménez has found that Ecuadorians

---

[22] Ecuadorian emigrants represented a new potential electoral base, and remittances were critical to the Ecuadorian economy (Herrera et al. 2005), so the strategy took advantage of a powerful political opportunity.

abroad are socialized into new political norms and strategies, and when they return home, they change the political engagement of their home communities, bringing more strategic thinking and willingness to engage in political activism (Jiménez 2018). In fact, this exposure to a new political culture can reshape the emigrants' identities and relationship with their own society and state once they return to Ecuador. This could help explain their importance in such a coalition of those affected by "human mobility." In addition, migrant coalitions have enlisted the support of Ecuadorians with personal ties to Colombians (Pugh et al. 2017), providing additional economic and political leverage in Ecuador and political cover to prevent a host population backlash.[23] As an IGO official explained, "In the border region, there are many [Ecuadorian] people who have Colombian friends and family. We are trying to take advantage of these connections to counterbalance the opposition of some local politicians for their own electoral purposes."[24] The director of an NGO in Quito said in a 2009 interview that his organization had deployed reciprocity arguments strategically to emphasize similarity and social capital between migrants *to* Ecuador and migrants *from* Ecuador. This strategy, he argued, has been effective in increasing the political space and perceived legitimacy of migrant rights.[25] As these examples show, the social and political sanctions against difference contained within the invisibility bargain can be modified and loosened by building new solidarity networks and emphasizing reciprocity. In the process, informal networks and coalitions can act as brokers through which migrants participate politically without incurring a nativist backlash.

Conclusion

This chapter has illustrated the complex social relations that are negotiated between migrants, the host society, and the state under the social invisibility expectation of the invisibility bargain. According to these expectations, social hierarchies of race, gender, class, and nationality shape the negotiation of identity and belonging between citizens and migrants, marking Colombian bodies as more or less easily accepted into the community of value and

---

[23] Interview 63IN 2014; Interview 22DM 2015.
[24] Interview 88QI 2015.
[25] Interview 166QN 2009.

influencing migrants' attempts to integrate peacefully and participate polit-ically in society. Since the norms legitimized in Ecuador reflect those of the historically dominant identity groups concentrated in cities, the price of ad-mission for Colombian migrants seeking full membership in the community of value seems to require approximation of mestizo traits, which creates par-ticular challenges for Afro-Colombians. Although indigeneity is not as vis-ible a marker of difference for Colombians in Ecuador, it certainly shapes the experiences of cross-border existence, ambiguous nationality and identity, and acceptance for the Cofan, Awa, and other indigenous groups that exist in both Ecuador and Colombia.

This case illustrates the invisibility bargain's utility for understanding how intersecting forms of difference complicate the negotiation of belonging in migrant-receiving states in the Global South. The argument introduced here provides a nuanced understanding of the informal expectations that produce vulnerability, the ways in which nationality, race, class, and gender can compound this marginalization, and the strategies migrants use to ac-cess the protection and resources they cannot claim directly from the state. Just as migrants and the host population negotiate categories of member-ship and the meanings given to them, they also negotiate rules and expecta-tions for the participation and social integration of migrant groups, whose claims to these forms of inclusion are not guaranteed by the formal status of citizenship.

Recognizing that identity and power shape both the community of value and migrants' strategies for entering it, this book has argued that in the Global South, migrants' relationship building through informal networks and their access to networks of nonstate institutions may be just as important as good policies and strong governmental institutions. In order to develop the evidence for this insight and illustrate the dynamics of this networked governance, chapter 7 examines the strategies of collective action and po-litical participation that migrants and their allies pursue in order to achieve greater human security in Ecuador in the context of the political invisibility expectation.

7

Political Invisibility and Migrants' Networked Governance Strategies in Ecuador

This chapter illustrates how Colombian migrants in Ecuador have adapted to the political invisibility expectation to exercise political agency and pursue access to the rights, resources, recognition, and protection that they need. It shows that the strategies that migrants pursue most often are those that are individual and do not require collective action, but that the strategies that are most effective are those (both individual and collective) that do not require overt, visible, public demand-making on the state that would invoke a backlash from the host population. Instead, informal negotiation at the local level, coalition building with allied groups within the host society, adapting cultural practices to better "fit in" with Ecuadorian society, and intentional, meaningful, task-oriented interaction between Ecuadorians and Colombians were all associated with better access to the governance network, and as a result, better human security outcomes.

In migrant-receiving communities of Ecuador, governance networks have played a major role in filling the gaps in state service provision and protection. The next section examines some of the specific ways that these governance networks link state and nonstate institutional actors with each other and provide access to human security for migrants (or fail to do so). The final section of the chapter delves into two major institutional processes—Enhanced Registration and the UN Interagency Program for Peace and Development in the northern border—as empirical cases that illustrate the powerful potential of networked governance to improve protection and participation for migrants and their host communities, while providing decentralized access points for migrants themselves to exercise agency in improving their own lives.

The Invisibility Bargain. Jeffrey D. Pugh, Oxford University Press (2021). © Oxford University Press.
DOI: 10.1093/oso/9780197538692.003.0007

Networked Governance: Pathways to Human Security

The specific pathways to human security and peacebuilding that are provided through networked governance in Ecuador include (*a*) expanding spaces for political participation and organizing to include migrants; (*b*) brokering access to resources for migrants in ways that do not cause a host society backlash by violating the "invisibility bargain"; (*c*) strengthening personal relationships and trust between Ecuadorians and Colombians; and (*d*) increasing access and protections of the rights guaranteed to migrants but often denied in practice, while avoiding overt violations of the invisibility bargain. It is also important to refrain from normative assumptions about the benevolence of nonstate actors or of the networks that link them with the state, as this form of governance also represents risks to human security that can lead to a failure to protect migrants and their Ecuadorian neighbors in some cases.

Political Participation

In many cases, migrants who fear or distrust the state may avoid engaging in official spaces for political participation, and they may be further excluded from having a say in decisions that affect them by social pressures demanding their political invisibility. As Ambrosini's (2017) "political pressure" category of intermediation suggests, these migrants may leverage their informal connections to individuals and institutions in the host population to negotiate decisions that will be in their interest and join coalitions to influence policies that benefit them, without necessarily taking an overt public stance on political issues. In a 2010 survey (MOS) of 128 Colombian migrants in Quito, respondents were asked whether they had used or could imagine using a series of strategies to improve their lives, and for those they had used, they were asked whether or not the strategy actually resulted in an improvement. Table 7.1 summarizes the results of this question, and shows that the strategies that migrants reported they had used or could imagine using tended to be individual actions like submitting a request for assistance to the UNHCR or the human rights ombudsman, or writing to the media, none of which require collective action or coordination with others.

Fewer respondents reported that they had or would negotiate with local officials, participate in public information campaigns, or join a protest. This

Table 7.1 Strategies employed by migrants in Quito

	Have done	Could do	(Have done + could do)	Would never do	DK/NA
Petition UNHCR	33%	49%	82%	7%	11%
Contact Defensoria del Pueblo (HR ombuds)	11%	63%	75%	16%	10%
Write to the media	7%	63%	70%	28%	1%
Contact the police	15%	52%	67%	29%	4%
Negotiate with local authorities	6%	61%	67%	29%	4%
Participate in a public information/ advocacy campaign	6%	49%	54%	43%	3%
Participate in a public protest to demand change	6%	27%	33%	61%	6%

Source: MOS 2010.

suggests that many migrants respond to the informal social pressures of the invisibility bargain by withdrawing from political spaces altogether. When asked what strategies that they tried had been most effective, however, a different pattern emerged, as seen in Table 7.2.

Those making direct claims on the *government*, seeking change within existing formal institutions, were the least effective in redressing their

Table 7.2 Perceived success of different strategies attempted by migrants

Strategy	% who perceived success
Negotiate with local authorities	100%
Participate in a public information/advocacy campaign	88%
Write to the media	82%
Petition UNHCR	44%
Participate in a public protest to demand change	43%
Contact the police	31%

Source: MOS 2010.

grievance. Those seeking to negotiate informally with local authorities, and those participating in public information campaigns to change general societal attitudes toward migrants, found these strategies to be more effective. Initiatives like the Coexist in Solidarity public information campaign, for example, coordinated efforts of dozens of NGOs, IGOs, and state agencies to combat xenophobia and helped to normalize a migration discourse that did not rely on national security or economic threat tropes. It also strengthened the different component organizations' knowledge of each other and participation in the articulation of shared goals. Of the seventy-nine organizations from seven provinces that signed the 2010 "manifesto" during a Coexist in Solidarity forum in Lago Agrio, one-third were state agencies from different levels, and two-thirds were nonstate actors, including NGOs, faith-based organizations, international organizations, businesses, and universities (Convivir 2011). At a local level, refugee-led organizations of Colombians were often helpful in negotiating with community leaders and in orienting new arrivals to ensure that recent migrants found the resources that they needed and were aware of their rights.[1] Although they required coordinating through social and institutional networks, both the negotiation and campaign strategies provided spaces for political participation that were more indirect and thus avoided violating the expectations of the invisibility bargain.

In contrast, overt protests by migrants and refugees in Ecuador have tended to be unsuccessful, and have led to repression, deportation, and unfavorable popular sentiment reflected in news media coverage. A group of Afro-Colombians in 2015, and another group of more than 100 in 2019, occupied a temporary camp set up in front of the UNHCR building in Quito where they demanded third-country resettlement (ACNUR Lamenta 2019; Al Menos 2019). In both cases the cardboard camp was eventually cleared away, they did not achieve their goals, and the media framed the incident in part as misguided or ungrateful migrants making demands that did not follow proper procedures.

In 2016, several hundred Cuban migrants occupied a space outside of the Mexican embassy in Quito, requesting humanitarian transit to the Mexico-US border in order to enter the United States. Police dismantled their camp, and (with the permission of the Quito mayor, who was a political opponent of Correa) they were moved to El Arbolito park. Here, their numbers swelled

---

[1] Interview 99QM 2008; Interview 104QM 2008; Interview 96QM 2008; Interview 94QM 2013; Interview 97QM 2013.

to more than 600, and this high-visibility protest was eventually met with brutal force during the night, with hundreds reportedly being arrested and detained without any legal transparency in "Hotel Carrion," a converted hotel that served as an immigrant-processing center. Eventually 121 Cubans were deported (Correa 2020; Picq 2016). In an instance of democratic elections actually hardening the potential backlash against political visibility, it is important to note that the interior minister at the time with responsibility for the operation, José Serrano, was the leader of the list of National Assembly candidates from the government's Alianza PAIS party in the election that was to take place five months later. Ahmed Correa (2020) observed about the response to the protest at El Arbolito, "In a pre-electoral context, this event personified expressions of national pride, xenophobic rhetoric, and territorial anxieties, while it reaffirmed the sovereignty over the bodies of a group of migrants converted into political enemies, ingrates who threatened the national order, with irrational aspirations of transit to U.S. soil" (74). This event illustrated vividly the backlash to a violation of the political invisibility expectation.

The MNS asked a similar set of questions to the MOS, so these findings can be extended across four other localities beyond Quito.[2] The results had many similarities with the smaller and earlier Quito study, but differed in several ways as well. The migrant respondents reported a greater tendency to employ strategies that were less visible and more individual, rather than visible strategies that required collective action. Likewise, they reported that strategies that involved allying with nonstate actors and targeting societal influencers worked better than those that made claims directly against the state. Figure 7.1 summarizes the results, illustrating the relative numbers of responses that had, could, or would never employ each strategy. For those who had used each strategy, the percentage who reported that it worked in improving their situation is illustrated in Figure 7.2.

Once again, the strategies migrants most frequently said they had used or could imagine using were those they could use individually—contact UNHCR, the police, and the human rights ombudsman. Interestingly, two of these involved interactions with the state, so it does not appear that migrants are unwilling to try state-directed strategies. However, when asked which

---

[2] These data include Quito, Lago Agrio, Esmeraldas, Ibarra, and Santo Domingo. Tulcán/Carchi is excluded from the analysis for this question because of a technical error in the administration of the questionnaire in that locality that caused uncertainty about the reliability of the results for this question.

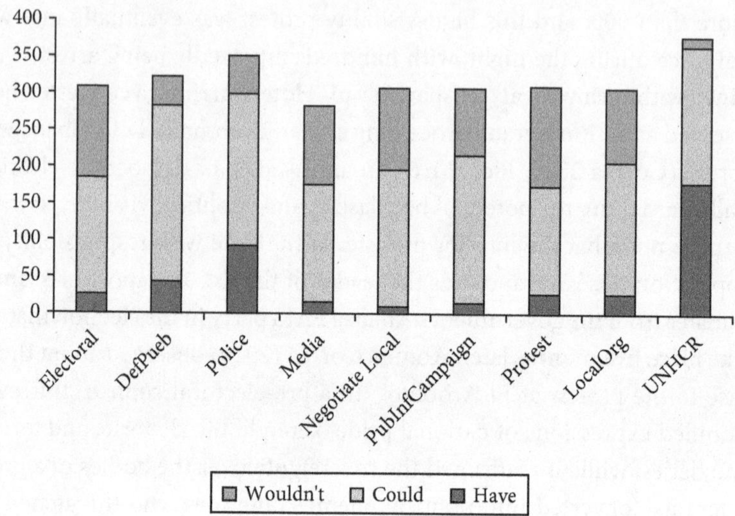

Figure 7.1 Migrants' use or willingness to use various political strategies
Source: MNS 2016.

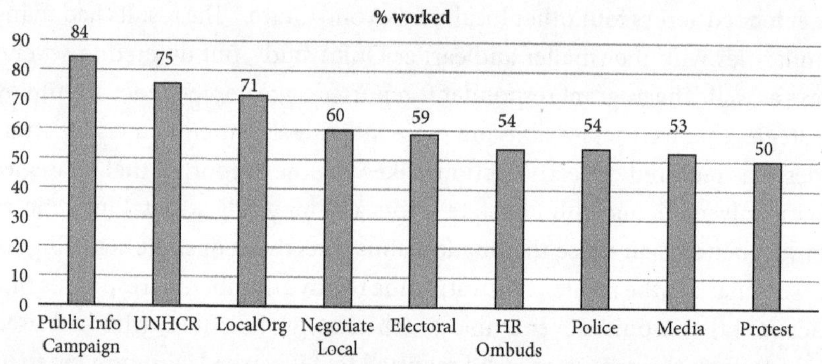

Figure 7.2 Reported success of various political strategies used by migrants
Source: MNS 2016.

strategies worked to improve their situation, the most visible strategies (protest, using the media) were seen as least effective, followed by those that involved making claims on the state (contacting the police, contacting the human rights ombudsman, and involvement in electoral politics). The most effective strategies were those—like involvement in a public information campaign, contacting the UNHCR, involvement in a local organization, and negotiating with local power brokers—that allowed them to build coalitions with nonstate actors and organizations, and to target Ecuadorians in society, rather than the state. They reported that even quite visible strategies were effective when done in coalition with nonstate actors as brokers, and when targeting influencers within society, which supports the expectations laid out in the previous chapter of the ways that migrants exercise agency and adapt their participation under the invisibility bargain. Summarizing the results a different way, Table 7.3 clarifies the comparison of these categories.

Colombians in Ecuador have been able to create and access spaces of political participation through a variety of entry points to the governance network. In 2006 and 2007, the international community was increasingly aware that policies and programs were being designed ostensibly for the benefit of migrants, but that the political voice and participation of migrants themselves was missing from the design of these programs. Fundación Esquel, a large Ecuadorian NGO, initiated a program to travel to remote communities in the border region, identify and invite Colombian migrants to participate in meetings, identify common goals, and develop organizational structures that would allow them to advocate for the resources and protections that they needed to accomplish these goals, targeting multiple types of institutions within the governance network. In the pueblo of Barranca Bermeja in Sucumbíos province, which was composed of some 80% Colombian inhabitants, the community defined access to clean water and education as primary goals, and strategically elected a leader, Miguel Lapo, who was Ecuadorian so that he could advocate for these resources without facing a backlash from community and government actors who might resent overt

Table 7.3 Relative success of more/less visible and state- versus nonstate-targeted strategies

	Worked	Did not work
Less visible strategies[a]	66%	34%
More visible strategies	60%	40%
Strategies targeting nonstate actor[b]	73%	27%
Strategies targeting state	54%	46%

[a] Includes contacting UNHCR, the police, and the human rights ombudsman, joining a local organization, or negotiating informally with local decision-makers.

[b] Includes participating in public information campaigns, negotiating with local decision-makers, contacting UNHCR, involving the media, and joining a local organization.

Source: MNS 2016.

Figure 7.3 Miguel Lapo welcomes Foreign Minister Fander Falconi to Barranca Bermeja, Sucumbíos

Photo credit: Cancillería del Ecuador, February 20, 2009. Available via Creative Commons (CC BY-SA 2.0) at https://www.flickr.com/photos/dgcomsoc/3296239600/in/photostream/.

political activism and claim-making by foreigners.[3] This was one of the first times that this community had access to larger institutional sources of assistance from the state and large NGOs, and as a result of self-organizing, it also was among the first communities to have access to the mobile refugee registration clinic known as Enhanced Registration, an initiative described later that was carried out by the UNHCR and the Ministry of Foreign Relations. Figure 7.3 shows Miguel Lapo greeting the Ecuadorian minister of foreign relations, Fander Falconi, and welcoming him to the community at the beginning of the Enhanced Registration initiative.

Brokering Access: The Ecuadorian Constitution of 2008

In one of the most striking (and consequential) examples of governance networks connecting Colombian migrants to state decision-making spaces

---

[3] Interview 126QN 2009.

through nonstate brokers, the 2008 Constituent Assembly that drafted Ecuador's new constitution produced some of the most favorable provisions guaranteeing protections for migrants and refugees in Latin America. While there was already a favorable political opportunity for this outcome after President Correa's campaign platform of human rights and universal citizenship, the constitutional text was largely shaped through intersecting and overlapping inputs from key civil society sectors (Ramírez 2016). A number of civil society organizations that were invited to participate in deliberative forums that informed the drafting of the constitution brought with them representatives of the refugee and migrant community as interlocutors and helped broker access for them to participate directly in these discussions.

The *mesa de mobilidad humana* was an official state-sanctioned space to discuss migration-related proposals, chaired by the Jesuit Refugee Service, and originally promoted by Ecuadorian emigrant associations. This working group, which included a number of church-affiliated groups, provided proposals targeted at broadening the scope of migration rights to an inclusive "human mobility" concept, which is indeed included in the final text of the constitution. This group, however, did not include refugee organizations, and some of the UNHCR partners and secular human rights organizations preferred to focus specifically on enshrining refugee rights because they thought it would be an easier "ask" than migration in general, and that the rights that were codified could thus be more extensive. They also were concerned about the lack of refugee representation in the official spaces.[4]

One of these organizations, Asylum Access, a small legal aid organization headed at that time by a young Ecuadorian woman who was a former Foreign Ministry official, hosted a workshop in which a prominent Ecuadorian returned emigrant leader, Dora Aguirre of Asociación Rumiñaui, inspired participants with her own experiences and shared strategies for political organizing and advocacy with refugees and other migrants in Quito. Fundación Esquel connected Asylum Access with the Colombian associations it had been organizing in the border regions and throughout the country and provided the budget to bring representatives of these associations to Quito for the one-day workshop. This was one of the first times that the smaller, diverse, Colombian refugee associations from around the country had been invited to a major strategizing and political participation space in Quito, as opposed to only the leader of the prominent politically active refugee

---

[4] Interview 111QN 2018.

organization based in Quito, Asociación de Refugiados Colombianos en Ecuador (ARCOE).

The participants identified priorities that guided Asylum Access's director in drafting proposed language for inclusion in the new constitution. She was invited to participate in constitutional deliberations at the Constituent Assembly in Montecristi on the strength of her personal connections in government and the expertise of the organization, and she was accompanied by four refugee leaders whom she worked with regularly in carrying out the business of the NGO, particularly those from the Asociación de Refugiados Colombianos (ASOREC). Through a friend who was the assistant to the president of the Constituent Assembly, she was able to secure a twenty-minute time slot to make a presentation to the assembly delegates, presenting the international law case for refugee provisions in the constitution, presenting the draft language proposal, and allowing the refugee leaders a direct opportunity to present their own stories. As a result, these Colombian refugees had a platform to articulate their views and goals, informing the ultimate outcome of the constitutional draft, which did incorporate several of the provisions that they proposed (see Table 7.4 for a comparison of elements of the proposal and provisions adopted in the final constitution).[5] According to the director of Asylum Access,

In a matter of, basically, the eight, nine hours that I was in Montecristi, we were able to get them to say, "Okay. We'll give these people twenty minutes." And once we had those twenty minutes, we brought in the four refugee leaders that came with me and we got them to tell their stories. We had a really good solid PowerPoint presentation that explains the human side and then the legal side. And then we said, "Call to action. Here are the articles. They're already prewritten. You don't have to really think too much about them or debate them much. It's basically already an international law. All you would be doing is enshrining it in our constitution." And because it was such a good combination of the technical work basically being done for them and plus the human side being so present in front of them that we had assembly people or assemblymen and women crying because of the testimony that they heard. So it was so touching that they all kind of made a commitment to include those articles. We had nothing else. And then once the constitution was published, we saw that the articles were there. That was that.[6]

[5] Interview 99QM 2008; Interview 104QM 2008.
[6] Interview 111QN 2018.

Table 7.4 Comparison of Asylum Access / refugee leader proposals and constitutional text

AAE/Refugee leader text	2008 Constitution
Recognizing the vulnerability of the refugee population and the international obligations that it has incurred; the Ecuadorian State; . . . Will respect at all levels as a basic right of the refugee population, the impossibility of return or deportation to the country of origin under any circumstance.	Art. 41: The rights of asylum and refuge are recognized, in accordance with the law and the international human rights instruments. Persons who are in a condition of asylum or refuge will enjoy special protection that guarantees the full exercise of their rights. The state will respect and guarantee the principle of non-refoulment, in addition to humanitarian assistance and emergency jurisdiction. Art. 416.7: We demand respect for human rights, particularly the rights of migrants, and encourage their exercise through compliance with the obligations incurred through ratification of international human rights instruments.
The right to non-deportation and non-refoulment, the prohibition against returning to their country of origin any person suffering persecution because of race, religion, nationality, determined social group, or political opinion. Freedom from arbitrary detention or punishment because of entrance or illegally remaining in [Ecuadorian] territory.	Art. 40: The right of all persons to migrate is recognized. No human will be identified or considered as illegal because of their migratory status. Art 41: Asylum seekers will not have any criminal sanctions applied to them because of having entered the country or remained in a situation of irregularity.
The state will ensure, through public policies and sanctions, that no refugee is discriminated because of nationality, place of origin, or migratory condition.	Art 11.2: All people are equal and will enjoy the same rights, duties and opportunities. No one will be discriminated because of ethnicity, **place of birth**, age, sex, gender identity, cultural identity, civil state, language, religion, ideology, political affiliation, judicial record, socio-economic condition, **migratory condition**. . . . The law will punish any form of discrimination.
Persons who have been recognized as refugees by the Ecuadorian State will be guaranteed the same rights and protections that Ecuadorian citizens possess with the exception of political rights.	Art. 9: Foreign persons who are in Ecuadorian territory will have the same rights and duties as Ecuadorians, in accordance with the Constitution.

Continued

Table 7.4 *Continued*

AAE/Refugee leader text	2008 Constitution
The state will establish public policies of information, promotion, and education for all public servants and the population in general regarding the particularities of the refugee population, their needs and vulnerabilities.	Art. 392: The state will protect the rights of persons in human mobility and will exercise the stewardship of migratory policy through the appropriate governmental agency in coordination with the different levels of government …
Together with society and Ecuadorians in general, the state should actively seek the integration and peaceful coexistence with the refugee population. The spirit of peace and solidarity will be observed as institutional principles that will govern all public actions with respect to the refugee population in Ecuador.	Art. 393: The state will guarantee human security through integrated policies and actions, to ensure the peaceful coexistence of people, to promote a culture of peace and to prevent forms of violence and discrimination and the commission of infractions and crimes. The planning and application of these policies will be delegated to specialized entities in different levels of government.
The freedom of circulation and to choose the place of residence in the territory of the host country.	Art 416.6: We propose the principle of universal citizenship, the free movement of all inhabitants of the planet and the progressive end to the condition of foreigner as a transformative element in the unequal relations among countries, especially North-South.

Source: ASOREC et al. 2008; Constitución de la República del Ecuador, Asamblea Constituyente 2008.

In this case, the budgetary resources of Fundación Esquel, the technical expertise and experience of Asylum Access and Dora Aguirre / Asociación Rumiñaui, the legitimacy and authentic representation of the refugee leaders, and the relationships and contacts of all three organizations combined into an effective advocacy strategy that mobilized social capital and "information politics" with "symbolic politics" to achieve progressive constitutional language that would later provide a basis for claim-making and advocacy by migrants and allies, including those involved in negotiating the Organic Law for Human Mobility. In an application of contact theory to political strategy, refugees used the sharing of their personal stories to combat the stigmatization and dehumanization of Colombians, encourage empathy by the assembly members, and tying this attitude change to a willingness to adopt favorable policy proposals presented at the same time. It is important to note that networks/relationships, expertise, and legitimacy were much more important resources than financial strength, power, or organizational size in this case—Asylum Access had existed in Ecuador for less than a year, and the director was only twenty-five years old. It later became a UNHCR partner and one of the most important refugee-serving organizations in the country, with physical presence in all of the major border provinces, until it closed in 2018. Dora Aguirre later was elected to the National Assembly as a representative for Ecuadorian emigrants abroad, and became one of the most vocal and powerful proponents of the Organic Law for Human Mobility, which was finally passed into law in 2017 after more than a decade of debate and negotiation.

Coalition Building

For some issue areas, refugees saw advantages to forging alliances with other sectors having overlapping interests, sometimes reframing their agenda in order to increase their ability to resonate politically with particular decision-makers. This strategy evokes Els de Graaw's tripartite model that emphasizes immigrant coalitions' issue-framing and agenda-setting functions (2016). In Tulcán and Santo Domingo, the local governments were not as receptive to discussing programs and policy changes related to refugees, given the resentment and pressure from their Ecuadorian constituents who viewed refugees as receiving disproportionate share of international assistance that was not shared with the broader community. Instead, refugees allied with Ecuadorian emigrants who had returned home from Spain and Italy, as well as some internal migrants from other provinces of Ecuador, organizing networks in support of "human mobility" policies. This reframing of the agenda was useful, since it emphasized that the political interests of refugees were shared by the more electorally significant returned-emigrant sector.[7]

In one specific example, local advocacy was emphasized first as part of a strategy to scale up to national level change in educational policy by activating local-national networks. By aligning their efforts, refugees, returned emigrants, and their allies were able to appeal to several state agencies in the governance network of Ibarra, while enlisting allies in the human rights ombudsman's office, UNHCR, the Hebrew Immigrant Aid Society (HIAS), and the Scalibrini mission, among others. These organizations

---

[7] Interview 22DM 2015; Interview CI4 2015.

formed an education forum in which they negotiated a change to a local education ordinance making it easier for children coming from other countries (whether refugees or Ecuadorians returning from abroad) to enroll in school even with incomplete transfer documentation, which had been a major barrier for refugees (Sánchez 2013; Rodríguez-Gómez 2019). Through their connections with their central offices in Quito, and with the national government, the local offices of these organizations in Ibarra promoted the local ordinance as a model that informed a national policy change in the Ministry of Education.[8] According to an IGO official in Ibarra,

> There was political will from everyone, from civil society and the government at the *local* level. . . . What happened is that in Quito things are more difficult, the bureaucracy is larger, but this is Zone 1 of Ecuador, where at that time certain powers were starting to be decentralized, and we took that as a strategy to push from here. This relied on a linkage with Patricio Benalcazar, in the human rights ombuds in Quito, who was an ally of the Scalibrini mission, so it was a matter of looking for a strategy . . . that was born here, to do advocacy from here. So the moment arrived when the national director answered the ombudsperson here, the provincial delegate, with the reform to this procedure. What we achieved with that is to include many children here in Imbabura and in all of Ecuador.[9]

The governance network in other locations used a similar issue-reframing strategy that linked refugee interests with those of returned emigrants. Rafael Correa's Plan Ecuador rested on a concept of universal citizenship that justified progressive protections of refugees and migrants in Ecuador, in large part in order to advance a reciprocity argument for protection of Ecuadorian emigrants in Europe, appealing to the interests of this diaspora in order to mobilize their economic and electoral support (Pugh 2017). This political calculation opened up a repertoire of justifications and narratives that non-state actors in the network mobilized in support of greater human security for migrants within Ecuador, holding the Correa government accountable for the consistent application of these principles even when it was politically

---

[8] Interview 73IS 2014.
[9] Interview 53II 2014.

difficult for the government to do so.[10] For example, the successful court challenge by the NGO Asylum Access and the Universidad San Francisco de Quito law clinic to Correa's regressive Decree 1182 explicitly invoked the concept of universal citizenship and the protections for refugees and nondiscrimination clauses in the constitution when accusing the decree of violating the law and being unconstitutional. The Constitutional Court agreed with its argument that the decree's abandonment of the Cartagena Declaration principles, its requirement that refugees must claim asylum within the first fifteen days of their arrival in Ecuador or forfeit their right to make this claim in the future, and other regressive provisions violated the government's obligations set out in the constitution, and as a result, the law was changed to extend the time window for asylum claims to three months and to reincorporate the Cartagena Declaration principles, among other changes (Ubidia Vasquez 2015; Correa 2016).

Resources

Human security is intricately linked to livelihoods and well-being (freedom from want), so satisfaction of basic needs like housing, employment, food, health, and education ultimately influence how vulnerable someone is to other types of harm. Since the perception of economic competition is one of the key drivers of xenophobia and antimigrant sentiment, publicly demanding economic assistance from the state is often seen as an illegitimate demand and is likely to result in a backlash from the host population that sees this as a violation of the invisibility bargain. Instead, economic strategies that emphasize the economic benefits to Ecuadorians (through increased international assistance and newly created jobs, for example) that would accompany better livelihoods for Colombians have been more successful. As suggested by Ambrosini's (2017) service provision category of intermediation, nonstate and informal brokers in the host society can link migrants with the resources and services they need to survive and improve their livelihoods.

Entrepreneurship and business plan competitions sponsored by the UNHCR and others have sometimes made start-up funding available to business partners that include an Ecuadorian and a Colombian launching a joint venture in order address these types of concerns and to use economic

---

[10] Interview 166QN 2009.

improvement to contribute to mutual understanding and a perception of interdependence. The UN system also learned, partly through early failures and partly through information provided by state and NGO counterparts in the governance network, that economic assistance provided exclusively to refugees in the border region often did more harm than good because it increased the resentment of equally poor Ecuadorian neighbors in the community. Over time, microenterprise loans, training, and other forms of economic assistance were targeted at priority communities where migrants were concentrating, but included Ecuadorian as well as Colombian beneficiaries in order to build resilience and capacity of the community as a whole.[11]

In 2007 NGOs and the UNHCR, which had frequent, direct contact with Colombian refugees, were made aware that the ID number appearing on the refugee *censo* identification card had a different number of digits than the number appearing on Ecuadorians' *cedula*, or national ID card. Although refugees had the right to open a bank account, work, and take out loans under Ecuadorian legislation, the extra digits on their *censo* were incompatible with the computer system used by the banks to authorize new accounts, and they were being systematically denied access to bank accounts and, by extension, to credit (and sometimes employment). When they showed their legal documents and explained the law, they confronted indifference and bureaucratic buck-passing from the banks as well as from the government regulators of financial institutions.

These NGOs and the UNHCR, however, began coordinating with the Ministry of Foreign Relations to raise awareness of the problem and advocate for a new credential with a compatible number of digits. They also enlisted the office of the Defensoría del Pueblo, the state human rights ombudsman, to investigate and issue a declaration asking the Superintendency of Banks to clarify that refugee status was not a legitimate reason for financial institutions to deny an applicant the opportunity to open a bank account.[12] Ultimately, such a statement was sent to banks, and (several years later) the Foreign Ministry began issuing a new type of refugee credential with digits that were compatible with the computer system.[13]

---

[11] Interview 143QS 2009; Interview 61IN 2014.

[12] Interview 143QS 2009.

[13] Maria de Lourdes Idrovo, Subdirector for Customer Service, Superintendency of Banks and Insurance for Ecuador, Letter #SAC-2009-1284 to Guillermo Rovayo, JRS, July 9, 2009; Interview 5CI 2015.

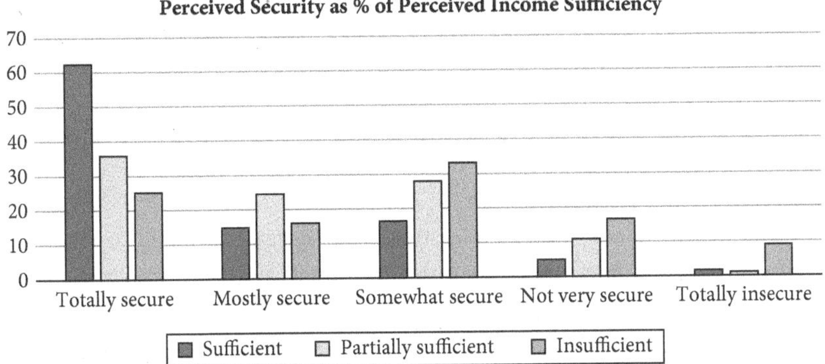

Figure 7.4 Comparison of perceived income sufficiency and perceived security Q13: Do you feel secure in the neighborhood where you live? Q10: With your monthly family income, are you able to cover your basic needs?
Source: MNS 2016.

These efforts to broker access to resources and enhance migrants' livelihoods are integrally linked to migrants' human security and integration in the host society. There was a highly significant correlation between MNS respondents reporting that their income was sufficient to cover their families' basic needs and those who reported that they felt safe where they live, as summarized in Figure 7.4.

When asked the biggest problem they have confronted since coming to Ecuador, the largest number of respondents mentioned access to employment (57%), and "not having sufficient economic resources" was the top response (21%) when respondents were asked what their biggest fear was while living in Ecuador. Note that economic deprivation as a factor in human security relates here to migrants' experience in Ecuador and is separate from the reasons why they left their country of origin. The vast majority of the survey respondents were forced migrants fleeing violence in Colombia, but once in Ecuador, economic concerns and structural violence became larger threats to their well-being than the risk of being killed by armed actors. This has important implications for the way that refugee status is determined. Migrants who deserve asylum and meet the criteria of the Refugee Convention are sometimes denied by the state's status determination process because they talk first about their current economic woes rather than the political violence that initially caused them to flee, and this is used to brand them as economic immigrants who are denied refugee status.[14]

Protection/Rights

As noted earlier, traditional state institutions to protect security and resolve conflicts involving migrants may not fulfill their functions, in part because of the distrust and fear that many migrants have of the state. This relationship is further complicated by the fact that invisibility is often used as a survival strategy by migrants, both those who have nefarious purposes and those who are simply trying to avoid potential threats and harm, and it is difficult for democratic states to apply their traditional legal instruments to provide order and keep the peace in this context (Ellerman 2010). Of MNS respondents who were aware of the existence of these institutions, only 22% reported having a lot of trust in the police, and 8% had a lot of trust in the courts. Beyond their distrust of formal state institutions, the power imbalance implicit in the invisibility bargain seemed to depress migrants' willingness to seek redress when victimized by an Ecuadorian aggressor, compared to when they were victimized by a fellow Colombian. Of those respondents who reported having been the victim of violent crime by an Ecuadorian aggressor since coming to the country, 42% said that they had "done nothing" in response (as opposed to the 34% who went to the police). In contrast, only 24% of those who had been attacked by a fellow Colombian "did nothing," indicating a greater willingness to reach out for help when they were not complaining about the actions of members of the host society. This institutional distrust continued over time, and seemed to be particularly concentrated among the Colombian population, compared to other migrant groups in Ecuador. In my 2019 survey comparing migrant groups in Quito, respondents were asked, "If you were the victim of a crime, how much confidence would you have that the judicial system would punish the guilty party?" Of the Colombian respondents, 32.5% reported "no confidence," compared to 16.5% of the other four immigrant population groups (Pugh et al. 2020; Jimenez and Pugh 2020).

The invisibility bargain's expectation of social invisibility creates an insidious silencing effect on migrants' attempts to seek help after being the victim

---

[14] Interview 110QN 2007.

of violent crime, especially from the police, courts, and other state agencies. The evidence from the MNS, summarized in Figure 7.5, shows that this effect is racialized, with white and mestizo migrants being more likely to seek help from state agencies and less likely to "do nothing" than black, mulatto, or indigenous migrants. This finding is consistent with the finding reported in the last chapter that black and indigenous migrants are connected to fewer institutional sources of assistance and protection than white and mestizo migrants. In both cases, visible markers of difference from the host population impede migrants' access to formal institutional protections, driving them either to rely on informal and nonstate institutions or to withdraw into isolation altogether.

Ambrosini's (2017) intermediation category of immediate help suggests that migrants may turn to nonstate and informal brokers in the host society when confronted with urgent needs like security threats. Indeed, the survey provides evidence to suggest that access to a diverse array of institutions in the governance network can be an important source of security that migrants reach out to when they are victimized, especially considering the limitations of the traditional state institutions and the disproportionate number of visibly different migrants who do not seek help from them. Migrants who had been the victim of violent crime in Ecuador reported a significantly larger number of institutional connections than those who had not been victimized. Sometimes, these connections allowed migrants to access life-saving

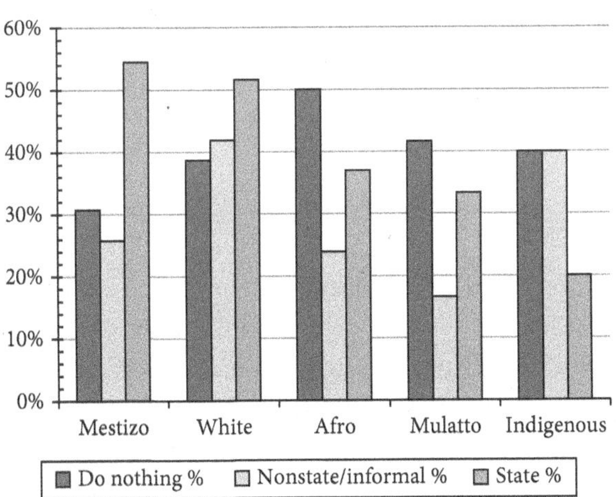

Figure 7.5 Responses of migrants to violent crime by race
Source: MNS 2016.

resources or protection that they had been denied when directly requesting it from the state.

In one such case, a refugee federation provided food and shelter for a recently arrived family fleeing from threats in Colombia. It also connected them with an Ecuadorian legal aid clinic that could educate them about their rights to refugee status and accompany them to the Foreign Ministry hearing to determine their status. Unfortunately, this put both the refugee federation and the legal aid clinic on the "target list" of a Colombian paramilitary splinter group that had threatened the family in the first place and had forced them to seek refuge in Ecuador. After the refugee organization's leaders received a written death threat, they asked the legal aid clinic (which had also been threatened) for help. The legal aid clinic had good working relationships with the government Ministry of Foreign Affairs, the UNHCR, the police, and other institutions, and it quickly filed for a protection order from the judiciary while arranging for the UN to move the family and the refugee organization leaders into protective hiding. Ultimately, the legal aid clinic filed a brief with the Inter-American Commission for Human Rights of the Organization of American States, which spurred the government to expedite refugee documents and resettle the family in a safer location.[15] This outcome might never have happened if the threatened migrants went directly to the police or courts. In this case, migrants were able to mobilize their relationships with nonstate actors in order to broker access to security provided by intergovernmental and state agencies. There are many cases, however, where other refugees and migrants in similar situations of insecurity are fearful of persecution or deportation and remain silent or are ignored when they do come forward.

Connection and Tolerance

Migrants' access to the network of state and nonstate institutions in the governance plays a key role in their integration into the host society, and the transformation of the relationship between migrants and native citizens into one of peaceful coexistence. When the *types* of institutions they are connected

---

[15] United Nations Human Rights Council, *Promotion and Protection of All Human Rights, Civil, Political, Economic, Social, and Cultural Rights, Including the Right to Development*, Report of the Special Rapporteur on the Situation of Human Rights Defenders, prepared by Margaret Sekaggya, Document A/HRC/13/22/Add.1, February 1, 2010, 113–14.

to are diverse and the *number* of ties is greater, resilience and autonomy tend to be greater, and it is less likely that the relationship will be an exploitative and dependent one of clientelistic exchange. In line with Ambrosini's (2017) categories of connection and tolerance, informal and nonstate brokers within the host society play a key role in connecting migrants with social networks that meet their needs for belonging and psychological support, and can help facilitate host-migrant relationship building that reduces social distance and decreases prejudice. These relationships form valuable "bridging social capital" (Allen Nan 2009; Putnam 2000) that helps redefine the notion of community into a more pluralistic and tolerant understanding that includes both foreigners and native-born citizens. On the flip side, the lack of such relationships and bridging social capital helps to explain the escalation of prejudice and dehumanization that can rationalize violence and exclusion of migrants by members of the host community.

When asked what they perceived to be the most important obstacle to resolving conflicts between Ecuadorians and migrants, the most frequent answers mentioned by MNS (2016) participants were discrimination/racism (18%) and not understanding each other as human beings (17%). Contact theory predicts that the frequency and depth of meaningful, equal-status interaction between migrants and native citizens directed toward a shared task is likely to contribute to less intergroup prejudice and more favorable perceptions of each other (Bohman 2015; Pettigrew and Tropp 2008). As detailed in the previous chapter, this interaction does make a significant difference in reducing negative attitudes between Ecuadorians and Colombian migrants. Nonstate actors can bring together Ecuadorians and Colombians in informal spaces that promote interaction, shared problem-solving, and learning about each other, and as a result reduce dehumanization and intergroup conflict. ASOREC, one of the refugee organizations in Quito, for example, regularly sponsored *mingas* that brought together Ecuadorians and Colombians in the community to address some shared need like building a public soccer field or placing sandbags to stop the erosion of the street. Following the Andean tradition, these workdays were followed by times of cultural sharing of Colombian dances, food, and so on, and a collective meal that helped build trust, in addition to the feeling of accomplishment from completing the shared task together.[16]

---

[16] Interview 99QM 2008; Interview 104QM 2008.

Going beyond individual-level trust-building, certain NGOs and IGOs whose central position in the governance network gave them access to and trust from refugees as well as with other NGOs and the state. Oxfam Italia in the Sucumbíos province of the Amazon, for example, was distinguished from other organizations by the fact that its technical staff stayed and lived full time Monday–Thursday in the far-flung rural communities it was serving with rural development assistance rather than staying in the capital city and making day trips to the community, like most other NGOs. As a result of this constant presence and interaction, and the concrete economic development assistance Oxfam offered, many of the migrants and refugees were willing to trust them enough to approach them to seek help with situations of insecurity or rights violations. According to the director, "Because of the trust that we have with them because of our constant presence, sometimes they tell us things, and if it is not within the areas that we work, we connect them with UNHCR or the Federation of Women of Sucumbíos, connecting them through the network of organizations that is here in Lago Agrio." He argued that their presence also offered a source of protection by having a trusted external NGO on the ground to witness threats and rights violation, including by the armed forces: "I think our presence has improved the security situation; we are like observers, and the people feel accompanied and not abandoned."[17] Oxfam also helped open doors, for example accompanying and introducing UNHCR personnel when that agency changed its strategy in 2009–10 to leave the cities and go out into the countryside.

By connecting refugees directly with other organizations and helping to broker the initial contacts to overcome distrust, Oxfam was contributing to the organizational strengthening of the community and the entrance of its members into the governance network, without maintaining clientelistic or paternalistic structures of dependency on its own programs. This example shows that even international organizations and large NGOs can develop a trusted ground presence and credible "practical authority" through presence and relationship-building over time, and by aligning their program and strategy with locally expressed needs. By doing so, they contribute to a "resilience" approach in which they identify resources, assets, leaders, and connectors within the community and work to strengthen them so that they can be mobilized to reduce the negative impact of adverse events, rather

---

[17] Interview 150SN 2013.

than assuming that they can "fix" the problems from the outside (Juncos 2018). This suggests policy recommendations that are consistent with the conclusions of other recent work on international peacebuilding in other regions (Autesserre 2017; Campbell 2018; Pugh 2016a).

Risks and Failures

It is important not to assume that governance networks automatically play a positive role for human security—they are structures of authority, resources, and recognition that may be mobilized or accessed to accomplish "good" purposes as well as "bad" ones (Chapman 2009). In some countries, informal institutions, vigilante groups, paramilitaries, and other actors draw on their access to migrants and local communities as well as the state to target particular people or groups with violence (Mulaj 2009; Helmke and Levitsky 2006; Baker and Scheye 2007; Staniland 2014). A growing literature on "rebel governance" has highlighted the way in which the exercise of authority by violent nonstate actors can both provide important service provision in far-flung localities and also contribute to high levels of violence not controlled by the state (Mampilly 2015; Arjona 2016; Jaskoski 2015; Idler 2019; Ballvé 2020; Mulaj 2009).

Governance networks can also work against people who occupy the key nodes that provide access to protection or resources by increasing their visibility and political salience, exposing them to harm by groups that do not share the goals of the governance network. The refugee organization and legal clinic targeted by the paramilitary splinter group discussed earlier in this chapter were fortunate that they were able to access protection in time, but their role as visible and exposed parts of the governance network does help explain why they were threatened in the first place. The same connections and informal referral networks that direct new migrants and refugees looking for help to sources of aid can also direct to their targets nefarious actors looking for information or trying to exercise coercive influence. Awareness of this phenomenon can have a chilling effect on Colombians' trust in their compatriots, and on their willingness to expose themselves to institutional sites associated with refugees. For example, a forum conducted by a Colombian victims/refugee organization in Ecuador at a major university was followed by threatening letters sent to the organizers by unknown armed actors who had apparently either infiltrated the forum or become aware of it through word of mouth. As a result, the organizers suspended further organizing activities out of fear.[18]

A social worker with HIAS in Ibarra reported in 2007 that many of the Colombian forced migrants in town were intentionally avoiding the refugee shelters provided by IGOs and the municipal government, because they were fearful that these sites were being monitored by agents of the Colombian illegal armed actors, and that taking advantage of the service might make the forced migrants more insecure. In both of these cases, information channels and connections between nonstate organizations (NGOs, IGOs, and sometimes illegal armed groups) represented a double-edged sword, and migrants feared accessing the governance network because of the risk of exposure. According to one Colombian, invisibility is not only a strategy to avoid social discrimination by Ecuadorians, but a survival mechanism motivated by fear of other Colombians, especially in border zones where illicit armed actors have significant presence and authority:

> Here, things are different, the food, the people, how they treat us . . . so we learnt to be invisible, to tone our voices, to look down, to act like anybody would do here. We have been able to settle down here taking care of a finca [farm] nearby. The owner is Ecuadorian and he lets us raise some chickens to sell at the market . . . but I avoid meeting other Colombians. I do not want to see anybody from my town or be seen by the people who killed my brother, who know me, who know who I am. In this place, we have been able to recover our lives back from them, but they say that they never forget . . . they do not leave pending tasks and probably, God forbid it, they may find us.[19]

Because of such fears, some Colombians chose organizations that were less central to the governance network (but whose composition involved more personal relationships and fewer strangers, who could increase risk), or they abandoned their attempts at political inclusion and accessing institutional assistance altogether, using invisibility as a survival strategy.

In other cases involving Colombian migrants in Ecuador, key leaders (especially Ecuadorians who worked closely with migrant organizations and linked them with other institutions) have been targeted and killed. Miguel

[18] Personal interview with person familiar with the event.
[19] Quoted in (Salcedo 2014: 164–65).

Lapo, the Ecuadorian leader elected by the primarily Colombian community of Barranca Bermeja mentioned earlier, is one such example. He was found dead after playing a role in negotiating access to resources and political participation with the state (Lari 2009; UNHCR 2009). Most likely, illegal armed groups saw this connection with official authorities as a threat to their own power in the region, which had traditionally ceded de facto authority to nonstate actors in the relative absence of the state (Jaskoski 2015). Similarly, a young community leader in Lago Agrio was assassinated in 2015 after playing a crucial role in organizing the Colombian and Ecuadorian young people of Sucumbíos province to articulate a common political agenda and launch peacebuilding efforts aimed at reducing stigmas and economic exclusion (Pugh 2016a).

When they are insufficiently diverse or rely too much on a few actors rather than links among a number of institutions, governance networks can also fail to accomplish their goals. The rise and fall of Colombian migrant/refugee organizations in Ecuador illustrates this problem. After forming and organizing with the help of Fundación Esquel, UNHCR, and others around 2006, refugee organizations like ARCOE, ASOREC, and the Asociación Comunitaria de Migrantes y Refugiados Colombianos grew with increasing numbers of both Colombian and Ecuadorian members (Burbano Alarcón 2017). They (particularly ARCOE) organized political advocacy strategies and accompanied parts of the Enhanced Registration process as observers, and they hosted *mingas* and cultural exchanges between Ecuadorians and Colombians.[20] In 2009, Colombian, refugee, and migrant associations from all over the country organized an umbrella federation called Federación Nacional de Refugiados (FENARE), which promised to increase the visibility and voice of migrants in national political conversations.

Unfortunately, however, these organizations, including FENARE, declined significantly in subsequent years, in part because of the challenge they posed to the expectations of the invisibility bargain, and because of concerns among allied NGOs that this strategy compounded the segregation rather than integration of migrants.[21] At least as importantly, most of the organizations relied on the energy and volunteer efforts of one or two leaders who were migrants themselves, sometimes without documentation (Palma

---

[20] Interview 96QM 2008; Interview 99QM 2008; Interview 102QM 2009; Interview 104QM 2008; Interview 108QM 2009.
[21] Interview 63IM 2014; Interview 61IM 2014.

2017). In one case, an organization withered after its leaders had to flee the country because of continued threats from armed actors in Colombia; in two or three others, health challenges and economic difficulties sapped the energy of the key leader and resulted in the paralysis of the organization. As one refugee leader explained, "It was not a ten-minute job, it was a twenty-four-hour and 365-day job; it was practically unpaid full-time labor. As [one colleague] expressed on many occasions, we are here, but we are not bringing home any food for our families, we are sacrificing our own families, and that was really hard for us. Because of that the organizations have not flourished, because the advocacy work that we did to be able to be a part of the Enhanced Registration was very hard, and that is why the organizations ended the way they did."[22]

As these factors compounded, FENARE also became less relevant, especially after economic support from NGOs and IGOs dried up.[23] In Tulcán and Santo Domingo, refugee/Colombian organizations that had previously been active declined when the leaders were accused of mishandling funds or using the organization to pursue their own economic interests, and they lost credibility in the eyes of the migrant population as well as the migrant-serving NGOs.[24] Likewise, one organization that had signed an agreement with UNHCR to carry out refugee rights trainings and had been provided with funding and computers to help with the task, sapped confidence when its leaders disappeared, along with the money and the computers.[25] This pattern reflects the uneasy coexistence and competition between structures of representation and of clientelistic brokerage.

Refugee and migrant organizations often claimed to be the best available option for representation, but without established and agreed-upon institutional channels, the necessity of relying on personal networks of contacts and influence for resources sometimes reproduced something more like patron-client networks. However, without stable salaried jobs or access to resources, and often relying on leadership that was also in a transient stage of life, the "patrons" at the head of these organizations did not have reliable access to jobs or resources to distribute in exchange for loyalty and mobilizational participation, so the networks were fragile and produced distrust both within the membership and with potential institutional allies. This pattern of decline

22 Interview 98IM 2014.
23 Interview 94QM 2013; Interview 97QM 2013.
24 Interview 21DM 2015; Interview 4CI 2015.
25 Interview 111QN 2018.

is reflected in the drop in levels of trust that migrant respondents reported having in Colombian organizations in Quito between 2010 and 2013. The percentage reporting that they had a lot of trust in Colombian organizations declined by half, from 34% in 2010 to 17% in 2013, the most negative change of any of the organizations in the survey. By 2019, very few Colombian migrant organizations remained viable, and in contrast to the robust and well-organized Venezuelan organizations that flourished from 2017 onward, Colombian organizations were not very visible in migrant-organizing and migrant participation spaces (Pugh et al. 2020).[26]

While governance networks are not universally positive, they have the potential to play an important role in improving human security for migrants. The ways in which migrants interact with state and nonstate actors that can provide access to political participation, protection, rights, and resources through governance networks are varied and often indirect. They involve negotiation and brokering that takes different forms depending on specific local, political, and temporal contexts. This section has traced some of these processes through which networks link together resources, expertise, trust and legitimacy, and access to relevant actors to improve the governance of migrant human security, even (especially) in areas of Ecuador where the state has been traditionally weak. The remaining section of this chapter illustrates the way governance networks have operated in practice to produce two important specific initiatives for the human security of migrants and refugees and their host communities—Enhanced Registration and the Peace and Development Program in the northern border zone—and also demonstrates the limitations and shortcomings of such networks.

Enhanced Registration

UNHCR's role in building state capacity gives it access and influence that often allow it to channel migrant grievances and negotiate greater protections, resulting in formal institutional changes. One of the most important UNHCR intervention in past years, the Enhanced Registration (Registro Ampliado) initiative, shows how innovations adapted through UNHCR interventions and negotiations with other domestic actors can over time shape formal state institutions. Throughout the decade of the 2000s,

---

[26] Interview 170QM 2019.

UNHCR pressed for greater state involvement in the registration of asylum seekers, but in the face of the state's lack of capacity, personnel, and resources, UNHCR carried out registration activities directly in the provinces outside of Quito, opening up field offices as well as carrying out occasional mobile brigades to reach isolated communities (UNHCR 2004). As a UNHCR official in Lago Agrio explained in 2006, "The closest government authorities are many miles away, [so] UNHCR goes out to remote communities to register asylum seekers, although the government is expected to take on this activity in the near future" (quoted in Fontanini et al. 2006).

Negotiation between UNHCR and the State

The 2006 survey of Colombians in the northern border mentioned earlier (Bilsborrow 2006), which was sponsored by UNHCR, provided unprecedented levels of detailed information on the location and scale of Colombian migrant populations in the northern border region, and their exclusion from state institutions in part because of lack of a formal legal status that confined them to an uncertain existence. UNHCR used this information and feedback from the participatory assessments to demonstrate to the state the presence of a large number of Colombians in need of protection who had not accessed the asylum system, indicating a need for an initiative that would adapt the status determination process to the needs of a dispersed, poor, and often fearful population who could not or would not come to Quito to apply for refugee status.[27]

In addition, UNHCR pointed out that by increasing the protections and rights for refugees through Enhanced Registration, the state would also gain significant amounts of information about the population living within its borders, which would increase its infrastructural power to provide security and control in the areas where these migrants lived. According to a former UNHCR staffer, "Registro Ampliado, in a sense, also provides a security, also provides information for the government. I mean, put it this way: before March 2009, the government had no idea about thousands of people in the country. Who were they, how did they get there? They didn't have a picture of them, and now they do. So it is an element, if you want, that the government has control."[28] This person recalled that the eventual strengthening of state

---

[27] Interview 81QI 2010.
[28] Interview 163WI 2010.

control through cooperation with the proposal was emphasized in UNHCR representative Martha Juarez's negotiations to convince the Ecuadorian government to sign onto Enhanced Registration. "Definitely, that was a selling point . . . when they were negotiating the registration. They said, 'Look, you provide registration, provide access to rights to thousands of people, and you also get information on who is in your country.'"[29]

This process of negotiation with the government underscores the point made earlier that the adaptation of nonstate institutions to ensure human security does not necessarily represent an erosion of the state, which is still primarily responsible for security within its borders. Although some institutions may indeed seek to undermine or replace formal state policies that are perceived to be reproducing insecurity, others facilitate negotiation and cooperation between the state, host society, and the interests of migrants in order to strengthen the overall infrastructural power and capacity for governance and security in the country, whether this is exercised by the state, nonstate actors, or some combination of both.

In addition to the functional reasons justifying the Enhanced Registration proposal, there were also political and organizational motives that provided a fertile political opportunity for both the state and the UNHCR. As international organizations gain more authority and have a larger budgetary or policy role, they develop greater autonomy and can sometimes respond more to their own independent organizational, budgetary, and turf interests than to a simple calculation of functional needs or the interests of states (Barnett and Finnemore 2004). According to a former government official,

> They had been discussing it since 2008, and the agreement was basically that UNHCR would put a lot of money for that Enhanced Registration because they needed to grow organically, in bureaucratic terms. At that time, UNHCR was having problems in Venezuela because the principal headquarters was in Caracas for this part of the region, and they were also having problems in Colombia. So one very bureaucratic strategy was to have a very strong active role in Ecuador, and from here they did make visible the humanitarian drama of Colombia at the international level, but putting themselves as the principal actors. . . . And the Ecuadorian state said, fine, let's

---

[29] Interview 163WI 2010. This characterization of the proposal reportedly made by Juarez was generally corroborated by a former internal security governmental official in Quito familiar with the negotiations. Interview 145QS 2017.

bring these resources. The state also had an interest in that time period in making itself visible as the protector state in the region, especially after the Colombian bombing in Ecuadorian territory. So from my perspective, it was a play to position the country's international image in humanitarian terms that also was useful to UNHCR because they raised a lot of money for the Colombian issue starting with that date.[30]

In the context of Rafael Correa's rhetorical commitments to Plan Ecuador as a development-oriented reaction against the more militaristic Plan Colombia (and his desire after the Angostura bombing to highlight the Colombian government's failure to provide security for its own citizens), Enhanced Registration was accepted as a joint initiative to be cofinanced and implemented between UNHCR and the Ecuadorian government. UNHCR was able to build on an additional political opportunity by presenting Ecuador as a pilot test case for a Global Needs Assessment, which unlocked an additional quantity of money for Enhanced Registration (UNHCR 2008). In January 2009, UNHCR signed an agreement with Ecuadorian minister of foreign relations, Fander Falconí, to implement the initiative together, aiming to register more than fifty thousand new refugees. Falconí acknowledged the state institutional gaps that he hoped the intervention would help to address, saying that the government hoped to "take steps toward a new vision in which the state can intervene, where it can institutionalize effective processes . . . and in this case achieve greater confidence in the state."[31]

During the year from March 2009 until the end of March 2010, a mobile, fifty-person brigade of government officials, plus UNHCR advisers and NGO observers, traveled to different locations in the northern border region, compressing the registration and status determination process that normally lasts three to six months into one day and registering 27,740 Colombians, who were given official refugee status (Escalante 2010). The Enhanced Registration officials applied status determination criteria based on the Cartagena Declaration of 1984, which recognized refugees fleeing "generalized violence" in the home country (which describes much of Colombia), rather than the more restrictive Refugee Convention criteria that are frequently used as the basis for decisions in the regular status determination

---

[30] Interview 145QS 2017.

[31] Quoted in "Ecuador firma convenio con ACNUR para fortalecer compromiso con refugiados," *Hoy* (January 19, 2009).

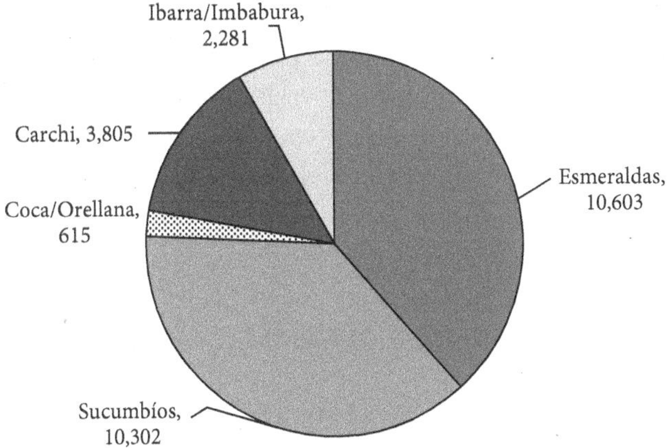

Figure 7.6 Refugee visas conferred during Enhanced Registration, March 2009–March 2010

Source: Molina 2010; Jaramillo 2010.

process in Quito. Compared to the average rate of about 32% at which the Ministry of Foreign Relations Refugee Office had recognized refugee status for asylum seekers during the period of 2000–2007, the acceptance rate during Enhanced Registration was much higher, with approximately two out of an average one hundred cases per day being deferred to the regular determination process for further investigation, and the rest of the cases being approved.[32] According to the Jesuit Refugee Service, which served as an observer during Enhanced Registration, some 10% of cases each day involved asylum seekers who had been denied refugee status in the regular status determination process, but were recognized as refugees during Enhanced Registration (Servicio Jesuita 2009: 10).

Figure 7.6 illustrates the breakdown by province of the number of Colombian refugees who were registered through the Enhanced Registration initiative. Esmeraldas and Sucumbíos, the two border provinces with the lowest levels of development and state presence, showed the greatest impact, with more than ten thousand new refugees registered in each province, while Carchi and Imbabura registered significant but smaller numbers. The Amazonian town of Coca, in Orellana province, which is not always included

---

[32] Servicio Jesuita 2009: 5; data for 2000–2007 derived from the Ministry of Foreign Relations Refugee Office, "Estadísticas: Solicitudes e refugio," http://www.mmrree.gov.ec/refugiados/html/___estadisticas.html (accessed August 15, 2010).

in northern border refugee initiatives, also benefited from the intervention, registering more than six hundred Colombians. By the completion of Enhanced Registration, the number of registered refugees in Ecuador had more than doubled, from fewer than twenty thousand registered refugees at the beginning of 2009 to more than fifty thousand in June 2010 (Jaramillo 2010; UNHCR 2010).[33]

Challenges

It is important to note also that, in addition to acting as an intermediary between the interests of the state, migrants, and migrant-receiving communities, UNHCR also provided a forum for negotiating intragovernmental disputes over the Enhanced Registration process. There were elements of resistance and opposition to Enhanced Registration, especially within the military, police, and Foreign Ministry (including some personnel from the Refugee Office), which viewed the process as lax and too generous in recognizing refugee status for Colombians who could later become security threats in Ecuador (Servicio Jesuita 2009: 10). During the 2008 national consultations prior to the initiation of the registration, in which UNHCR brought together stakeholders from different agencies to negotiate and consult on the design of the intervention to address the invisibility of Colombians in the border region, these suspicions within certain state agencies already had resulted in the planned duration of the Enhanced Registration drive for 2009–10 being reduced from eighteen months to twelve months.[34] After the design of the intervention had been agreed, the tensions among state agencies and officials continued.

For example, various media reports appeared in regional press while Enhanced Registration was taking place, in which police officials held out a few examples of Colombians who had committed a crime while possessing refugee recognition, using these examples as justification to express strong reservations about the Enhanced Registration process, which they viewed as enabling criminals. For example, two Colombian men, Wilmer C., alias

---

[33] UNHCR, "Estadisticas sobre refugiados, solicitantes de asilo, y otras personas bajo la competencia del ACNUR en America Latina," website of Plan de Acción de México (December 31, 2008), http://www.acnur.org/t3/pam/informacion-general/. See also "El Registro Ampliado de Refugiados Culminó Ayer," *El Comercio* (April 1, 2010).

[34] Interview 163WI 2010.

"El Cholo," and William P., were detained in Esmeraldas province in May 2009 for alleged extortion of money from local business owners. The commander of the San Lorenzo sector police, Bolívar Obando, complained that the case illustrated the role of Enhanced Registration in exacerbating insecurity, saying, "They even gave [refugee] papers to people who act outside the law."[35] Officials in both the Foreign Ministry's Refugee Office and in UNHCR argued in response to this type of statement that refugee status does not exempt wrongdoers from being subject to the criminal justice system of Ecuador, and that the entire Colombian population should not be stigmatized based on the actions of a few individuals, considering that within both Ecuadorian and Colombian populations, not everyone is a saint (Roldán 2009).[36]

In addition to the external tensions over Enhanced Registration, some of these same concerns were expressed by those directly involved in it. An evaluation report by the JRS, which maintained an observer presence throughout the Enhanced Registration process,[37] warned, "It is extremely worrisome that on repeated occasions we have seen, even in the Eligibility Commission, that certain officials of the DGR [General Directorate for Refugees] in the Ministry of Foreign Affairs maintain a very negative perception toward Enhanced Registration and a marked resistance to the idea of starting to apply in Quito the same acceptance criteria that were applied in Enhanced Registration, because they perceive this process as very lax. One gets the sense that these officials are looking to take advantage of any little misstep in the process that they can find in order to cancel it" (Servicio Jesuita 2009: 5). These tensions did not completely derail the process, and Enhanced Registration continued to its end as planned, although the reduction from eighteen to twelve months and funding shortfalls did result in only half as many people being registered as originally projected.[38] This political context required continued negotiation and adaptation throughout the year-long registration process.

---

[35] "La visa de refugiado no exime a los foráneos que delinquen," *El Comercio* (June 14, 2009), https://www.elcomercio.com/actualidad/visa-refugiado-no-exime-foraneos.html.

[36] See the responses of Alfonso Morales, director of the Office of Refugees, and Martha Juarez, UNHCR representative in Ecuador, quoted in "La visa de refugiado"; Interview 140QS 2008.

[37] Nonstate institutions that sent observers to participate in Enhanced Registration included JRS, Asylum Access, and for an initial period, Colombian organizations like ARCOE, although funding constraints prohibited the participation of this last group for most of the process. These NGOs observed Enhanced Registration, offered specialized technical assistance, and carried out trainings for the waiting asylum seekers.

[38] Interview 163WI 2010; see also "Ecuador firma convenio con ACNUR."

One of the ongoing sources of tension throughout the process was between the central government and UNHCR on the one hand as the decision-makers behind Enhanced Registration, and the local governments and Ecuadorian population in the proposed registration sites on the other hand. Part of this tension can be understood through the lens of the invisibility bargain, in which the prospect of more empowered migrants and refugees with increased visibility claiming rights and services was perceived as threatening by some Ecuadorians. This segment of the population placed pressure on their local leaders, who in some cases expressed opposition to Enhanced Registration. In a centralized governmental structure like Ecuador's, however, these local leaders did not have the political standing to stop the process, nor a unified basis for opposition, given that other sectors of their constituencies were supportive of Enhanced Registration. In the words of one international organization observer,

> There were a lot of people within the government [for whom] Enhanced Registration wasn't always popular, considering the rise of xenophobia and the stigma of Colombians within the country. So there were people, some of the mayors and the governors in the provinces who asked the DGR [General Directorate for Refugees], "Please stop this." . . . The days where the turns would be given out, there were rivers of people, there were hundreds of people outside the coliseum. You know, it was visible. In terms of politics, that is not good. It's not good for the electorate, if you want.[39]

In San Lorenzo, Esmeraldas, local government officials often felt that they were left to deal with the consequences of the spillover from the Colombian conflict with little support or coordination from the central government, and little financial compensation to assist with the effort. Despite the fact that Enhanced Registration was scheduled to begin in March 2009 in Sucumbíos (where UNHCR, the government, and others had been carrying out a long-term communication and awareness campaign to prepare the population), the plan was changed by presidential order, for unexplained reasons, a few weeks before the scheduled start of the registration drive, making Esmeraldas the new location where the initiative would begin. Local officials in Esmeraldas province complained that this change was made with little consultation or coordination by the central government.[40] The change in timing

---

[39] Interview 163WI 2010.
[40] Interview 163WI 2010.

for Enhanced Registration in Esmeraldas was particularly problematic for mayors in the towns of Muisne, Quinende, and San Lorenzo, who were in the middle of local election campaigns, making them especially sensitive to local public sentiment.[41] During the initial phase of Enhanced Registration, this lack of coordination and insufficient preparation of the local population had a negative impact on the process at first. According to JRS observers,

> The publicity for Enhanced Registration in this phase has been deficient, giving rise to rumors and speculations about the process, both among the beneficiary population and among the local population. . . . There is no clear information about what a refugee is, what is the purpose of Enhanced Registration, who are its beneficiaries, dates and places of the brigades, the free cost of the process, etc. In addition, it is necessary to inform the Ecuadorian population about these and other issues involved in the process due to the rejection that this is generating among the local population. (Servicio Jesuita 2009: 8)

In San Lorenzo, local officials viewed the visibility of the Colombian applicants at Enhanced Registration with apprehension. According to a former international organization official in Esmeraldas, "Authorities definitely had their claws out, during the Enhanced Registration, particularly in San Lorenzo, due to rising levels of violence. . . . The fact that outside a church there were hundreds of Colombians waiting in line to be given a turn, that really got authorities on their toes."[42] The growing frustration with rising crime, which many Ecuadorian constituents associated with the Colombian conflict, led to a protest in June 2009 by fifteen hundred residents of San Lorenzo, demanding greater efforts by the central government to ensure security and order in the town.[43] Similar protests in other coastal cities followed, also demanding a response to perceived insecurity and blaming Colombians for delinquency (Toro 2010).

This feeling of frustration over perceived insecurity, straining of public services, and lack of sustained central government assistance in the context of an increasing Colombian population was an important part of the political

---

[41] "Disturbios en inscripciones," *Hoy* (February 6, 2009), http://www.hoy.com.ec/noticias-ecuador/disturbios-en-inscripcionesdisturbios-en-inscripciones-332671.html.

[42] Interview 163WI 2010.

[43] "San Lorenzo exige seguridad," *Hoy* (June 3, 2009), http://www.hoy.com.ec/noticias-ecuador/san-lorenzo-exige-seguridad-2-351598.html.

context that shaped the interaction and negotiations among local officials, UNHCR, and the central government during Enhanced Registration. This antiforeigner impulse was exacerbated by the news media, which tended to cover forced migration using frames of threatening outsider, helpless victim, or massive flows bringing delinquency, all of which dehumanized and denied agency to refugees (Rivera 2013; Crawley et al. 2016). In a separate study, I found that about one-third of sampled news stories on Ecuadorian television pertaining to migration featured a "villain" frame emphasizing security threats and burdens of migrants, while 55% of the TV news stories featured a "victim" frame (Pugh and Moya 2020).

One NGO representative in Lago Agrio observed about the perception of the Enhanced Registration process, "At first it was an international example. . . . The problem was that it made the problem visible, and the news media magnified this even more."[44] The response of local politicians to political pressure from their Ecuadorian constituents (and the narratives developed in the news media), which was in some cases to oppose the refugee registration drive, also highlights, in contrast, the importance of nonstate actors for guaranteeing the rights of Colombian members of the community, who cannot vote.

Protection Results and State Capacity Building

Despite the messy political disputes that shaped the process before and during Enhanced Registration, this intervention had a major impact on the protection of rights and on building state capacity. According to a UNHCR statement, "Many refugees have been living in remote border areas of the north for years, unable to access asylum procedures in urban areas either because of lack of resources and information or because of fear. Without legal status a majority of these refugees became vulnerable and marginalized. Documentation makes a real difference in the lives of refugees, who can use it to move freely in Ecuador and to gain access to health centers, schools and other services" (Escalante 2010). One refugee in San Lorenzo, for example, explained that her refugee documentation was an essential part of survival for her family, given health problems that necessitated access to healthcare and given the risk of deportation by suspicious police: "The refugee

---

[44] Interview 150SN 2013.

identification card that they gave us has been a blessing for us. We can show it to the police so they can see that we are legally in this country."[45] Former UNHCR Ecuador representative Martha Juarez argued that, although Enhanced Registration was primarily focused on the protection of rights, it should be used as an important step toward improving economic resources and mutual recognition within refugee-receiving communities:

> Enhanced Registration involves a legal integration. It is about protecting [refugees] so that they are not returned to their country. But afterward comes the process that actually gives them access to their rights, so that the children have access to education, health, so that people can work, so they can rent a place to live without being discriminated against. That is integration in the area of rights. Later, of course, it is important that people have a livelihood, and all of this helps them to integrate economically. Next is the integration with their neighbors, in this case so that Ecuadorians and Colombians live in peaceful coexistence.[46]

In addition to its direct benefits in providing legal documentation and rec-ognition to refugees in remote areas, Enhanced Registration also improved state capacity to handle status determination procedures for the growing Colombian population in a transparent and efficient manner. A former UNHCR staffer pointed out that Enhanced Registration's deployment of a fifty-person brigade of government workers over the period of a year, with close consultation and technical assistance from UNHCR, provided an ideal capacity-building opportunity, and these personnel were then trained, expe-rienced, and available to staff field offices of the Ministry of Foreign Relations Refugee Office as they expanded their provincial reach. The significant amount of capital and equipment, such as computers, printers, and vehicles, that were purchased for the Enhanced Registration effort were also used to equip government field offices to handle increased refugee claims, rather than continuing to rely on UNHCR for these registration functions.[47]

In fact, the Ministry of Foreign Relations Refugee Office used this increased capacity to open field offices in Esmeraldas, Tulcán, and Guayaquil

---

[45] Quoted in "Ecuador: Refugiados y realidades locales," *Evaluación de necesidades globales,* UNHCR website, http://www.acnur.org/t3/eng/testimonios/ (accessed August 16, 2010).

[46] Martha Juarez, "Los refugiados quieren aportar algo positivo a quien los acoge," interview in *El Comercio* (July 24, 2009).

[47] Interview 163WI 2010.

in the next couple of years after the initiative ended.[48] With the conclusion of Enhanced Registration, UNHCR turned over all asylum seeker registration functions to the newly strengthened Refugee Office.[49] The Refugee Office planned to implement some of the more streamlined procedures that were developed during Enhanced Registration into its regular status determination process at the national level in order to decrease its asylum seeker backlog and regularize the use of the more permissive Cartagena Declaration criteria for deciding refugee status. In practice, however, the political pushback on the government resulted in these changes not being implemented permanently, and with Decree 1182 in 2012, a regression in the openness of the status determination process (Correa 2016; Ubidia Vásquez 2015). Enhanced Registration illustrates UNHCR's dual role in directly providing public goods such as security, peace, and protection, while also negotiating with, pressuring, and strengthening the state to enforce its existing formal institutions.

Ultimately, the concrete result of the initiative for increasing security and peace in migrant-receiving communities was mixed: it did result in greater legal certainty for many Colombians in Ecuador, and the state did increase its capacity to register and administer the status determination process, decentralizing its services into border province offices to a greater extent than before. Despite the promise and potential of the initiative, the fact that much of Enhanced Registration's success came from the political will and commitment of particular government officials created worries about the future institutionalization and implementation of the initiative's innovations (Servicio Jesuita 2009: 4, 10).[50]

In fact, although its ambitious scope, innovative structure, and impressive numbers of refugees registered caused Enhanced Registration to gain international attention,[51] its success in raising the profile of the refugee issue in Ecuador sparked a backlash that ultimately eroded political and social support for open borders and universal citizenship, leading to the Regression stage (Pugh 2017). For example, former president and Correa opponent Lucio Gutierrez claimed in 2012, "Because of the open-door policies of Rafael Correa, which throw the borders wide open, criminals are

---

[48] Interview 81QI 2010.

[49] Interview 163WI 2010.

[50] UNHCR, "Ecuador," *UNHCR Global Report 2009* (June 2010), 322.

[51] "ACNUR tilda de ejemplo la iniciativa del Ecuador para formalizar la situación de refugiados Colombianos," Reuters / EuropaPress (April 6, 2010).

entering to rob us, assassins are entering to kill us, and narcotraffickers are entering to take the lives of our children" (Oposición 2012). One could point to Enhanced Registration as the apex of the Coordination stage led by the UNHCR and NGOs, and its aftermath as the beginning of the regression in refugee protections during the state-led stage of institutional hollowing out.

Interagency Program for Peace and Development in the Northern Border Zone

After Ecuadorian president Lucio Gutierrez invited UN secretary-general Kofi Annan to visit Ecuador in 2003 and send an assessment team in 2004 to "help with the Colombian security problem," the UNHCR office in Ecuador designed a series of institutional adaptations to address the gaps in state institutions and policies that were identified during the visit. Among the failures that UNHCR pointed out were the "limited capacity for management and weak coordination by the executive and disconnection between national and local levels partially due to the lack of a shared plan agreed upon with the participation of all key players. Notable weakness of UDENOR [Unit for Northern Border Region Development] as the cooperation coordination entity has been observed, [as well as] ineffective decentralization and low local technical capacity."[52]

In order to improve coordination among UNHCR and government agencies and develop a more integrated peacebuilding approach to the provision of human security in the Ecuadorian border region, a UN Interagency Program for Peace and Development for the northern border zone was created, which included representatives of sixteen UN agencies, under the leadership of UNHCR and the UNDP. According to the program's chief technical adviser for peace and development, Michael Brown, this adaptation improved local UN capacity to promote develop and peace for migrants and Ecuadorian receiving communities in the context of a lack of state capacity. He explained, "We've been promoting economic development projects, and specifically trying to target the communities along the actual borderline itself, right across the river from Colombia, in order to fill the gaps that if you

---

[52] United Nations, "Interagency Assessment of Ecuador's Northern Border Region: Summary," presentation by the United Nations System in Ecuador, Quito, 2004, web3.coehs.siu.edu/SSW/ecuador/UN_North_Border_Ecuador.ppt (accessed August 12, 2018).

don't have these projects these communities are kind of left there on their own."[53]

In an illustration of the important role of UNHCR institutional adaptations in strengthening state institutions, the Interagency Program for Peace and Development also facilitated greater coordination with the secretariat of the government's Plan Ecuador to introduce into state policy implementation a greater level of sensitivity to the conflict dynamics facing Colombians and Ecuadorians in the border region (Brown 2009). According to Brown, "Working with the national Ecuadorian Secretariat responsible for border relations with Colombia, the Programme also facilitated mutual understanding of the cross-border challenges between decision-makers of both countries. Since its establishment in 2006, the Programme has provided advice to the Government of Ecuador in the development of a peace and development strategy for the northern border" (Brown 2009).

This Interagency Program also intervened to facilitate dialogue between Ecuadorian and Colombian high-level civil society leaders when diplomatic relations and tensions between official state leaders made official negotiation impossible.[54] After Ecuador and Colombia cut off official diplomatic ties with each other after the Colombian raid on the FARC camp at Angostura in March 2008, the UN facilitated an unofficial dialogue, entitled the Colombia-Ecuador Dialogue Group, together with the Carter Center and with input from the Organization of American States (Meacham 2008; Huerta Montalvo 2009). This effort brought together influential decision-makers from the civil society of both countries, such as former ministers of foreign relations, prominent academics, NGO representatives, journalists, and business leaders, to move toward a restoration of relations.[55] According to a former minister of foreign relations who was part of the binational dialogue group, the value of the initiative lay exactly in its unofficial nature, which allowed for creative space to build trust, networks, and relationships without the pressure of defending a national position: "From the official side, the governmental side, you have to be very tough . . . but in these types of meetings that are informal, not secret, but very free, you learn a lot, and you

---

[53] Recorded interview by UNDP with Michael Brown, Chief Technical Adviser, Peace and Development, United Nations Development Program (UNDP), Quito, Ecuador, http://www.undp.org/cpr/audio/Ecuador_conflict_prevention.mp3 (accessed August 8, 2010).

[54] Interview 91QI 2008.

[55] Interview 92QI 2009.

know each other, and you can do many things to create more understanding, in this case between Ecuador and Colombia."[56]

The tensions between the governments of the two countries had paralyzed the Ecuadorian and Colombian governments' bilateral cooperation on projects, from river decontamination to the repair of roads at border crossings and an agreement on limiting radio frequencies along the border, according to a local official who was part of the dialogue group.[57] According to Manuel Chiriboga, a member of the dialogue group from Ecuador, "Having face-to-face relation helps you very much understand the other's position, and we have achieved a lot. We've tried to construct a common view on a number of issues and to transmit that to the public to assure that people change their traditional views or stereotypes of how they see others, in our case, Colombians, and help them see us" (Carter Center 2009). Chiriboga and one of his Colombian counterparts, for example, used the dialogue as an opportunity to share experiences and to launch a joint initiative based on Chiriboga's successes organizing Ecuadorian peasant farmers, replicating the program in the Colombian department of Nariño. After meetings in the region and two meetings at the Carter Center in Atlanta, the dialogue group successfully convinced the presidents of both countries in October 2009 to restore bilateral diplomatic relations at the lower working level of chargés d'affaires (Wilentz 2008). This required the members of both nationalities to use their informal leverage, networks, and influence to prod their respective governments toward restoration of relations, providing face-saving political cover for the leaders to consider new alternative positions.[58]

The Interagency Program for Peace and Development has also facilitated more effective policy implementation (and more coordinated interventions into national agenda-setting processes) by local governments and nonstate actors in the northern border. For example, a Provincial Round Table that the program sponsored in 2008 in Sucumbíos brought together local mayors, provincial governors and prefects, and representatives of nonstate organizations to create one unified agenda of local needs to send to the national government in order to encourage a policy process that responded effectively to the needs of Ecuadorians and Colombians in the border zone. According to UNDP adviser Michael Brown, in a region with little state presence and

---

[56] Interview 137QS 2017.
[57] Interview 18CS 2015. See also "En la frontera norte se pararon los proyectos," *El Comercio* (October 2, 2009).
[58] Interview 121QN 2016.

divided regional interests, the round table brought together local leaders who "had never got together before and in fact had consistently been working at cross purposes."[59] Reflecting on the added value of the round-table dialogue (and the interagency approach of the northern border zone program itself) for promoting more effective human security and peacebuilding outcomes, Brown added, "In a lot of conflict situations, it's not only what you do but how you do it, and doing it in a way that is open, participatory, and based on consensus brings you an enormous way forward to help local people to be able to have the space to overcome some of their differences."[60]

As illustrated here, the UN agencies like UNHCR may sometimes be more flexible than the state in bringing together different national groups and dealing with cross-border/transnational challenges. The diverse missions of these different IGOs can also be a strength, as UNHCR's mandate-driven mission based on Ecuador's treaty obligations gives it more independence to pressure the state or call out wrongdoing, whereas UNDP's need to sign annual agreements and work closely with the state sometimes gives it greater access and trust for delicate diplomatic tasks.[61] A UNDP official said that the Interagency Program was especially successful in building local government and NGO capacity to mitigate conflict and in opening spaces for dialogue.[62] Particularly in the political context of hostility between the Ecuadorian and Colombian presidents, or in the face of dysfunctional communication channels between central and local governments, trusted independent actors with presence in the region, like the UNDP, UNHCR, and other agencies that are represented within the Interagency Program for Peace and Development may sometimes adapt more effectively than the state to local-level human security needs.[63]

One example is a "quick response fund" that gives the Interagency Program the flexibility to respond to urgent needs in the face of local-level conflict, supporting proposals by local communities to carry out dialogue, advocacy, and joint problem-solving programs. This intervention, initiated in 2005 and continued since that time, addressed the long decision-making and processing times involved in attaining support from state or large donors for projects to resolve local conflicts. The fund was designed to introduce

[59] Recorded interview with Michael Brown.
[60] Recorded interview with Michael Brown.
[61] Interview 91QI 2008.
[62] Interview 92QI 2009.
[63] Interview 33EI 2012.

greater flexibility of funds to support local peacebuilding initiatives before conflicts escalated beyond repair:

> The time required for securing and processing funds from the vast majority of institutional donors does not respond to the urgency of the response required by an escalating socio-environmental conflict. From the point when an institution or cooperation agency receives a request to intervene in a conflict, it takes no less than four months—at the very least—to receive the necessary money to intervene to manage the conflict. By that time, the conflict may well have escalated to such a point that it is impossible or much more costly to find an adequate response. In addition, once an environmental or social damage has been caused, it may not be possible to return things to their previous condition. (Dumas 2006: 8)

The community peacebuilding initiatives that were funded through this mechanism helped to empower community members (including Colombians and Ecuadorians) and local organizations in Esmeraldas to build conflict resolution capacity around shared problems, such as pollution from an electrical plant, difficulties in securing land tenure, and conflicts between community members and a palm oil agricultural company that exercised significant local power. The process of engaging in dialogue over these specific social-environmental problems in turn fostered mutual recognition among local residents (Dumas 2006). According to Michael Brown (2009), "In each case, the community developed a common understanding of the conflict and defined joint actions to prevent the situation from deteriorating."

Conclusion

This chapter has explored the role of networks to explain how different types of institutions leverage "practical authority" to carry out governance functions, especially the provision of conflict resolution and human security in migrant-receiving communities in Ecuador. The invisibility bargain and its restrictive expectations for migrants' political and social behavior place limits on their ability to access protection, rights, and resources through traditional state institutions. The state, in turn, confronts political incentives that do not necessarily encourage it to vigorously defend the rights of migrants or offer meaningful protections from victimization. In this context, tracing the informal channels through which migrants negotiate access to the resources and protection that they need contributes a more nuanced understanding of the many ways that security provision depends on a range of nonstate actors beyond the state. Having reviewed over the past four chapters the evidence provided by subnational comparisons of governance networks, longitudinal tracing of the evolution and interactions among key institutional actors, and patterns identified in survey data and interviews to demonstrate the effects of the invisibility bargain and the way it shapes migrant agency and political participation and human security, the final chapter offers a concluding summary of the argument. It also suggests pathways for further research, including ways that my argument can be extended to other regions of the world and to other populations to better explain the interactions of integration, political participation, and human security as they are negotiated among migrants and their host communities.

8

Conclusion

The vast majority of the world's refugees live in the Global South, and even in the case of economic immigrants, more than half of the population has a developing country destination. At the same time, the majority of academic work on migration has focused on receiving countries in the Global North. This disjuncture represents a significant barrier to understanding how most migrants and refugees integrate into their host countries, the strategies that they use to ensure survival, rights, livelihoods, and peaceful coexistence, and the policies and social structures with which they negotiate their protection, and even their existence. In Latin America, and in many other parts of the Global South, power is more a function of personal relationships than formal titles or institutional mandates, and one's networks and contacts contribute more to one's effectiveness in getting things done than the letter of the law or one's formal job description.

Practical authority and the informal institutions that structure and regulate interactions in predictable ways that are separate from formal state institutions and laws explain much of how decisions are made, compliance is gained, and people are mobilized for particular purposes. These networks and informal institutions that comprise a broader governance network can reinforce and complement shared goals with the state, or they can subvert or compete with state policies. The diversity and connectedness of different types of institutions—state, nonstate, and international—helps us to understand when the governance network offers multiple access points that migrants and refugees trust enough to reach out to. It also explains when these initial entry points have the relationships to coordinate and refer migrants to other parts of the governance network in order to ensure that they are able to achieve the rights, resources, protection, and mutual recognition to enjoy human security and peaceful coexistence with the host population.

This book has argued that the "invisibility bargain" structures the experience and opportunities of migrants in host countries; the strategies they employ to secure access to rights, resources, and protection; and the ways that state and nonstate actors respond to and interact with them, whether through impediment and control, brokering, or receptivity. The precarity that migrants confront when their physical presence and acceptance in the host country are conditional on their economic contributions, social invisibility, and depoliticization results in indirect negotiation becoming a survival strategy.

Migrants often seek indirect pathways to gain access to rights that they are guaranteed in domestic or international law, or to seek protection, peaceful coexistence and mutual recognition, and resources sufficient for a dignified livelihood in the host country. Because democratic governments are politically accountable primarily to their own citizens (i.e., those who vote) and not to foreigners who reside in their territory (who in the case of Ecuador often do not vote), the state may be less than ideal as the primary actor guaranteeing the safety and rights of migrants and refugees in the host country. The political incentives faced by politicians may prod them to ignore or actively subvert those legal protections that benefit migrants if they perceive them to take away time, resources, political dominance, or other benefits from native citizens. Even if there is not such a zero-sum relationship in reality, some state actors might find it politically expedient to pretend that there is, blaming or scapegoating migrants for problems faced by the host population as one way of deflecting responsibility away from themselves (Savun and Gineste 2019). At the same time, because the state has a dual role as both a protector of rights/security and a coercive enforcer of laws, its willingness to offer protection as opposed to persecution and exclusion is the result of social construction of threat, securitization of the migration issue, and who is perceived to be a "threatening outsider" who must be stopped and controlled versus a "deserving insider" in need of protection (Braithwaite et al 2019; Sandoval-Garcia 2004). Because this construction happens through negotiation and the sometimes arbitrary everyday practices of social actors and "street level bureaucrats," migrants are often more distrustful of state agencies that could become threats to their freedom or livelihoods if the particular state actor is more influenced by securitizing narratives and a threat perception than by the protections and rights that are embodied in laws, treaties, and the constitution.

In the face of this uncertainty and distrust and the political incentives of the state, a dense and diverse governance network that connects state agencies with nonstate actors, including IGOs, NGOs, firms, informal networks, and others, provides alternative access points that migrants can approach to improve their own security, livelihood, and relationships with their Ecuadorian neighbors. NGOs and IGOs certainly have their own limitations, including questions of donor-driven agendas, lack of local context or legitimacy in the case of international organizations recently coming into Ecuador, insufficient capacity, democratic deficit critiques for IGOs, and a potential lack of public accountability/transparency. For these reasons, simply replacing state efforts with nonstate ones is not an effective or desirable strategy; rather, strengthening the relationships and connections among all three types in a dense and diverse governance network helps to ensure that more trusted initial access points are available, and that once connected, migrants can be referred or accompanied through the network to protectors and service providers that are able to meet their needs and ensure that their rights are recognized. The limitations and strengths of each type of organization are thus balanced and complemented by the others, increasing the ultimate likelihood of migrants gaining access to the rights, resources, and protections that they seek, and that their efforts at political participation are brokered by allies with the legitimacy and contacts in the host society to help them avoid a backlash against political visibility.

Reviewing the Evidence

Ecuador provides a useful and complex base of empirical material for understanding the dynamics that influence the integration, protection, and coexistence of migrants. The largest recipient of refugees and asylum seekers in Latin America (primarily from Colombia) at roughly the same time that many Ecuadorians were leaving to try to improve their fortunes in Europe and the United States, Ecuador has confronted intersecting facets of human mobility. During a relatively short and clearly demarcated time period from 2000 to 2017, the country experienced three distinct phases: (1) state neglect and national security orientation (2000–2006), in which the Catholic Church and the UNHCR were the predominant protective institutions in the governance network, (2) coordinated partnership (2007–2011), in which the UNHCR was the predominant actor in partnership with the state, which was actively trying to build its capacity and become an internationally recognized progressive state for migration and integration, and (3) regression/decline (2012–2017), in which the state took primary control of migration policy and institutions. In reaction to political pressure, it increased restrictions for refugees, reduced drastically the number of refugees it accepted, shifted to the language of "human mobility" rather than refugees (which allowed it to base its practices on executive decrees rather than international treaty obligations), promoted the use of Mercosur visas rather than asylum claims, and cut staff and budget for refugee and immigration government agencies even as UNHCR and nonstate actors also scaled down.

The findings emerging from the analysis of the Colombian migration experience during this time period indicate the critical importance of nonstate actors as the key component of the governance network providing the easiest and most trusted entry point for migrants to access rights, resources, and protections, fulfilling the responsibilities embodied in international law and the domestic constitution. Comparing the three different temporal phases also provides evidence for a "strength of weak states" argument: when the state was the predominant actor in the governance network, there seemed to be less security and less peaceful integration in migrant-receiving communities compared to the phase in which the UNHCR and state were strong and coordinated partners, along with a range of NGOs.

It is important to emphasize that the effects of the invisibility bargain are not felt equally across all categories of migrants. Race, sex, socioeconomic class, nationality, and legal status all form intersecting hierarchies through which power and privilege are exercised, resources and networks are made available to or excluded from certain migrants, and "communities of value" are defined. Afro-Colombians, women, forced migrants, undocumented migrants, and those with fewer economic resources often confront steeper challenges in navigating the invisibility bargain and achieving social integration and political participation compared to other migrants. At the same time, migrants exercise agency in navigating these complex realities, choosing coping strategies that they hope will allow them to gain access to the rights, resources, and protections that they need to attain dignified livelihoods and live in peaceful coexistence with their neighbors in Ecuador. As chapter 6 described, different migrants may choose strategies to (1) reduce social distance by developing meaningful relationships with Ecuadorians, (2) minimize differences by trying to become more like Ecuadorians or by avoiding Ecuadorians altogether, and (3) form coalitions and networks with Ecuadorian NGOs and returned emigrant allies. Their success in using these strategies depends both on their own characteristics and action and on the availability, diversity, and density of social and governance networks in their particular locality.

The channels through which influence and authority are generated and exercised, and through which innovative practices to achieve better security for all inhabitants and more peaceful relations between Colombians and Ecuadorians coexisting in the country are carried out, often reflect informal institutions, flexible networks, and personal relationships more than formal institutional mandates and legal jurisdiction. This is certainly true in "brown areas" in the border region where the state is a peripheral player and "shadow citizenship" the main type of authority structure (O'Donnell 2004; Idler 2019). Even in the capital cities of Ecuador, where the state may *choose* to have an ambivalent and ambiguous role in enforcing laws and providing migrant protections, however, "practical authority" (Abers and Keck 2013) and navigation of the social expectations in the invisibility bargain provide a more useful explanation for outcomes than a formal legal or institutional analysis.

The empirical chapters identified several of the key mechanisms through which the often informal linkages between state and nonstate actors may lead to constructive policies and protections in migrant-receiving communities: (*a*) building coalitions of actors with different sources of political leverage and motivations that can provide brokers and allies to advocate for change from within the host society, thus helping migrants avoid violating the invisibility bargain by using more overt claims-making strategies directed toward the state; (*b*) providing reciprocal resource-sharing of money, expertise, and political will in the Andean tradition of the *minga*, reducing the pressure of scarce resources in motivating state neglect and scapegoating of migrants in Ecuador; and (*c*) using the frequent mobility and overlap of skilled personnel who move between positions in the UN system, NGOs, and state agencies, resulting in a rich social capital when these people bring their preexisting personal relationships with them, which then help to strengthen working relations and the likelihood of referrals and coordination across the governance network.

The three most important state policy innovations extending protections and rights for migrants in Ecuador all resulted from an iterative process of deliberation, advocacy, and negotiation in which nonstate and international actors brokered negotiations with migrants and the state, while adding their own separate interests and perspectives to achieve their organizational goals. The 2008 constitution, which was drafted by the state but incorporated migration and refugee provisions that were shaped largely by a coalition of civil society organizations, returned migrant groups, and invited refugee participation, produced progressive and far-reaching protections that were later used as a basis for advocacy to improve state practices and codify these protections more specifically in law.

The 2009–2010 Enhanced Registration more than doubled the number of registered refugees, and it was the result of the UNHCR-funded survey (Bilsborrow 2006) that allowed for stronger information politics by UNHCR (in addition to significant funding when the UNHCR aligned its strategy to access Global Needs Assessment funding to offer the state). This initiative took advantage of the political opportunity offered by Correa's election and human rights-focused Plan Ecuador platform, but it drew additional legitimacy and practical authority from the participation of observers from refugee organizations and NGOs, and technical assistance from UNHCR. Although it may have overreached in raising the visibility of the Colombian population in a way that triggered a backlash leading to the "decline" era and state regression in 2012, the initiative did contribute to greater state capacity and decentralization of refugee registration into border areas where asylum seekers were already living.

Finally, the adoption of the Organic Law on Human Mobility by the National Assembly in 2017 was the culmination of more than a decade of NGO and IGO organizing and advocacy, negotiation, and coalition building. Here a key component was the alliance of returned Ecuadorian emigrants with Colombian migrant/refugees to reframe the debate from refugee protection to an integrated "human mobility" bill that would spell out detailed protections for all categories of people in mobility so that outdated and less legally binding executive decrees weren't being adapted (and loosely interpreted) to apply to new situations. The concurrent announcement that the public defender's office would be required to guarantee legal representation to all asylum seekers going through the status determination further enshrined as a state responsibility a protection that had been provided previously by nonstate actors (with inevitable unevenness due to limited resources and presence). In all three of these instances of increasing state protection, nonstate actors were key driving forces behind the change, and the governance network that connected IGOs, NGOs, and the state were important to their success, legitimacy, and ability to exercise "practical authority" to achieve greater peace and human security.

Next Steps and Areas of Further Research within Ecuador

While this book provides the results of more than a decade of fieldwork and analysis and makes both theoretical and empirical contributions, Ecuador has much more still to explore in understanding dynamics of migration and refugees, especially as the influx of Venezuelans has brought a new era of forced migration management. Two promising areas for further research—comparing temporal periods and comparing populations—are suggested in what follows.

Comparing Temporal Periods

One of the benefits of using a single case study is that national political conditions are treated as a constant, in order to better sharpen the comparisons of other factors across localities, issue areas, institutional types, or other divides. However, the ability to measure the impact of national political conditions on human security outcomes in migrant-receiving areas within a single case can only be accomplished by measuring change over time, and Ecuador provides an excellent opportunity to do so. President Rafael Correa saw as a central part of his political agenda a desire to challenge the hegemonic neoliberal model of North-dominated globalization and trade in goods and services (often accompanied by security-oriented restrictions on migration from South to North). Because of this, his promotion in 2007 of a range of concepts and policies, including universal citizenship, Plan Ecuador, human mobility, and *buen vivir* provides a clear "before and after" point to determine whether and how this national political agenda influenced (and was influenced by) local and international discourses and practices and the human security experienced by migrants themselves. The gradual decline and hollowing out of this agenda after 2011, and ultimately the transition from Correa to President Lenin Moreno (who reverted to a more traditional and securitized migration policy and a less confrontational international position) provides additional temporal variation along which to measure differences and analyze causal arguments about why these changes occurred.

Key security-related events in the border region—the Colombian bombing of the FARC camp at Angostura in 2008 and the kidnapping and murder of journalists by a dissident FARC splinter cell commanded by "El Guacho" in 2018—represent promising critical junctures to examine the securitization of migration discourse and the narratives that link or distinguish international relations between Colombia and Ecuador with social relations between Colombians and Ecuadorians. Studies employing a constructivist framework and discourse analysis of political leaders' speech acts (Pugh

2017) or content analysis of media stories (Rivera 2013; Farris and Silber Mohamed 2018; Pugh and Moya 2020) and those comparing migration policy under Correa versus Moreno would be promising avenues for further research on these questions.

Comparing Populations

The collapse of the economy and effective governance in Venezuela has led to one of the largest humanitarian tragedies and fastest escalations of displacement across borders in the Americas. Estimates range from 1.4 to 4.7 million displaced Venezuelans abroad as of 2018, with some of the primary destinations being regional neighbors like Colombia, Peru, Ecuador, Chile, and Brazil (Freier and Parent 2018; Selee and Bolter 2020). Given the complex nature of the crisis, and the mixture of poverty and economic deprivation with violence and government repression as the "push factors" motivating the displacement, this population has confronted a trickier legal context than previous Colombian forced migrants, whose claims to refugee status was more straightforward. Although many regional neighbors are signatories of the Cartagena Declaration of 1984, which recognizes "generalized violence" as a legitimate basis for claiming asylum, Venezuelans are often opting for economic visas or other pathways to legal recognition outside of the refugee system. Peru is the exception, where seeking asylum is often quicker than pursuing other types of visas (hence Peru is the largest recipient of people claiming refugee status), but most countries have either issued special humanitarian visas or, like Ecuador, are integrating the Venezuelan migrants through existing migratory institutions and policies while imposing additional visa restrictions (Freier and Parent 2018; Selee and Bolter 2020). The COVID-19 crisis made the situation even more complex, with curfews, border shutdowns, collapsed labor markets and economies, and suspicion of disease making life harder for many Venezuelans in Ecuador and elsewhere in the region. Many have made the difficult decision to try to return to Venezuela (Van Praag and Arnson 2020). Beyers and Nicholls (2020) argue that this exit resulted from a governmental rationality of inaction that fulfilled the strategic goal of "herding" Venezuelans out of the country, even if it was not coordinated or achieved through a formal policy.

Comparing this new flow of Venezuelan migrants to the previous waves of Colombian refugees provides an opportunity for scholars to better understand the impact of a clear legal status determination based on refugee criteria versus a more generalized mixed migration flow on the likelihood of robust protection and social integration in Ecuador, and the social acceptance of such receptive policies and practices. Given that Venezuelan migrants are often better educated and are traditionally accustomed to a wealthier standard of living than many of the Colombian refugees who cross into Ecuador (Faiola 2018),[1] comparing these populations' experience in Ecuador provides an interesting opportunity to also examine the role of economic class and expectations on migrants' integration under the invisibility bargain (Pugh et al. 2020).

There are tentative indications that these factors have sometimes made it more difficult for Venezuelans to pursue some of the invisibility strategies that Colombians used, and their social visibility has worked against them, as overt nationalistic symbols (i.e., Venezuelan flag clothing) and disappointment with modest economic standards of living in their host community have violated the "logic of gratitude" that underlies the invisibility bargain (Moulin 2012), triggering sometimes intense backlash against Venezuelans by some Ecuadorians (García 2020). In fact, the combination of Venezuelans' higher socioeconomic level and average education, and their greater "social visibility" compared to Colombians provides an interesting way to untangle how much relative weight the "economic contribution" expectation has versus the "social invisibility" expectation in the invisibility bargain. For example, in September 2017, a video circulated on social media of a Venezuelan news broadcaster in Ecuador offering disparaging comments about Ecuadorians, pointing to economic class, indigeneity, and physical attractiveness of Ecuadorians as reasons for her perception of Venezuelan superiority.[2] This video infuriated many Ecuadorians and led to harassment, boycotts, and violent attacks on Venezuelan informal street sellers, some of whom found it necessary to distance themselves from the offending news broadcaster, and even to create a video apologizing on behalf of all Venezuelans to the Ecuadorian people.[3] Later, the murder of a pregnant Ecuadorian woman in front of police and cameras by her Venezuelan

---

[1] Anthony Faiola, "From Riches to Rags: Venezuelans Become Latin America's New Underclass," *Washington Post*, July 27, 2018, https://www.washingtonpost.com/news/world/wp/2018/07/27/feature/as-venezuela-crumbles-its-fleeing-citizens-are-becoming-latin-americas-new-underclass/?utm_term=.79f7a02d754e.

[2] See https://www.youtube.com/watch?v=77XLrpeyELUandfeature=youtu.be.

[3] "Estos son los cuatro casos más sonados de discriminación a ecuatorianos en 2017," *Diario Extra*, October 25, 2017.

boyfriend in Ibarra triggered a backlash against Venezuelan migrants. Angry mobs targeted migrants and chased them from their residences in Ibarra and elsewhere, egged on by a tweet from President Moreno threatening to impose visa restrictions and unleash "brigades" to "control" Venezuelans. These episodes perfectly illustrated the risks of violating the social invisibility expectation. In contrast, other strategies, such as the conational association Chamos Venezolanos en Ecuador equipping a "halfway house" in 2018 to receive recent Venezuelan arrivals, in collaboration with other civil society organizations, seemed to provide better results in improving human security and protections for Venezuelans while avoiding sparking a xenophobic backlash from the Ecuadorian host society.[4]

One other population that is remarkably understudied in Ecuador, but which could provide a fruitful basis for further research to extend the research agenda initiated by this book, is the East Asian, and especially the Chinese, population. Given that Colombians are marked as different primarily by accent, despite sharing many similarities with Ecuadorians like language, dominant racial similarities, religion, food, geography, shared history, and more, Chinese migrants are obviously much more distinct and visibly different from Ecuadorians. However, Zepeda and Carrion (2015) find generally more positive views among Ecuadorians of Chinese migrants than Colombians, Peruvians, or other Latin American migrants. Given that Chinese migrants are associated with economic investment and the extractive industries, and not with being refugees or being associated with violence, studies could explore the relative strength of the "economic contribution" expectation versus the "social invisibility" expectation. Following Hopkins (2015), and as elaborated in chapters 2 and 6, the social invisibility expectation is not violated by mere phenotype/linguistic difference, but by this difference violating the norms and expectations of the host community. Chinese migrants could also provide an interesting test of Adida's (2014) theory that migrants who are more ethnically similar to the host community may trigger greater xenophobic backlash than those who are more obviously different because they represent a more realistic threat to the in-group's power position, having greater possibilities for social/ethnic mobility across group boundaries, which increases the incentives for in-group members to police the identity group boundaries more strongly. This theory would expect that Chinese migrants would face less discrimination and social/political exclusion than

[4] Interview 171QM 2019.

Colombians, which finds some support in preliminary evidence from a new comparative survey (Jiménez and Pugh 2020).

Finally, there is an opportunity to deepen and complicate the idea of the "valued contribution" in the invisibility bargain. Given that different people might value different sorts of factors or contributions, and the same thing that seems like a contribution to some may seem like a threat to others, further research and theorizing could develop a more nuanced argument about the power position of the host population sectors who view migrants' contributions as valuable versus those who see them as a burden or a threat. In the case of Chinese migrants in particular, Ecuadorians have relied heavily on Chinese investment, expertise, and migration for the development of infrastructure and extractive industry, and the public perception of these contributions varies quite distinctly by ethnicity (indigenous vs. mestizo), region, and whether the respondent lives in a locality that is directly affected by the environmental effects of the extractive industry (Eisenstadt and West 2017). National marches by environmentalists and indigenous activists have sometimes employed framing that blames Chinese people and companies in Ecuador for enabling environmentally destructive policies of the state (Aidoo et al. 2017). In addition, allegations of extrajudicial assassination of labor and social leaders who questioned extractive projects have also sometimes been used to articulate group threat discourses toward Chinese people (Ray and Chimienti 2017). In this context, additional research could examine the conflict resolution strategies that governance networks employ to improve constructive relations between Ecuadorians and Chinese firms and migrants (Hager et al. 2017), examining how they change with the relatively stronger economic power position of Chinese migrants compared to Colombian ones.

Extending Theory to Other Cases

Scope of Comparison and Migration in Global Context

The past decades have produced a massive increase in political engagement with migration issues on the part of the world's governments, and of scholarly engagement with the issue by academics. Once a marginalized topic within international relations and seen as a "low politics" issue in foreign policy circles, migration has become the predominant political division of our time and the source of much creative and high-quality research. As an indication of the explosion of scholarly research on the topic over the past twenty years, the number of scholarly articles has increased from around six hundred per year in 2000 to over fifteen hundred per year for most of the past decade. The number of think tanks working on migration and publishing in English has also skyrocketed, from around thirty in 1995 to nearly two hundred two decades later (IOM 2018).

At the same time as (and related to) this increase in knowledge production, governments have begun engaging proactively via migration policies, most of which are designed to promote migration and constructive integration of migrants in their host communities. This trend has increased over time, and it reflects a sharp divide between the Global North and the Global South. The number of governments with policies designed to *reduce* immigration has declined from 40% of the global total in 1996 to 16% in 2011. The decline in the Global North was most pronounced, dropping from 60% in 1996 to 10% in 2011, while governments with restrictive policies in the Global South declined from 34% in 1996 to 18% in 2011 (IOM 2014).

Going beyond mere tacit tolerance, the number of governments with policies to integrate non-nationals in their countries increased during this same time period from 44% to 60%. In the Global North, integration policies were adopted in 91% of countries, compared with 47% of Global South countries, and 29% of least developed countries (IOM 2014). These numbers illustrate a striking context for making sense of the findings in this book and thinking about next steps for research, policy, and practice. There is a political moment in which decision-makers and thinkers have recognized the importance of migration for the identities, well-being, peace, and security of all residents, and greater understanding and policy solutions are being developed in response. However, as this book has argued, formal policy solutions are a better predictor of outcomes for migrants and their host societies in the Global North, whereas understanding what drives outcomes in the Global South often requires a more nuanced understanding of a diversity of power brokers and holders of "practical authority," both formal and informal institutions, and the complex ways in which governance networks connect state, nonstate, and international actors with migrants and their neighbors to regulate and improve access to rights, recognition, resources, and protection. These networks, of course, are more difficult to operationalize, measure, and track systematically, and incorporate into planning than formal policies and institutions.

Significance for Other Receiving Contexts

The theoretical argument developed in this book offers a powerful framework for understanding the intersection of migrant integration, participation, and human security, with the potential to illuminate these dynamics in other migrant-receiving countries around the world, especially in Africa, the Middle East, and Asia. In these regions are middle-income countries that, like Ecuador, have been major sending countries of migrants, but also have become important host countries, for economic and/or forced migrants. Since South-South migration of all types exceeds South-North migration, and 86% of all refugees live in the Global South (IOM 2014), it is important to understand these complex mixed contexts. Turkey, South Africa, India, Bangladesh, the Gulf States, and others have emerged as major receiving countries in the Global South, even as many of their own citizens have migrated in the past or concurrently. Turkey, as the largest host of refugees in the world, is governed by a populist president who has employed ambiguous rhetoric that is welcoming while simultaneously hollowing out protections in practice, similar to the experience in Ecuador (Tolay 2016). In some Gulf States, long-term migrant workers exist in an intentional liminal state of juridical precarity, contributing their labor while being subjected to bureaucratic processes and informal expectations that deprive them of any political agency, belonging, or incorporation into the "community of value" (Lori 2019; Tsourapas 2019). In these and other cases, the shifting and often informal expectations of migrants and the possibilities for interest alignment and political coalitions creates interesting opportunities to apply and test the invisibility bargain framework in very different contexts that nonetheless share many similar characteristics and patterns. In many cases, these new receiving states use "indifference as policy" to cope with the influx, outsourcing the operational responsibilities for refugee protection to UNHCR or NGOs in ways that are quite similar to the patterns introduced in this book (Norman 2018).

Implications for Policy and Practice

Beginning in 2005 when my participation in facilitating a series of dialogues among Ecuadorian and Colombian women in Ibarra with UNHCR and the United Nations Development Fund for Women sparked my interest in this topic, my research agenda has always reflected a firm commitment to policy relevance and to studying questions that matter to practitioners, NGO workers, UN officials, and migrants and refugees themselves. Along the way, preliminary results have been used to brief officials at the United Nations in New York, in Quito, and in the border provinces, as inputs in various *mesas* in which the Ecuadorian state and civil society was debating migration policy (including the Organic Law for Human Mobility), as data summaries provided to NGOs throughout Ecuador that provide insight into the experiences of the population they are working with, and in trainings with refugees in Ecuador and mediators and Amnesty International activists in the United States for how to engage in effective advocacy and conflict resolution work on immigration and refugee issues. Following in that tradition, this section summarizes some of the key lessons learned and recommendations for stakeholders that emerge from the research presented in this book.

For Migrants and Refugees

- Building strong coalitions with other migrants and with strategic groups within the host population is critical for organizing.
- Not all tactics are equally effective. Marches and protests can energize in-group solidarity and awareness of rights, but these high-visibility strategies that make claims directly on the host government can backfire by sparking a host society backlash that actually worsens the security and well-being of migrants. Negotiation with strategic brokers, coalition building, and social interaction toward shared goals may be more effective.
- Migrants should be active participants and drivers of their own protection and well-being. There is a risk of paternalism and disempowerment when migrants accept a reified label of victim to be protected by host society saviors. Donor agendas, the possibility of exploitation, and policy/programmatic proposals that do not actually respond to the priorities and needs that are most important to migrants are all risks when migrants cede their own agency to others. Although the invisibility bargain often incentivizes indirect approaches to advocacy and participation, this does not mean that migrants can or should be passive. They should be strategic actors in partnership with other coalition allies.

For Civil Society Organizations and Activists

- Including migrants as shared decision-makers and agenda-setters from the beginning of program planning and strategy/visioning processes helps to ensure that programs actually respond to the needs and lived experiences of those they purport to serve.
- At the same time, a broad base of participation is important, with attention paid to inclusion of multiple voices, because choosing one or two spokespersons as "representatives" of a diverse and fluid community like migrants is risky. This is a mobile community, and individuals may move on or have life challenges, so building spaces for dialogue and participation based in particular communities and places is more sustainable than having these spaces depend on the organizing and will of a couple of leaders.
- Politics of migration includes a cognitive element and an emotional one, "information politics" and "symbolic politics," as well as leverage through powerful allies. NGOs can improve their case for change by basing arguments on good, convincing data, but at least as importantly, they should demand that deliberative spaces to make decisions *about* migrants and refugees should *include* migrants and refugees, and that they be given a chance to voice their views and tell their stories. The symbolic politics of these first-person narratives can be quite influential, as the case of the constitution illustrates.

For Receiving Governments

- Although this book shows that civil society can complement and sometimes compensate for weak state protections of migrants, strong and effective institutions and legal protections are a crucial starting point. States should realize that a population in the shadows is not in their interest, and that offering meaningful protections and a chance for dignified livelihoods for all inhabitants reduces conflicts and potentially violence later on.
- Coordinating constructively with nonstate and international organizations and managing these relationships strategically should be seen as best practices for good governance, rather than seeing these other institutions as competitive threats. Strengthening a diverse network

of different types of actors to share costs, divide tasks so that the actor with the most relevant "practical authority" leads, and extend trusted access points to a variety of potential beneficiaries who otherwise would not approach the state all improves the state's ability to ensure security and peaceful coexistence of its inhabitants. This makes all residents—citizens and migrants—better off.

- In order to manage potential constituent backlash from direct state intervention to protect and help migrants, strategic messaging can emphasize topical protections (i.e., labor rights for all who work, preventing discrimination against all minorities, including but not only migrants, etc.) or a territorial/community focus to include both migrants and host population in receiving communities. This way the same protection is offered, but it less explicitly singles out and divides migrant beneficiaries from citizen constituents, who might react by putting negative pressure on the political leader to impose greater migrant restrictions in general.

For International Organizations and International Donors in the Migration/Peace Space

- Relationship building and network creation should be seen as high-priority activities worthy of funding. Paying international consultants to carry out a workshop or produce a report is less likely to produce sustainable change or transform social relations than investing in long-term strategies by local actors that are deeply immersed in existing governance networks to strengthen the connections with other local actors, and their ability to facilitate access by previously excluded and marginalized populations. Even when this approach is messier, more difficult to measure in neat and tidy outcomes and indicators within a two-year project cycle, it is important to change funding models to make it possible, rather than simply fund the types of problems and projects that fit within the existing funding models.
- Social capital has value; when hiring personnel, NGOs and IGOs should not only consider the skills and experiences reflected on a résumé, but also the communities that people can access, decision-makers that they have in their phone contacts, and the groups that trust them. These resources and relational attributes are among the most important factors in allowing a person to do a job well when working on migration issues.

This is especially true for large international/external organizations whose "street credibility" may be borrowed primarily from the local individuals they hire to implement programs.

- Do No Harm must be enshrined as a basic principle underlying international programs and interventions related to migrants and refugees. Given the overlapping identities and density of relationships between migrants and their host communities, economic resources are best targeted at the community level—this way they help the targeted migrant population but also their neighbors, reducing resentment and backlash and helping members of the host community to realize direct, explicit benefits that come from hosting this population.

Summing Up

Relationships—both social and institutional—matter, and the connections they form among actors in the migration governance network are important channels through which resources, information, cooperation, referrals, and understanding can flow. In the context of the invisibility bargain, migrants' acceptance, belonging, and participation in decision-making processes that affect their livelihoods and security are often contingent on their adherence to host-population expectations to refrain from overt claim-making or visible social presence that violates host-society norms and expectations. However, rather than accepting the precarity and vulnerability of being confined to the shadows of society, there are many ways in which migrants can exercise agency, build coalitions, use symbolic politics and their own stories and relationships to increase intergroup empathy, and use indirect strategies to gain brokered access to decision-making and negotiation spaces with the state. This book has outlined a framework for understanding how these complex intersections of formal and informal institutions, state and nonstate actors produce peace and human security for migrants and their host societies in the Global South. In an era of increasing displacement and human mobility, in which formal laws and institutions do not always explain the outcomes experienced by migrants and the host population, this type of nuanced understanding is critical in order to understand who has relevant practical authority and how it can be leveraged to strengthen policies and practices that lead to greater peace and human security for all inhabitants.

Migration Networks Survey Instrument

Survey of Experiences and Networks of Migrants and Refugees in Ecuador (English translation)

(Frequencies for the full results can be found online at http://invisibilitybargain.com.)

Thanks for participating in the survey. Please mark your response to each question below.

1. In which country were you born?
Ecuador
Colombia
Other country: _______________________________________

2. In what year did you enter Ecuador? Year: ___ ___ ___ ___

3. Sex (please select one):
Woman
Man
Other

4. In what year were you born? Year: ___ ___ ___ ___

5. What is the highest level of formal education that you have finished?
Did not complete primary school
Completed primary school
Completed secondary school
Obtained a university degree
Obtained a graduate degree

6. With what race or ethnicity to you identify?
Mestizo
Black/Afro-descendent
Mulatto
White
Indigenous

7. What is your current employment situation?
Working full time
Working part time
Working sporadically (from time to time, but not regularly)
Not working

[If the response is "not working," please continue to question #9. If it is any of the other answers, please continue to question #8.]

8. Do you have a written contract?
Yes
No

9. Which of the following ranges includes your average monthly income?
$0–$60
$60–$200
$200–$318
$318–$400
$400+

10. Are your family's monthly earnings enough to cover your basic necessities?
Sufficient
Partly sufficient
Insufficient

11. Trust in institutions. For each of the following institutions in Ecuador, please select the level of trust that you have in that institution, whether it is a lot of trust, a little trust, or no trust. If you do not have enough information or do not have an opinion, you can respond "I don't know":
Institution   A lot of trust (1) A little trust (2) No trust (3) Don't know (4)
Defensoría del Pueblo
Fundación Asylum
Access/ASELER
HIAS
La Iglesia
Las cortes
ACNUR (Naciones Unidas)
Chancillería del Ecuador (DR)
Organizaciones de colombianos
Policía
Servicio Jesuita
Casa de Movilidad Humana
FEPP
FAS (Fundación Ambiente y Sociedad)
Misión Scalabriniana
RET
Programa Mundial de Alimentos (PAM)
Gobierno colombiano

12. What is your general perception toward each of the following groups?:
a. Ecuadorian people?
Positive
Negative
No opinion

b. Colombian people?
Positive
Negative
No opinion
c. The Ecuadorian state?
Positive
Negative
No opinion
d. The Colombian state?
Positive
Negative
No opinion

13. Do you feel secure in the neighborhood where you live?
Completely secure
Secure most of the time
Somewhat secure
Not very secure
Completely insecure

14. Since you came to Ecuador, have you been the victim of a violent crime?
Yes
No

[If you answered yes, please continue to questions #15 and #16 below. If you answered no, please skip to question #17.]

15. What nationality was the aggressor?
Ecuadorian
Colombian
Other nationality: _______________________
Don't know

16. What action did you take after this crime?
Action   [After attack by Ecuadorian] [After attack by Colombian or other]
Go to the police
Submit complaint to the Commission, Human Rights observer, courts, or other agency of the state
Use private security company/guards
Neighborhood watch/ self-protection group
Handle the matter yourself or with friends/family
Do nothing
Go to a religious organization/pray
Request help from an NGO or other organization
Other: _______________________________

17. From which organizations have you received assistance since you arrived in Ecuador? Write up to five of the most important. If you have not received help from any organizations, mark the appropriate space below.

A. ____

B. ____

C. ____

D. ____

E. ____

_____ I have not receive help from any organization.

Beside the letters that correspond to the organizations that you mentioned above, please mark what type of assistance you received from each organization:

Food/housing/supplies
Money or loans
Help finding a job
Help with legal documents, visa, etc.
Emotional support
Security or protection
Other type of help:
A.
B.
C.
D.
E.

18. How frequently do you communicate with Ecuadorian people?
Daily
Weekly
Monthly
Several times per year
Almost never

19. Please look at the following list of places where sometimes people of other nationalities talk with Ecuadorians. In which of these places do you generally talk the most with Ecuadorian people?

[Please choose only one]

School/university
Market
Neighborhood
Work
Street
Sports
Family
Organization
Other: ____

20. Please read the in the table below several strategies that people sometimes use and indicate whether you have done any of them, if you could imagine doing any of them, or if you would never do them.

[For each strategy that you select, please indicate whether that action worked in improving some problem or not]

Strategy /Have done / Could imagine doing / Would never doing / Improved? Yes No
Support the election of representatives who agree with your preferred policies
Contact the Human Rights ombudsman / Defensoría del Pueblo.
Contact the police
Write to the media
Negotiate with local political authorities to protect your interests
Participate in a public information campaign and advocacy
Participate in a local organization
Participate in a public protest to demand a change
Contact UNHCR

21. What are the main problems that you have faced in Ecuador?

[Please select all that apply:]

Access to health services
Access to education
Lack of security
Access to employment/job
Lack of voting rights
Obtaining legal documentation
Rights to travel freely
Separation from family
Discrimination
Other: _________________________________

22. What is the biggest fear that you have living here in Ecuador? [please select only one]
Being detained/arrested
Being attacked physically
Being robbed
Being accused
Being deported
Being threatened by armed groups
Being the victim of discrimination or having your rights denied
Not having sufficient economic resources
Other: _________________________________

23. Have you felt discriminated against since coming to Ecuador?

Yes   No
[If you selected yes, please continue to question #24. If you selected no, skip to question #25 below.]

24. On what basis did you feel discriminated against in Ecuador? Please mark all the reasons that apply.
Accent / speaking style
Refugee status
Economic status
Color of skin
Because of being Colombian
Because of being a woman
Other: _______________________

25. What do you think is the most important obstacle to resolving difficulties between Ecuadorians and people from other countries like you? [please mark only one]
Lack of legal rights
Not understanding others as human beings
Cultural differences
Opposing economic interests
Lack of state protection for people from your country
Lack of economic resources
Lack of common interests
Racism/discrimination
Conflict between governments
Other:_______________________

26. Thinking about the future, in five years, where do you imagine you will be living?
Still living in Ecuador
Returned to your country of origin
Moved to another country

27. What nationality are the majority of the neighbors who live in your neighborhood?
Majority are Ecuadorians
Majority are Colombians
There is a mix of approximately equal numbers of both groups
Other:

27. What is your legal status in Ecuador? Please select one.
Approved refugee
Asylum seeker (have applied for a refugee visa and are awaiting response)
Immigrant with a different visa (not a refugee)
Refugee visa has been denied
Without official documentation
Other: _______________________
[If you selected that you are without official documentation, please continue to question #28 below:]

28. Please read the following reasons, and select why you currently do not have official documentation.

I have not tried to apply for a visa

I could not apply for a visa because I did not know how

I could not apply for a visa because of the cost

My documents were stolen

I had a visa, but it expired or was revoked

My documents were taken by the police or government officials

Other: ________________________________

Thank you for your participation! Please turn in your completed survey to the interviewer.

Bibliography

"3 sentenciados por asesinato de Walker Vera, alcalde de Muisne." 2015. *El Universo* (May 13): https://www.eluniverso.com/noticias/2015/05/13/nota/4867196/3-sentenciados-asesinato-walker-vera-alcalde-muisne.

Abello Colak, Alexandra, and Jenny Pearce. 2009. "'Security from Below': Humanizing Security in Contexts of Chronic Violence." *IDS Bulletin* 40, no. 2 (March): 11–19.

Abers, Rebecca, and Margaret Keck. 2013. *Practical Authority: Agency and Institutional Change in Brazilian Water Politics*. New York: Oxford University Press.

Abrahamsen, Rita, and Michael C. Williamson. 2009. "Security beyond the State: Global Security Assemblages in International Politics." *International Political Sociology* 3, no. 1 (March): 1–17.

Ackerman, Peter, and Hardy Merriman. 2015. "The Checklist for Ending Tyranny." In Matthew Burrows and Maria J. Stephan, eds., *Is Authoritarianism Staging a Comeback?* 63–80. Washington, DC: Atlantic Council.

"ACNUR Lamenta Falta de Acuerdo con Ciudadanos Colombianos que Pedían Refugio en Europa." 2019. *El Comercio* (August 2). https://www.elcomercio.com/actualidad/acnur-acuerdo-ciudadanos-colombianos-traslado.html.

Adamson, Fiona. 2006. "Crossing Borders: International Migration and National Security." *International Security* 31, no. 1 (Summer): 165–99.

Adida, Claire. 2014. *Immigrant Exclusion and Insecurity in Africa*. New York: Cambridge University Press.

Ager, Alastair, and Alison Strang. 2008. "Understanding Integration: A Conceptual Framework." *Journal of Refugee Studies* 21, no. 2: 166–91.

Aidoo, Richard, Pamela Martin, Min Ye, and Diego Quiroga. 2017. "Footprints of the Dragon: China's Oil Diplomacy and Its Impacts on Sustainable Development Policy in Ecuador and Ghana." *International Development Policy* 8, no. 1 [Online] doi: https://doi.org/10.4000/poldev.2408.

Allen Nan, Susan. 2009. "Social Capital in Exclusive and Inclusive Networks: Satisfying Human Needs through Conflict and Conflict Resolution." In Michaelene Cox, ed., *Social Capital and Peace-Building: Creating and Resolving Conflict with Trust and Social Networks*, 172–85. New York: Routledge.

"Al Menos 100 Refugiados Permanecen al Exterior de Oficinas de ACNUR en Quito." 2019. *El Universo*, (June 19). https://www.eluniverso.com/noticias/2019/06/19/nota/7385496/menos-100-refugiados-permanecen-exterior-oficinas-acnur-quito.

Alvarez, Sonia. 2017. "Beyond the Civil Society Agenda? Participation and Practices of Governance, Governability, and Governmentality in Latin America." In Sonia Alvarez et al., eds., *Beyond Civil Society: Activism, Participation, and Protest in Latin America*, 316–30. Durham, NC: Duke University Press.

Álvarez Velasco, Soledad. 2020. "From Ecuador to Elsewhere: The (Re)configuration of a Transit Country." *Migration and Society* 3: 34–49.

Ambrosini, Maurizio. 2013. *Irregular Migration and Invisible Welfare*. London: Palgrave Macmillan.

Ambrosini, Maurizio. 2017. "Why Irregular Migrants Arrive and Remain: The Role of Intermediaries." *Journal of Ethnic and Migration Studies* 43, no. 11: 1813–30.

Andersen-Rodgers, David, and Kerry F. Crawford. 2018. *Human Security: Theory and Action*. Lanham, MD: Rowman & Littlefield.

Anderson, Benedict. 1983. *Imagined Communities: Reflections on the Origin and Spread of Nationalism*. New York: Verso Books.

Anderson, Bridget. 2013. *Us and Them? The Dangerous Politics of Immigration Control*. New York: Oxford University Press.

Andreas, Peter. 2000. *Border Games: Policing the U.S.-Mexico Divide*. Ithaca, NY: Cornell University Press.

Andreas, Peter, and Timothy Snyder. 2001. *The Wall around the West: State Borders and Immigration Controls in North America and Europe*. Lanham, MD: Rowman & Littlefield.

Andrews, B. Lacey. 2003. "When Is a Refugee Not a Refugee? Flexible Social Categories and Host/Refugee Relations in Guinea." New Issues in Refugee Research Working Paper no. 88. Geneva: UNHCR Evaluation and Policy Analysis Unit.

Angostura, María. 2011. "Ecuador: El Vaticano asalta la iglesia de Sucumbíos." *La Haine*, February 1. https://www.lahaine.org/ecuador-el-vaticano-asalta-la-iglesia-de.

Arjona, Ana. 2016. *Rebelocracy: Social Order in the Colombian Civil War*. New York: Cambridge University Press.

ASOREC et al. 2008. "Propuesta a la Constituyente." Proposal co-signed by ASOREC, ASOCOMIRCE, ASERES, Grupo RENACER, Caminos de Vida, ASEREX, ASELER (February 23). Quito.

Autesserre, Séverine. 2017. "International Peacebuilding and Local Success: Assumptions and Effectiveness." *International Studies Review* 19, no. 1: 114–32.

Baker, Bruce, and Eric Scheye. 2007. "Multi-layered Justice and Security Delivery in Post-conflict and Fragile States." *Conflict, Security, and Development* 7, no. 4 (December): 503–28.

Ballvé, Teo. 2020. *The Frontier Effect: State Formation and Violence in Colombia*. Ithaca, NY: Cornell University Press.

Balyk, Lana, and Jeff Pugh. 2013. "Governance Networks in Ecuador's Border Region." *Forced Migration Review* 43 (May): 47–49.

Barnett, Michael, and Martha Finnemore. 2004. *Rules for the World: International Organizations in Global Politics*. Ithaca, NY: Cornell University Press.

Bayón, Manuel, Gustavo Durán, Alejandra Bonilla, Daniel Zárate, Javier González, Margarete Araujo, and Johanna Villavicencio. 2020. "Lago Agrio: Barrios petroleros en el casco urbano que claman por sus derechos." In *Contested Cities Ecuador*, Ch. 6, 1–31. Quito: FLACSO-Ecuador.

Beck, Scott, Kenneth Mijeski, and Meagan Stark. 2011. "¿Qué es racismo? Awareness of Racism and Discrimination in Ecuador." *Latin American Research Review* 46, no. 1: 102–25.

Becker, Marc. 2016. "The Correa Coup." *Latin American Perspectives* 43, no. 1: 71–92.

Becker, Marc. 2019. "Ecuador's Social Movements, Electoral Politics, and Military Coups." In William R. Thompson, ed., *Oxford Research Encyclopedia of Politics*. New York: Oxford University Press.

Benhabib, Seyla. 2004. *The Rights of Others: Aliens, Residents, and Citizens.* New York: Cambridge University Press.

Berry, J. W. 2005. "Acculturation: Living Successfully in Two Cultures." *International Journal of Intercultural Relations* 29: 697–712.

Bersani, Bianca, Thomas Loughran, and Alex Piquero. 2014. "Comparing Patterns and Predictors of Immigrant Offending among a Sample of Adjudicated Youth." *Journal of Youth and Adolescence* 43, no. 11: 1914–33.

Betts, Alexander, ed. 2011. *Global Migration Governance.* New York: Oxford University Press.

Beyers, Christiaan, and Esteban Nichols. 2020. "Government through Inaction: The Venezuelan Migratory Crisis in Ecuador." *Journal of Latin American Studies* 52, no. 3: 633–57. https://doi.org/10.1017/S0022216X20000607.

Bilsborrow, Richard. 2006. *The Living Conditions of Refugees, Asylum Seekers, and Other Colombians Living in Ecuador.* Geneva: Netherlands Interdisciplinary Demographic Institute, October.

Bloch, Alice. 1999. "Carrying Out a Survey of Refugees: Some Methodological Considerations and Guidelines." *Journal of Refugee Studies* 12, no. 4: 367–83.

Bloch, Alice, and Sonia McKay. 2016. *Living on the Margins: Undocumented Migrants in a Global City.* Chicago: Policy Press.

Blumer, Herbert. 1958. "Race Prejudice as a Sense of Group Position." *Pacific Sociological Review* 1, no. 1: 3–7.

Bogardus, Emory S. 1925. "Measuring Social Distance." *Sociology & Social Research* 9: 299–308.

Bohman, Andrea. 2015. "It's Who You Know: Political Influence on Anti-immigrant Attitudes and the Moderating Role of Intergroup Contact." *Sociological Research Online* 20, no. 3, Article 6: 1–17.

Bosniak, Linda. 2006. *The Citizen and the Alien: Dilemmas of Contemporary Membership.* Princeton, NJ: Princeton University Press.

Boulding, Kenneth E. 1978. *Stable Peace.* Austin: University of Texas Press.

Brader, Ted, Nicholas A. Valentino, and Elizabeth Suhay. 2008. "What Triggers Public Opposition to Immigration? Anxiety, Group Cues, and Immigration Threat." *American Journal of Political Science* 52, no. 4: 959–78.

Braithwaite, Alex, Idean Salehyan, and Burcu Savun. 2019. "Refugees, Forced Migration, and Conflict: Introduction to the Special Issue." *Journal of Peace Research* 56, no. 1 (January): 5–11.

Briscoe, Ivan. 2008. "Trouble on the Borders: Latin America's New Conflict Zones." *Comment.* Report, Fundación para las Relaciones Internacionales y el Diálogo Exterior (July 11).

Brown, Michael. 2009. "Making Peace across Borders a Reality." *Crisis Prevention and Recovery Newsletter,* no. 1 (January).

Burbano Alarcón, Mauricio. 2017. "Las asociaciones de inmigrantes extranjeros en Quito: Capital social y liderazgo." *Cuadernos Deusto de Derechos Humanos.* No. 89. Bilbao, Spain: Universidad de Deusto.

Buzan, Barry, Ole Waever, and Jaap de Wilde. 1998. *Security: A New Framework for Analysis.* Boulder, CO: Lynne Rienner.

Caldwell, Kia Lilly. 2006. *Negras in Brazil: Re-envisioning Black Women, Citizenship, and the Politics of Identity.* New Brunswick, NJ: Rutgers University Press.

Camacho Zambrano, Gloria. 2005. *Mujeres al borde: Refugiadas colombianas en el Ecuador*. Quito: UNIFEM.

Campbell, Susanna. 2018. *Global Governance and Local Peace: Accountability and Performance in International Peacebuilding*. New York: Cambridge University Press.

Carter Center. 2009. "Ecuador and Colombia: We Can Achieve Much Together." Carter Center Statement, (October 20) http://www.cartercenter.org/news/publications/peace/americas_publications/profile-chiriboga-navarro.html [accessed August 12, 2018].

Carter Center. 2011. *Assessing the Binational Dialogue: Colombia-Ecuador 2007–2009*. Panama City, Panama: UNDP/Carter Center.

Cebulko, Kara. 2014. "Documented, Undocumented, and Liminally Legal: Legal Status during the Transition to Adulthood for 1.5-Generation Brazilian Immigrants." *Sociological Quarterly* 55: 143–67.

Cebulko, Kara, and Maroa Galvão. 2016. "The Criminalization of Brazilian Immigrants." In Rich Furman, Greg Lamphear, and Douglas Epps, eds., *The Immigrant Other: Lived Experiences in a Transnational World*, 151–65. New York: Columbia University Press.

Cervone, Emma. 1999. "Racismo y vida cotidiana: Las tácticas de la defensa étnica." In Emma Cervone and Fredy Rivera, eds., *Ecuador racista: Imágenes e identidades*, 137–58. Quito: FLACSO.

Chapman, Terrence. 2009. "The Pacific Promise of Civic Institutions? Causal Ambiguity in the Study of Social Capital." In Michaelene Cox, ed., *Social Capital and Peace-Building: Creating and Resolving Conflict with Trust and Social Networks*, 157–71. New York: Routledge.

Chenoweth, Erica. 2015. "Trends in Civil Resistance and Authoritarian Responses." In Matthew Burrows and Maria J. Stephan, eds., *Is Authoritarianism Staging a Comeback?* Ch. 5. Washington, DC: Atlantic Council.

Cherrez, Cecilia. 2012. "Ecuador: Criminalización de la protesta social en tiempos de revolución ciudadana." *Aportes andinos* 30 (April). Available online at http://portal.uasb.edu.ec/padh_contenido.php?cd=3910&pagpath=1&swpath=infb&cd_centro=5&ug=pu.

Chin, Christine B. N. 2003. "Visible Bodies, Invisible Work: State Practices toward Migrant Women Domestic Workers in Malaysia." *Asian and Pacific Migration Journal* 12, nos. (1–2): 49–73.

Chiriboga, Manuel. 2014. *Las ONG ecuatorianas en los procesos de cambio*. Quito: Ediciones Abya-Yala.

Choo, Hae Yeon, and Myra Marx Ferree. 2010. "Practicing Intersectionality in Sociological Research: A Critical Analysis of Inclusions, Interactions, and Institutions in the Study of Inequalities." *Sociological Theory* 28, no. 2 (June): 129–49.

Churchill, Leon. 2011. "Networks and Hierarchies Can Coexist." In Jack W. Meek and Kurt Thurmaier, eds., *Networked Governance: The Future of Intergovernmental Management*, 224–26. Washington, DC: CQ Press.

Citrin, Jack, Donald P. Green, Christopher Muste, and Cara Wong. 1997. "Public Opinion toward Immigration Reform: The Role of Economic Motivations." *Journal of Politics* 59, no. 3: 858–81.

Cleary, Edward. 2009. *How Latin America Saved the Soul of the Catholic Church*. New York: Paulist Press.

Collins, Patricia Hill. 1990. *Black Feminist Thought: Knowledge, Consciousness and the Politics of Empowerment*. New York: Routledge.

"Condenan a 25 años de prisión a exalcalde de Muisne por asesinato del alcalde." 2015. *La República* (May 12): https://www.larepublica.ec/blog/politica/2015/05/12/condenan-a-25-anos-de-prision-a-exalcalde-de-muisne-por-asesinato-del-alcalde/.

Conaghan, Catherine, and Carlos de La Torre. 2008. "The Permanent Campaign of Rafael Correa: Making Ecuador's Plebiscitary Presidency." *International Journal of Press/Politics* 13, no. 3: 267–84.

Consultoría para los Derechos Humanos y el Desplazamiento (CODHES). 2015. *Continuidades de la desprotección: Migraciones forzadas y satisfacción de derechos sociales en la frontera entre Colombia y Ecuador.* Bogotá: CODHES.

Convivir en Solidaridad: Diagnóstico y propuestas de trabajo de la campaña contra la discriminación y la xenofobia. 2011. Lago Agrio, Ecuador: UNHCR.

Cooley, Alexander, and James Ron. 2002. "The NGO Scramble: Organizational Insecurity and the Political Economy of Transnational Action." *International Security* 27(1): 5–39.

Correa, Ahmed. 2016. "Ciudadanía universal y libre movilidad: Comentarios sobre una utopía ecuatoriana." *LASA Forum* 47, no. 2: 12–17.

Correa, Ahmed. 2020. "Deportación, tránsito y refugio: El caso de los Cubanos de El Arbolito en Ecuador." *PÉRIPLOS: Revista de Investigación sobre Migraciones* 3, no. 2: 52–88.

Coutin, Susan. 2003. "Illegality, Borderlands, and the Space of Nonexistence." In Richard Warren Perry and Bill Maurer, eds., *Globalization under Construction: Governmentality, Law, and Identity,* 171–202. Minneapolis: University of Minnesota Press.

Cox, Michaelene, ed. 2009. *Social Capital and Peace-Building: Creating and Resolving Conflict with Trust and Social Networks.* New York: Routledge.

Crawley, Heaven, Simon McMahon, and Katharine Jones. "Victims and Villains: Migrant Voices in the British Media." Centre for Trust, Peace, and Social Relations. 1–8. 2016.

Crenshaw, Kimberlé Williams. 1991. "Mapping the Margins: Intersectionality, Identity Politics, and Violence against Women of Color." *Stanford Law Review* 43, no. 6: 1241–99.

Dai, Xinyuan. 2007. *International Institutions and National Policies.* New York: Cambridge University Press.

Dancygier, Rafaela. 2010. *Immigration and Conflict in Europe.* New York: Cambridge University Press.

Dancygier, Rafaela M., Naoki Egami, Amaney Jamal, and Ramona Rischke. 2019. "Hating and Mating: Fears over Mate Competition and Violent Hate Crime against Refugees" (March 23). Available at SSRN: http://dx.doi.org/10.2139/ssrn.3358780.

d'Appollonia, Ariane Chebel. 2012. *Frontiers of Fear: Immigration and Insecurity in the United States and Europe.* Ithaca, NY: Cornell University Press.

Das, Veena, and Deborah Poole, eds. 2004. *Anthropology in the Margins of the State.* Santa Fe, NM: School of American Research Press.

Das Gupta, Monisha. 2006. *Unruly Immigrants: Rights, Activism, and Transnational South Asian Politics in the United States.* Durham, NC: Duke University Press.

De Graauw, Els. 2016. *Making Immigrant Rights Real: Nonprofits and the Politics of Integration in San Francisco.* Ithaca, NY: Cornell University Press.

De la Torre, Carlos. 2002. *Afroquiteños: Ciudadanía y racismo.* Quito: CAAP.

De la Torre, Carlos. 2006. "Ethnic Movements and Citizenship in Ecuador." *Latin American Research Review* 41, no. 2: 247–59.

De la Torre, Carlos. 2017. Populist Citizenship in the Bolivarian Revolutions. *Middle Atlantic Review of Latin American Studies* 1, no. 1: 4–32.

De la Torre, Carlos. 2020. "Rafael Correa's Technopopulism in Comparative Perspective." In Francisco Sánchez and Simón Pachano, eds., *Assessing the Left Turn in Ecuador*, 91–114. New York: Springer.

De la Torre, Carlos, and Steve Striffler, eds. 2008. *The Ecuador Reader: History, Culture, Politics*. Durham, NC: Duke University Press.

De la Torre, Margarita. 2009. "Obstáculos a la protección internacional de refugiados: Estudio de caso, Refugiados Colombianos en Ecuador (1997–2007)." Graduation monograph, Universidad Colegio Mayor de Nuestra Señora del Rosario, Bogotá, Colombia.

DeLeon, Cedric. 2013. *Party and Society*. Polity Press.

Diaz-Briquets, Sergio, and Sydney Weintraub, eds. 1991. *The Effects of Receiving Country Policies on Migration Flows*. Boulder, CO: Westview Press.

Donahue, John, and Richard Zeckhauser. 2011. *Collaborative Governance: Private Roles for Public Goals in Turbulent Times*. Princeton, NJ: Princeton University Press.

Dulitzky, Ariel. 2005. "A Region in Denial: Racial Discrimination and Racism in Latin America." In Anani Dzidzienyo and Suzanne Oboler, eds., *Neither Enemies nor Friends: Latinos, Blacks, Afro-Latinos*, 39–59. New York: Palgrave Macmillan.

Dumas, Juan. 2006. *Fondo respuesta: Apoyando intervenciones eficaces en conflictos socio-ambientales. Sistematización de la primera experiencia en Ecuador*. Quito: UNDP.

Duoos, Tori. 2015. "The MERCOSUR Visa: A Band-Aid for Ecuador's Rejected Colombian Asylum Seekers." *Refugees International* (December 10). Available online at https://www.refugeesinternational.org/blog/2015/12/10/ecuador [Accessed August 23, 2018].

Eisenstadt, Todd, and Karleen Jones West, 2017. "Public Opinion, Vulnerability, and Living with Extraction on Ecuador's Oil Frontier: Where the Debate between Development and Environmentalism Gets Personal." *Comparative Politics* 49, no. 2: 231–51.

Ellerman, Antje. 2010. "Undocumented Migrants and Resistance in the Liberal State." *Politics and Society* 38, no. 3: 408–29.

Engbersen, Godfried, and Dennis Broeders. 2009. "The State versus the Alien: Immigration Control and Strategies of Irregular Immigrants." *West European Politics* 32, no. 5: 867–85.

Enloe, Cynthia. 2011. "The Mundane Matters." *International Political Sociology* 5, no. 4: 447–50.

Erfani, Julie A. Murphy. 2007. "Whose Security? Dilemmas of U.S. Border Security in the Arizona-Sonora Borderlands." In Emmanuel Brunet-Jailly, ed., *Borderlands: Comparing Border Security in North America and Europe*, 41–74. Ottawa: University of Ottawa Press.

Escalante, Andrea. 2010. "Ecuador Issues ID to 27,000 Refugees in Remote Northern Areas of the Country." UNHCR News Stories, April 10.

Ewing, Walter, Daniel Martínez, and Rubén Rumbaut. 2015. "The Criminalization of Immigration in the United States." Special Report. American Immigration Council.

Faiola, Anthony. 2018. "From Riches to Rags: Venezuelans Become Latin America's New Underclass." *Washington Post* (July 27). https://www.washingtonpost.com/news/world/wp/2018/07/27/feature/as-venezuela-crumbles-its-fleeing-citizens-are-becoming-latin-americas-new-underclass/.

Falconí, Fander. 2010. *¡Con Ecuador por el mundo!* Quito: Editorial El Conejo.

Farris, Emily, and Heather Silber Mohamed. 2018. "Picturing Immigration: How the Media Criminalizes Immigrants." *Politics, Groups, and Identities.* https://doi.org/10.1080/21565503.2018.1484375.

Fernández, José M., and Matteo Pazzona. 2019. "Evaluating the Spillover Effects of the Colombian Conflict in Ecuador." *Defence and Peace Economics* 30, no. 3: 324–48.

Fontanini, Francesca, Giovanni Monge, and Nazli Zaki. 2006. "Fear Prevents Paperless Colombians in Ecuador from Seeking Help." *UNHCR News*, September 29. https://www.unhcr.org/en-us/news/latest/2006/9/451d1f964/fear-prevents-paperless-colombians-ecuador-seeking-help.html.

Foote, Nicola, and Michael Goebel, eds. 2014. *Immigration and National Identities in Latin America.* Gainesville: University Press of Florida.

Fox, Jonathan. 1994. "The Difficult Transition from Clientelism to Citizenship: Lessons from Mexico." *World Politics* 46, no. 2: 151–84.

Freier, Luisa Feline, and Nicolas Parent. 2018. "A South American Migration Crisis: Venezuelan Outflows Test Neighbors' Hospitality." In *Migration Information Source.* July 18. Migration Policy Institute.

Galama, Anneke, and Paul van Tongeren, eds. 2002. *Towards Better Peacebuilding Practice: On Lessons Learned, Evaluation Practices and Aid and Conflict.* Utrecht, the Netherlands: European Centre for Conflict Prevention.

Gallego Coto, Pablo. 2014. "Historia de la provincia de Sucumbios." Prefectura de Sucumbíos. http://www.sucumbios.gob.ec/index.php/2015-10-20-00-03-09/2014-10-11-16-35-05/2014-10-11-16-54-02.

Galtung, Johan. 1969. "Violence, Peace, and Peace Research." *Journal of Peace Research* 6, no. 3: 167–91.

Garces, Alicia. 2009. *La historia de Sucumbíos desde las voces de las mujeres.* Quito: Ediciones Abya-Yala.

Garcia, Gabriela. 2020. "Venezolanos en Ecuador: Prácticas de seguridad, criminalización y control." *Border Criminologies* (blog). March 20, 2020. https://www.law.ox.ac.uk/research-subject-groups/centre-criminology/centreborder-criminologies/blog/2020/03/venezolanos-en-0.

Garland, David. 2001. *The Culture of Control.* Oxford: Oxford University Press.

Gerlach, Allen. 2003. *Indians, Oil, and Politics: A Recent History of Ecuador.* Wilmington, DE: Scholarly Resources.

Gómez Martín, Carmen, and Gabriela Malo. 2020. "Salir de la noción economicista y despolitizada del refugiado: Una visión crítica sobre el refugio colombiano en Ecuador." *Périplos: Revista de Estudos sobre Migrações* 3, no. 2: 17–145.

González Carranza, Laura. 2008. *Fronteras en el limbo: El Plan Colombia en el Ecuador.* Serie Investigación no. 13. Quito: Fundación Regional de Asesoría en Derechos Humanos.

González-Murphy, Laura Valeria. 2013. *Protecting Immigrant Rights in Mexico: Understanding the State-Civil Society Nexus.* New York: Routledge.

Gottwald, Martin. 2004. "Protecting Colombian Refugees in the Andean Region: The Fight against Invisibility." *International Journal of Refugee Law* 16, no. 4: 517–46.

Graham, Christopher. 2019. "The Political Economy of Migration Governance: How Political Actors, Networks, Institutions, and Policies Impact the Migration-Development Nexus in the Global South." Ph.D dissertation, University of Massachusetts Boston.

Granovetter, Mark. 1973. "The Strength of Weak Ties." *American Journal of Sociology* 78, no. 6: 1360–80.

Greer, Christina. 2013. *Black Ethnics: Race, Immigration, and the Pursuit of the American Dream*. New York: Oxford University Press.

Guimond, Serge, Pierre De Oliveira, Rodolphe Kamiesjki, and Jim Sidanius. 2010. "The Trouble with Assimilation: Social Dominance and the Emergence of Hostility against Immigrants." *International Journal of Intercultural Relations* 34: 642–50.

Gurr, Ted Robert. 1970. *Why Men Rebel*. New York: Routledge.

Gutiérrez, Gustavo. 1988. *A Theology of Liberation*. Translated and edited by Sister Caridad Inda and John Eagleson. Rev. ed. Maryknoll, NY: Orbis Books.

Hager, Ann Marie, James Larson, Nene Kumashe Ugbah, and Vijay Ramesh. 2017. "Oil Extraction in the Ecuadorian Amazon: Incorporating Conflict Resolution Theory and Practice." *Conflict Resolution Quarterly* 35, no. 2: 243–67.

Hainmueller, Jens, and Michael J. Hiscox. 2010. "Attitudes toward Highly Skilled and Low-Skilled Immigration: Evidence from a Survey Experiment." *American Political Science Review* 104, no. 1: 61–84.

Hainmueller, Jens, and Daniel J. Hopkins. 2015. "The Hidden American Immigration Consensus: A Conjoint Analysis of Attitudes toward Immigrants." *American Journal of Political Science* 59, no. 3: 529–48.

Hall, Edward T. 1990. *The Hidden Dimension*. New York: Anchor.

Hammar, Tomas. 1990. *Democracy and the Nation State: Aliens, Denizens, and Citizens in a World of International Migration*. London: Routledge.

Hancock, Ange-Marie. 2016. *Intersectionality: An Intellectual History*. New York: Oxford University Press.

Hancock, Landon, and Christopher Mitchell, eds. 2018. *Local Peacebuilding and Legitimacy: Interactions between National and Local Levels*. New York: Routledge.

Handelsman, Michael. 2019. *Representaciones de lo Afro y su recepción en Ecuador. Encuentros y desencuentros en tension*. Quito: UASB and Abya-Yala.

Hankivsky, Olena, and Julia S. Jordan-Zachery, eds. 2019. *The Palgrave Handbook of Intersectionality in Public Policy*. Cham, Switzerland: Springer International Publishing.

Hellgren, Zenia. 2014. "Negotiating the Boundaries of Social Membership: Undocumented Migrant Claims-Making in Sweden and Spain." *Journal of Ethnic and Migration Studies* 40, no. 8: 1175–91.

Helmke, Gretchen, and Steven Levitsky, eds. 2006. *Informal Institutions and Democracy*. Baltimore, MD: Johns Hopkins University Press.

Herrera, Gioconda, Carrillo María Cristia, and Torres Alicia. 2005. *La migración ecuatoriana: Transnacionalismo, redes e identidades*. Quito: FLACSO.

Herz, Monica, and João Pontes Nogueira. 2002. *Ecuador vs. Peru: Peacemaking amid Rivalry*. Boulder, CO: Lynne Rienner.

Hilgers, Tina. 2012. *Clientelism in Everyday Latin American Politics*. New York: Palgrave Macmillan.

Hochschild, Jennifer, Jacqueline Chattopadhyay, Claudine Gay, and Michael Jones-Correa. 2013. *Outsiders No More? Models of Immigrant Political Incorporation*. New York: Oxford University Press.

Hollifield, James. 2008. "The Politics of International Migration." In Caroline Brettell and James Hollifield, eds., *Migration Theory: Talking across Disciplines*, 2nd ed., 183–237. New York: Routledge.

Honig, Dan. 2018. *Navigation by Judgment: Why and When Top-Down Management of Foreign Aid Doesn't Work*. New York: Oxford University Press.

Hopkins, Daniel J. 2010. "Politicized Places: Explaining Where and When Immigrants Provoke Local Opposition." *American Political Science Review* 104, no. 1 (February): 40–60.

Hopkins, Daniel J. 2015. "The Upside of Accents: Language, Skin Tone, and Attitudes toward Immigration." *British Journal of Political Science* 45, no. 3: 531–57.

Huerta Montalvo, Francisco. 2009. *Informe Comisión de Transparencia y Verdad Angostura* Quito: Comisión de Transparencia, Presidencia del Ecuador, December 10.

Huntington, Samuel. 2004. *Who Are We: The Challenges to America's National Identity*. New York: Simon & Schuster.

Hurtado, Osvaldo. 1977. *Political Power in Ecuador*. Albuquerque: University of New Mexico Press.

Hyden, Goran, Julius Court, and Kenneth Mease. 2004. *Making Sense of Governance: Empirical Evidence from 16 Developing Countries*. Boulder, CO: Lynne Rienner.

Idler, Annette. 2019. *Borderland Battles: Violence, Crime, and Governance at the Edges of Colombia's War*. New York: Oxford University Press.

Ikeda, Anna. 2018. "Exploring a Civil Resistance Approach to Examining U.S. Military Base Politics: The Case of Manta, Ecuador." *Middle Atlantic Review of Latin American Studies* 2, no. 1: 112–24.

INEC 2010. *Censo de Población y Vivienda*. Quito: Instituto Nacional de Estadística y Censos.

INEC. 2011. *Encuesta de Victimización y Percepción de Inseguridad 2011*. Quito: Instituto Nacional de Estadística y Censos. https://www.ecuadorencifras.gob.ec/estadisticas/.

International Crisis Group (ICG). 2012. "Colombia: Peace at Last?" Latin America Report No. 45- 25, September.

International Organization for Migration (IOM). 2014. *Global Migration Trends: An Overview*. Geneva: IOM.

International Organization for Migration (IOM). 2018. "Migration Research and Analysis: Growth, Reach and Recent Contributions." World Migration Report, Information Sheet no. 4.

Jacobsen, Karen. 2002. "Livelihoods in Conflict: The Pursuit of Livelihoods by Refugees and the Impact on the Human Security of Host Communities." *International Migration* 40, no. 5: 95–123.

Jaramillo, Andrés. 2010. "El 98,4% de refugiados en Ecuador tiene nacionalidad colombiana." *El Comercio*, May 15.

Jaramillo, Grace. 2020. "Rafael Correa's Foreign Policy Paradox: Discursive Sovereignty, Practical Dependency." In Francisco Sánchez and Simón Pachano, eds., *Assessing the Left Turn in Ecuador*, 325–49. New York: Springer.

Jaskoski, Maiah. 2012. "Public Security Forces with Private Funding: Local Army Entrepreneurship in Peru and Ecuador." *Latin American Research Review* 47, no 2: 79–99.

Jaskoski, Maiah. 2015. "The Colombian FARC in Northern Ecuador: Borderline and Borderland Dynamics." In Maiah Jaskoski, Arturo Sotomayor, and Harold Trinkunas, eds., *American Crossings: Border Politics in the Western Hemisphere*, 171–88. Baltimore, MD: Johns Hopkins University Press.

Jiménez, Luis. 2018. *Migrants and Political Change in Latin America*. Gainesville: University of Florida Press.

Jiménez, Luis, and Jeffrey D. Pugh. 2020. "Comparing Migrant Populations in Ecuador." Available at SSRN: https://ssrn.com/abstract=3684739.

Johnston, Les. 2006. "Transnational Security Governance." In Jennifer Wood and Benoit Dupont, eds., *Democracy, Society, and the Governance of Security*, 33–51. New York: Cambridge University Press.

Jordan, Miriam. 2020. "Farmworkers, Mostly Undocumented, Become 'Essential' during Pandemic." *New York Times*, April 2.

Juncos, Ana. 2018. "Resilience in Peacebuilding: Contesting Uncertainty, Ambiguity, and Complexity." *Contemporary Security Policy* 39, no. 4: 559–74. https://doi.org/10.1080/13523260.2018.1491742.

Kastoryano, Riva. 2002. *Negotiating Identities: States and Immigrants in France and Germany*. Translated by Barbara Harshav. Princeton, NJ: Princeton University Press.

Keck, Margaret, and Kathryn Sikkink. 1998. *Activists beyond Borders: Advocacy Networks in International Politics*. Ithaca, NY: Cornell University Press.

Kinder, Donald R., and Cindy D. Kam. 2010. *Us Against Them: Ethnocentric Foundations of American Opinion*. Chicago: University of Chicago Press.

King, Gary, and C. J. Murray. 2001. "Rethinking Human Security." *Political Science Quarterly* 116: 585–610.

Koinova, Maria. 2014. "Why Do Conflict-Generated Diasporas Pursue Sovereignty-Based Claims through State-Based or Transnational Channels? Armenian, Albanian and Palestinian Diasporas in the UK Compared." *European Journal of International Relations* 20, no. 4: 1043–71.

Korovkin, Tanya. 2008. "The Colombian War and 'Invisible' Refugees in Ecuador." *Peace Review* 20: 321–29.

Kushner, Jacob. 2012. "Haitians Face Persecution across Dominican Border." *NACLA Report on the Americas* 45, no. 2: 50–58.

Kyle, David. 2000. *Transnational Peasants: Migrations, Networks, and Ethnicity in Andean Ecuador*. Baltimore, MD: Johns Hopkins University Press.

Lalander, Rickard, and Pablo Ospina Peralta. 2012. "Movimiento indígena y revolución ciudadana en Ecuador." *Cuestiones politicas* 28, no. 48: 13–50.

Landau, Loren. 2015. "Recognition, Solidarity, and the Power of Mobility in Africa's Urban Estuaries." In Darshan Vigneswaran and Joel Quirk, eds., *Mobility Makes States: Migration and Power in Africa*, 218–36. Philadelphia: University of Pennsylvania Press.

Landau, Loren, and Marguerite Duponchel. 2011. "Laws, Policies, or Social Position? Capabilities and the Determinants of Effective Protection in Four African Cities." *Journal of Refugee Studies* 24, no. 1: 1–22.

Lari, Andrea. 2009. "Ecuadorian Leaders' Assassination Shows Spillover of Colombian Conflict." Statement by Refugees International. https://reliefweb.int/report/ecuador/ecuadorian-leaders-assassination-shows-spillover-colombian-conflict.

Latinobarómetro. 2007. Santiago, Chile: Corporación Latinobarómetro. http://www.latinobarometro.org/. Accessed March 8, 2010.

Lawrence, Duncan. 2015. "Crossing the Cordillera: Immigrant Attributes and Chilean Attitudes." *Latin American Research Review* 50, no. 4: 154–77.

Lederach, John Paul. 1997. *Building Peace: Sustainable Reconciliation in Divided Societies*. Washington, DC: US Institute of Peace.

Lederach, John Paul. 2005. *The Moral Imagination: The Art and Soul of Building Peace.* New York: Oxford University Press.

Lewis, Tammy. 2016. *Ecuador's Environmental Revolutions: Ecoimperialists, Ecodependents, and Ecoresisters.* Cambridge, MA: MIT Press.

Lipschutz, Ronnie, ed. 1995. *On Security.* New York: Columbia University Press.

Lipsky, Michael. 1980. *Street-Level Bureaucracy: Dilemmas of the Individual in Public Service.* New York: Russell Sage Foundation.

Lischer, Sara Kenyon. 2006. *Dangerous Sanctuaries: Refugee Camps, Civil War, and the Dilemmas of Humanitarian Aid.* Ithaca, NY: Cornell University Press.

López, Kathleen. 2014. "In Search of Legitimacy: Chinese Immigrants and Latin American Nation Building." In Nicola Foote and Michael Goebel, eds., *Immigration and National Identities in Latin America,* 182–204. Gainesville: University Press of Florida.

Lori, Noora. 2019. *Offshore Citizens: Permanent Temporary Status in the Gulf.* New York: Oxford University Press.

Losier, Jessica. 2020. "The Colombian Peace Agreement with the FARC: Its Impact on the Lives of Colombian Asylum Seekers in Ecuador". MA thesis, University of Ottawa.

Luckham, Robin. 2007. "The Discordant Voices of 'Security.'" *Development in Practice* 17, nos. 4–5 (August): 682–90.

Luis, Luciniano. 1994. *La Misión Carmelita en Sucumbíos.* Quito: Abya-Yala and ISAMIS.

Mac Ginty, Roger. 2011. *International Peacebuilding and Local Resistance: Hybrid Forms of Peace.* New York: Springer.

Macipe, Javier, dir. 2013. *Adiós padrecitos.* Video documentary. Asociación Huauquipura.

MacLean, Lauren M. 2010. *Informal Institutions and Citizenship in Rural Africa: Risk and Reciprocity in Ghana and Côte d'Ivoire.* New York: Cambridge University Press.

Madrid, Raúl. 2012. *The Rise of Ethnic Politics in Latin America.* Cambridge: Cambridge University Press.

Malhotra, Neil, Yotam Margalit, and Cecilia Hyunjung Mo. 2013. "Economic Explanations for Opposition to Immigration: Distinguishing between Prevalence and Conditional Impact." *American Journal of Political Science* 57, no. 2: 391–410.

Mampilly, Zachariah Cherian. 2015. *Rebel Rulers: Insurgent Governance and Civilian Life during War.* Ithaca, NY: Cornell University Press.

Marinakis, Andrés, ed. 2014. *Incumplimiento con el salario mínimo en América Latina: El peso de los factores económicos e institucionales.* Santiago, Chile: International Labour Office.

Martin, Pamela L. 2011. *Oil in the Soil: The Politics of Paying to Preserve the Amazon.* Lanham, MD: Rowman & Littlefield.

Martinez Novo, Carmen. 2004. "Los misioneros salesianos y el movimiento indígena de Cotopaxi." *Ecuador Debate* 63 (December): 235–68.

Martínez Novo, Carmen. 2014. "Managing Diversity in Postneoliberal Ecuador." *Journal of Latin American and Caribbean Anthropology* 19, no. 1: 103–25.

Martz, John D. 1987. *Politics and Petroleum in Ecuador.* New Brunswick, NJ: Transaction.

Mas Giralt, Rosa. 2011. "Colombian Migrant Families in the North of England: Sociocultural Invisibility and Young People's Identity Strategies." In Cathy McIlwaine, ed., *Cross-Border Migration by Latin Americans: European Perspectives and Beyond,* 197–215. New York: Palgrave Macmillan.

Massey, Douglas S., and Magaly Sanchez. 2010. *Brokered Boundaries: Immigrant Identity in Anti-immigrant Times.* New York: Russell Sage Foundation.

McIlwaine, Cathy, ed. 2011. *Cross-Border Migration by Latin Americans: European Perspectives and Beyond*. New York: Palgrave Macmillan.

McLaren, Lauren. 2003. "Anti-immigrant Prejudice in Europe: Contact, Threat Perception, and Preferences for the Exclusion of Migrants." *Social Forces* 81, no. 3: 909–36.

Meacham, Carl. 2008. *Playing with Fire: Colombia, Ecuador, and Venezuela*. Report to Members of the Committee on Foreign Relations, United States Senate, 110th Congress, April 28.

Meloni, Francesca, Cécile Rousseau, Alexandra Ricard-Guay, and Jill Hanley. 2016. "Invisible Students: Institutional Invisibility and Access to Education for Undocumented Children." *International Journal of Migration, Health and Social Care* 13, no. 1: 15–25.

Méndez, Elizabeth. 2013. *Migraciones fronterizas de Afrocolombianos: Una realidad vista desde el cumplimiento de la normativa internacional de protección al refugiado en la frontera norte de Esmeraldas en el período 2005–2010*. Quito: FLACSO.

Menjívar, Cecilia. 2000. *Fragmented Ties: Salvadoran Immigrant Networks in America*. Berkeley: University of California Press.

Meseguer, Covadonga, and Achim Kemmerling. 2018. "What Do You Fear? Anti-immigrant Sentiment in Latin America." *International Migration Review* 52, no. 1: 236–72.

Migdal, Joel. 2001. *State in Society: Studying How States and Societies Transform and Constitute One Another*. New York: Cambridge University Press.

Misago, Jean Pierre. 2017. "Politics by Other Means? The Political Economy of Xenophobic Violence in Post-apartheid South Africa." *Black Scholar* 47, no. 2: 40–53.

Molina Bolívar, Juan Camilo. 2010. "El Registro Ampliado: Implicaciones solidarias y oportunidades del refugio en Ecuador." *Boletín del Conyuntura del Sistema de Información sobre Migraciones Andinas* 2 (May): 1–4.

Møller, Bjørn. 2000. "The Concept of Security: The Pros and Cons of Expansion and Contraction." Paper for joint sessions of the Peace Theories Commission and the Security and Disarmament Commission at the 18th General Conference of the International Peace Research Association, Tampere, Finland, August 5–9.

Moncada, Eduardo, and Richard Snyder. 2012. "Subnational Comparative Research on Democracy: Taking Stock and Looking Forward." *Comparative Democratization* 10, no. 1: 1, 4–9.

Montufar, Cesar. 2013. "Rafael Correa and His Plebiscitary Citizens' Revolution." In Carlos de la Torre and Cynthia Arnson, eds., *Latin American Populism in the Twenty-First Century*, 295–322. Baltimore, MD: Johns Hopkins University Press.

Moore, Will, and Stephen Shellman. 2007. "Whither Will They Go? A Global Study of Refugees' Destinations, 1965–1995." *International Studies Quarterly* 51, no. 4 (December): 811–34.

Moravcsik, A. 2004. "Is There a 'Democratic Deficit' in World Politics? A Framework for Analysis." *Government and Opposition* 39, no. 2: 336–63.

Moreno Parra, María. 2019. "Environmental Racism: Slow Death and the Displacement of Ancestral Afro-Ecuadorian Territory in Esmeraldas." *Íconos: Revista de ciencias sociales* 64 (August): 89–109.

Moscoso, Raul, and Nancy Burneo. 2014. *Más allá de las fronteras: La población refugiada en Quito y sus redes de integración*. Quito: UNHCR and Instituto de la Ciudad.

Moulin, Carolina. 2012. "Ungrateful Subjects? Refugee Protests and the Logic of Gratitude." In Peter Nyers and Kim Rygiel, eds., *Citizenship, Migrant Activism and the Politics of Movement*, 54–72. New York: Routledge.

Moulin, Carolina, and Peter Nyers. 2007. "'We Live in a Country of UNHCR': Refugee Protests and Global Political Society." *International Political Sociology* 1, no. 4: 356–72.

Mouly, Cécile, and Esperanza Hernández Delgado, eds. 2019. *Civil Resistance and Violent Conflict in Latin America: Mobilizing for Rights*. New York: Springer.

Mulaj, Kledja. 2009. *Violent Non-state Actors in World Politics*. New York: Oxford University Press.

Mundt, Marcia, Karen Ross, and Charla M. Burnett. 2018. "Scaling Social Movements through Social Media: The Case of Black Lives Matter." *Social Media + Society* 4, no. 4: 1–14.

Munro, Murray. 2003. "A Primer on Accent Discrimination in the Canadian Context." *TESL Canada Journal / Au Revue TESL du Canada* 20, no. 2 (Spring): 38–51.

Murphy, Craig N. 2013. "The Role for 'Human Security' in an IR That Can Learn from Difference." In Mustapha Kamal Pasha, ed., *Globalization, Difference and Human Security*, 17–26. New York: Routledge.

Murray, Jean-Pierre. 2020. "Beyond the 'Women-and-Children' Bias in Human Trafficking: A Study of Haitian Migrants in the Dominican Republic." *Oxford Monitor of Forced Migration* 8, no. 2: 132–50.

Naber, Nadine. 2000. "Ambiguous Insiders: An Investigation of Arab American Invisibility." *Ethnic and Racial Studies* 23, no. 1: 37–61.

Navas, Albertina, Jose Francisco Sieber, and Martin Gottwald. 2004. *La protección internacional de refugiados: El caso Ecuador, perspectiva histórica 1976–2004*. Venezuela: ACNUR and CEE.

Neocosmos, Michael. 2006. *From "Foreign Natives" to "Native Foreigners": Explaining Xenophobia in Post-apartheid South Africa. Citizenship and Nationalism, Identity and Politics*. Dakar, Senegal: CODESRIA.

Norman, Kelsey P. 2018. "Inclusion, Exclusion or Indifference? Redefining Migrant and Refugee Host State Engagement Options in Mediterranean 'Transit' Countries." *Journal of Ethnic and Migration Studies* 45, no. 1: 42–60. https://doi.org/10.1080/1369183X.2018.1482201.

Nyers, Peter, and Kim Rygiel, eds. 2012. *Citizenship, Migrant Activism and the Politics of Movement*. New York: Routledge.

Ochoa, Paulina. 2016. "Taking Place Seriously: Territorial Presence and the Rights of Immigrants." *Journal of Political Philosophy* 24, no. 1: 67–87.

O'Donnell, Guillermo. 2004. "The Quality of Democracy: Why the Rule of Law Matters." *Journal of Democracy* 15, no. 4: 32–46.

Ohanyan, Anna. 2015. *Networked Regionalism as Conflict Management*. Stanford, CA: Stanford University Press.

Okamoto, Dina, and Kim Ebert. 2016. "Group Boundaries, Immigrant Inclusion, and the Politics of Immigrant-Native Relations." *American Behavioral Scientist* 60, no. 2: 224–50.

Olzak, Susan. 1992. *The Dynamics of Ethnic Competition and Conflict*. Stanford, CA: Stanford University Press.

"Oposición del Ecuador Busca que se Pida Visa a Extranjeros." 2012. *TeleAmazonas*. Posted as YouTube video on El Ciudadano channel (June 16). https://www.youtube.com/watch?v=3OMRekVLg1I.

Ortega, Carlos, and Oscar Ospina. 2012. *No se puede ser refugiado toda la vida*. Quito: FLACSO.

Ortega, Hernando. 2007. "Ibarra." In Fredy Rivera, Hernando Ortega, Paulina Larreátegui, and Pilar Riaño Alcalá, eds., *Migración forzada de Colombianos: Colombia, Ecuador, Canadá*, 92–115. Medellín, Colombia: Corporación Región.

Oviedo, Sara, Consuelo Sánchez, Santiago Cruz, and Ahmed Correa. 2013. *Mejor acceso a los derechos de personas en contextos de movilidad humana en la zona norte del Ecuador.* Ibarra, Ecuador: Gobierno Provincial de Imbabura, European Union, Fundación Esperanza, and UNHCR.

Palma, Maritza. 2017. *Refugiados: Relatos de vida de Colombianos en Ecuador.* Colombia: Universidad Católica de Pereira.

Park, John S. W., and Shannon Gleeson. 2014. *The Nation and Its Peoples: Citizens, Denizens, Migrants.* New York: Routledge.

Pedroza, Luicy. 2019. *Citizenship beyond Nationality: Immigrants' Right to Vote across the World.* Philadelphia: University of Pennsylvania Press.

Peñaranda, Bibiana, and David Sulewski. 2018. "Las mariposas de Buenaventura, Colombia: Sostienen la vida, construyen la paz." *Middle Atlantic Review of Latin American Studies* 1, no. 2: 36–42.

Pessina, María. 2011. *La protección internacional de refugiados en las Américas.* Quito: UNHCR.

Peters, Anne, Lucy Koechlin, Till Forster, and Gretta Fenner Zinkernagel, eds. 2009. *Non-state Actors as Standard Setters.* Cambridge: Cambridge University Press.

Pettigrew, Thomas. 1998. "Intergroup Contact Theory." *Annual Review of Psychology* 49: 65–85.

Pettigrew, Thomas, and Linda Tropp. 2008. "How Does Intergroup Contact Reduce Prejudice? Meta-analytic Tests of Three Mediators." *European Journal of Social Psychology* 38, no. 6: 922–34.

Picq, Manuela Lavinas. 2016. "El caminar de las manuelas." *Crítica Contemporánea: Revista de Teoría Política* 6 (December): 124–38.

Poe, Abigail, and Adam Isaacson. 2009. *Ecuador's Humanitarian Emergency: The Spillover of Colombia's Conflict.* International Policy Report. Washington, DC: Center for International Policy.

Polga-Hecimovich, John. 2020. "Reshaping the State: The Unitary Executive Presidency of Rafael Correa." In Francisco Sánchez and Simón Pachano, eds., *Assessing the Left Turn in Ecuador,* 15–39. New York: Springer.

Polzer, Tara. 2009. "Negotiating Rights: The Politics of Local Integration." *Refuge* 26, no. 2: 92–106.

Ponton, Daniel. 2013. "Perfiles de los Victimarios en el Distrito Metropolitano de Quito." In Blanca C. Armijos V., ed., *Estudios de Seguridad Ciudadana, Compilacion 2010–2012,* 68–96. Quito: Observatorio Metropolitano de Seguridad Ciudadana.

Ponton, Daniel, coord. 2016. *Negociación de paz: Escenarios para el desarrollo y la integración fronteriza Ecuador-Colombia.* Quito: Editorial IAEN.

Portes, Alejandro, ed. 1995. *The Economic Sociology of Immigration: Essays on Networks, Ethnicity and Entrepreneurship.* New York: Russell Sage Foundation.

Portes, Alejandro, and Rubén G. Rumbaut. 2006. *Immigrant America: A Portrait.* Berkeley, CA: University of California Press.

Portes, Alejandro, and Min Zhou. 1993. "The New Second Generation: Segmented Assimilation and Its Variants." *Annals of the American Academy of Political and Social Science* 530, no. 1: 74–96.

Pugh, Jeffrey D. 2008. "Vectors of Contestation: Social Movements and Party Systems in Ecuador and Colombia." *Latin American Essays* 21 (Summer): 46–65.

Pugh, Jeffrey D. 2015. *Redes de migrantes y refugiados en Ecuador: Un estudio de Quito, Lago Agrio, Ibarra, y Esmeraldas.* Quito: CEMPROC.

Pugh, Jeffrey D. 2016a. "Peacebuilding among Transnational Youth in Migrant-Receiving Border Regions of Ecuador." *Journal of Peacebuilding and Development* 11, no. 3: 83–97.

Pugh, Jeffrey. 2016b. "What Displaced Colombians Living Abroad Think about the Peace Efforts." *The Conversation*, October 5.

Pugh, Jeffrey D. 2017. "Universal Citizenship through the Discourse and Policy of Rafael Correa." *Latin American Politics and Society* 59, no. 3 (Fall): 98–121.

Pugh, Jeffrey D. 2018. "Negotiating Identity and Belonging through the Invisibility Bargain: Colombian Forced Migrants in Ecuador." *International Migration Review* 52, no. 4: 978–1010.

Pugh, Jeffrey D., Luis Jimenez, and Bettina Latuff. 2020. "Welcome Wears Thin for Colombians in Ecuador as Venezuelans Become More Visible." Migration Information Source, January 9.

Pugh, Jeffrey D., and Jennifer Moya. 2020. "Words of (Un)welcome: Securitization and Migration Discourses in Ecuadorian Media." Available at SSRN: https:// ssrn.com/ abstract=3679341

Pugh, Jeffrey D., and Karen Ross. 2019. "Mapping the Field of International Peace Education Programs and Exploring Their Networked Impact on Peacebuilding." *Conflict Resolution Quarterly* 37, no. 1: 49–66.

Pugh, Jeffrey D., David Sulewski, and Julie Moreno. 2017. "Adapting Community Mediation for Colombian Forced Migrants in Ecuador." *Conflict Resolution Quarterly* 34, no. 4 (Summer): 409–30.

Putnam, Robert. 2000. *Bowling Alone: The Collapse and Revival of American Community.* New York: Simon & Schuster.

Quillian, Lincoln. 1995. "Prejudice as a Response to Perceived Group Threat: Population Composition and Anti-immigrant and Racial Prejudice in Europe." *American Sociological Review* 60, no. 4: 586.

Rahier, Jean Muteba, ed. 2012. *Black Social Movements in Latin America: From Monocultural Mestizaje and "Invisibility" to Multiculturalism and State Corporatism/ Co-optation.* New York: Palgrave Macmillan.

Ramakrishnan, S. Karthick, and Tom Wong. 2010. "Immigration Policies Go Local: The Varying Responses of Local Governments to Low-Skilled and Undocumented Immigration." In Monica W. Varsanyi, ed., *Taking Local Control: Immigration Policy Activism in US Cities and States*, 73–93. Palo Alto, CA: Stanford University Press.

Ramírez, Jacques. 2016. "Migration Policy in the New Ecuadorean Constitution: Toward the Formation of a Transnational Nation-State." *Latin American Perspectives* 43, no. 1: 175–86.

Ramirez Gallegos, Franklin, ed. 2020. *Octubre y el derecho a la resistencia: Revuelta popular y neoliberalismo autoritario en Ecuador.* N.p.: CLACSO.

Rapoport Center. 2009. *Forgotten Territories, Unrealized Rights: Rural Afro-Ecuadorians and their Fight for Land, Equality, and Security.* Austin, TX: Rapoport Center for Human Rights & Justice.

Ray, Rebecca, and Adam Chimienti. 2017. "A Line in the Equatorial Forests: Chinese Investment and the Environmental and Social Impacts of Extractive Industries in Ecuador." In Rebecca Ray, Kevin Gallagher, Andres Lopez, Cynthia Sanborn, and Andres López, eds., *China and Sustainable Development in Latin America: The Social and Environmental Dimension*, 107–44. London: Anthem Press.

Rigoni, Isabelle. 2012. "Intersectionality and Mediated Cultural Production in a Globalized Post-colonial World." *Ethnic and Racial Studies* 35, no. 5: 834–49.

Rincón, Adriana, Consuelo Sánchez, and Jeffrey Pugh. 2019. "Transnational Governance and Peace Processes: The Case of the UN and ICC in Colombia." In Aigul Kulnazarova and Christian Ydesen, eds., *Handbook of Global Approaches to Peace and International Institutions*, 561–84. New York: Palgrave Macmillan.

Riofrancos, Thea. 2020. *Resource Radicals: From Petro-nationalism to Post-extractivism in Ecuador.* Durham, NC: Duke University Press.

Risse, Thomas. 2011. *Governance without a State? Policies and Politics in Areas of Limited Statehood.* New York: Columbia University Press.

Rivera, Fredy. 2013. *La seguridad perversa: Política, democracia y derechos humanos en Ecuador, 1998–2006.* Quito: Flacso-Sede Ecuador.

Rivera, Fredy, Hernando Ortega, Paulina Larreátegui, and Pilar Riaño Alcalá, eds. 2007. *Migración forzada de Colombianos: Colombia, Ecuador, Canadá.* Medellín: Corporación Región.

Roberts, Kenneth. 2002. "Party-Society Linkages and Democratic Representation in Latin America." *Canadian Journal of Latin American and Caribbean Studies* 27, no. 53: 9–34.

Rodríguez-Gómez, Diana. 2019. "Bureaucratic Encounters and the Quest for Educational Access among Colombian Refugees in Ecuador." *Journal on Education in Emergencies* 5, no. 1: 62–93.

Roldán, Johanna. 2009. "Mitos y realidades del Registro Ampliado de refugiados en el Ecuador." *EntreTierras: Boletín de políticas migratorias y derechos humanos*, April, 5.

Romo Pérez, Andrea. 2019. "The Experiences of Black and Colombian Female Offenders with the Police in Ecuador: Understanding Minorities' Intersecting Identities." *Feminist Criminology* 14, no. 3: 330–48. https://doi.org/10.1177/1557085117744875.

Romo Pérez, Andrea. 2020. "'We Colombian Women Are Damned No Matter What We Do': An Analysis of Police Officers' Perceptions and Colombian Women's Experiences during Their Arrest in Ecuador." In Raanan Rein, Stefan Rinke, and David M. K. Sheinin, eds., *Migrants, Refugees, and Asylum Seekers in Latin America*, 309–25. Leiden: Brill.

Rovayo, Guillermo, and Silvia Colem. 2007. *El conflicto colombiano en el Ecuador: Apuntes para un posible agenda de trabajo structural.* Quito: Comité Ecuménico de Proyectos, October.

Ryburn, Megan. 2018. *Uncertain Citizenship: Everyday Practices of Bolivian Migrants in Chile.* Berkeley: University of California Press.

Saas, Claire. 2001. "Muslim Headscarf and Secularism in France." *European Journal of Migration and Law* 3: 453–56.

Sajjad, Tazreena. 2018. "What's in a Name? 'Refugees,' 'Migrants' and the Politics of Labelling." *Race & Class* 60, no. 2: 40–62.

Salcedo, Ruth Adriana. 2014. "Frontiers of Identity: Transnational Displacement, Clandestinity, and Conflict in the Ecuadorian-Colombian Borderlands and Inner Cities in Ecuador". PhD dissertation, George Mason University.

Salem, Paul. 1993. "A Critique of Western Conflict Resolution from a Non-Western Perspective." *Negotiation Journal* 9, no. 4 (October): 361–68.

Sánchez, Consuelo. 2013. *Narrativas de exclusión: Niñas, niños y adolescentes migrantes en Quito.* Quito: FLACSO Ecuador.

Sánchez, Francisco, and Simón Pachano, eds. 2020. *Assessing the Left Turn in Ecuador.* New York: Springer.

Sandoval-García, Carlos. 2004. *Threatening Others: Nicaraguans and the Formation of National Identities in Costa Rica.* Athens, OH: Ohio University Press.

Sang, H. Kil, Cecilia Menjívar, and Roxanne L. Doty. 2009. "Securing Borders: Patriotism, Vigilantism and the Brutalization of the US American Public." In William F. McDonald, ed., *Immigration, Crime and Justice,* 297–312. Bingley, England: Emerald Group Publishing.

San Roman, Rafael. 2011. "De la liberación descalza a los heraldos con botas." *Alandar,* February 1. http://www.alandar.org/hemeroteca/iglesia/de-la-liberacion-descalza-a-los/.

Santacruz, Lucy, and Alexandra Vallejo. 2012. "Vivir en la ciudad: El proceso de inserción sociocultural; condiciones y estrategias de vida." In Carlos Ortega and Oscar Ospina, eds., *No se puede ser refugiado toda la vida,* 57–124. Quito: FLACSO.

Santacruz Benavides, Lucy. 2013. *Expectativas de futuro de la población colombiana refugiada en las ciudades de Ibarra, Lago Agrio, y Esmeraldas.* Quito: FLACSO.

Sassen, Saskia. 1999. *Guests and Aliens.* New York: New Press.

Sassen, Saskia. 2006. *Territory, Authority, and Rights: From Medieval to Global Assemblages.* Princeton, NJ: Princeton University Press.

Sassen, Saskia. 2014. *Expulsions: Brutality and Complexity in the Global Economy.* Cambridge, MA: Harvard University Press.

Savun, Burcu, and Christian Gineste. 2019. "From Protection to Persecution: Threat Environment and Refugee Scapegoating." *Journal of Peace Research* 56, no. 1 (January): 88–102.

Schlesinger, Arthur. 1992. *The Disuniting of America: Reflections on a Multicultural Society.* New York: Norton.

Schneckener, Ulrich. 2011. "State Building or New Modes of Governance? The Effects of International Involvement in Areas of Limited Statehood." In Thomas Risse, ed., *Governance without a State? Policies and Politics in Areas of Limited Statehood,* 232–61. New York: Columbia University Press.

Schussler, Stuart. 2009. *Entre sospecha y ciudadanía: Refugiados colombianos en Quito.* Quito: Ediciones Abya-Yala.

Selee, Andrew, and Jessica Bolter. 2020. "An Uneven Welcome: Latin American and Caribbean Responses to Venezuelan and Nicaraguan Migration." Migration Policy Institute Report, February 3. https://www.migrationpolicy.org/research/latam-caribbean-responses-venezuelan-nicaraguan-migration.

Servicio Jesuita. 2009. *Informe del Servicio Jesuita a refugiados y migrantes del Ecuador sobre el proceso del Registro Ampliado en Muisne, Quinendé, y San Lorenzo: 23 de marzo al 8 de mayo, 2009.* Quito: Servicio Jesuita, May.

Sides, John, and Jack Citrin. 2007. "European Opinion about Immigration: The Role of Identities, Interests and Information." *British Journal of Political Science* 37, no. 3: 477–504.

Silber Mohamed, Heather. 2017. *The New Americans? Immigration, Protest, and the Politics of Latino Identity.* Lawrence: University Press of Kansas.

Skidmore, Thomas, Peter Smith, and James Green. 2009. *Modern Latin America.* New York: Oxford University Press.

Snyder, Richard. 2001. "Scaling Down: The Subnational Comparative Method." *Studies in Comparative International Development* 36, no. 1: 93–110.

Solomon, Hussein. 2003. *Of Myths and Migration: Illegal Immigration into South Africa.* Pretoria: University of South Africa Press.

Staniland, Paul. 2014. *Networks of Rebellion: Explaining Insurgent Cohesion and Collapse.* Ithaca, NY: Cornell University Press.

Stolle-McAllister, John. 2019. *Intercultural Interventions: Politics, Community, and Environment in the Otavalo Valley.* Amherst, NY: Cambria Press.

Stone-Cadena, Victoria, and Soledad Álvarez Velasco. 2018. "Historicizing Mobility: *Coyoterismo* in the Indigenous Ecuadorian Migration Industry." *Annals of the American Academy of Political and Social Science* 676, no. 1: 194–211.

Sullivan, Michael John. 2014. "By Right of Service: The Military as a Pathway to Earned Citizenship." *Politics, Groups, and Identities* 2, no. 2: 245–59.

Sullivan, Michael John. 2019. *Earned Citizenship.* New York: Oxford University Press.

Tarrow, Sidney G. 1998. *Power in Movement: Social Movements and Contentious Politics.* New York: Cambridge University Press.

Telles, Edward. 2014. *Pigmentocracies: Ethnicity, Race, and Color in Latin America.* Chapel Hill: University of North Carolina Press.

Telles, Edward, and Christina Sue. 2019. *Durable Ethnicity: Mexican Americans and the Ethnic Core.* New York: Oxford University Press.

Theiss-Morse, Elizabeth. 2009. *Who Counts as an American? The Boundaries of National Identity.* New York: Cambridge University Press.

Thomsen, Lotte, Eva G. T. Green, and Jim Sidanius. 2008. "We Will Hunt Them Down: How Social Dominance Orientation and Right-Wing Authoritarianism Fuel Ethnic Persecution of Immigrants in Fundamentally Different Ways." *Journal of Experimental Social Psychology* 44, no. 6: 1455–64.

Tolay, Juliette. 2016. "Mass Migration and Images of State Power: Turkey's Claim to the Status of a Responsible Rising Power." *Rising Powers Quarterly* 1, no. 2: 135–49.

Toro, Manuel. 2010. "Policía de Esmeraldas inició el año con emergencia operativa." *El Universo,* January 31. https://www.eluniverso.com/2010/01/31/1/1447/policia-esmeraldas-inicio-ano-emergencia-operativa.html.

Tsai, Kellee. 2006. "Adaptive Informal Institutions and Endogenous Institutional Change in China." *World Politics* 59 (October): 116–41.

Tsai, Kellee. 2007. *Capitalism without Democracy.* Ithaca, NY: Cornell University Press.

Tsourapas, Gerasimos. 2018. *The Politics of Migration in Modern Egypt: Strategies for Regime Survival in Autocracies.* Cambridge: Cambridge University Press.

Ubidia Vásquez, Daniela. 2015. "La inconstitucionalidad parcial del Decreto 1182 sobre el derecho a solicitar refugio en el Ecuador: Análisis y efectos." *USFQ Law Review* 2, no. 1: 145–72.

Ulloa Tapia, César. 2013. "Discurso político de los gobiernos bolivarianos." *Cuestiones políticas* 29, no. 50: 96–119.

United Nations Development Program (UNDP). 1994. *Human Development Report 1994.* New York: Oxford University Press.

United Nations Development Program (UNDP) and Carter Center. 2011. *Assessing the Binational Dialogue: Colombia-Ecuador 2007–2009.* Panama City, Panama: UNDP and Carter Center.

United Nations High Commissioner for Refugees (UNHCR). 2004. *Reporte 2004.* Quito: ACNUR Ecuador.

United Nations High Commissioner for Refugees (UNHCR). 2008. GNA Ecuador: Q&A with Marta Juarez, UNHCR Representative in Ecuador. Interview. http://www.unhcr.org/en-us/subsites/gna/48e492642/gna-ecuador-qa-marta-juarez-unhcr-representative-ecuador.html (accessed August 22, 2018).

United Nations High Commissioner for Refugees (UNHCR). 2009. "Ecuador: ACNUR repudia asesinato de presidente comunitario." UNHCR news release, October 7. http://www.un.org/spanish/News/story.asp?NewsID=16740#.VuOIbOZLKVA   (accessed August 12, 2018).

United Nations High Commissioner for Refugees (UNHCR). 2010. *UNHCR in Ecuador* Report (September).   https://www.acnur.org/fileadmin/Documentos/RefugiadosAmericas/Ecuador/EN/UNHCR_in_Ecuador._September_2010_-_ENGLISH.pdf.

United Nations High Commissioner for Refugees (UNHCR). 2016. ACNUR Hoja Informativa, April. Quito: ACNUR Ecuador. http://www.acnur.org/fileadmin/Documentos/RefugiadosAmericas/Ecuador/2016/ACNUR_Ecuador_2016_General_ES_Abril.pdf.

United Nations Office of Internal Oversight Services (OIOS). 2017. "Audit of the Operations in Ecuador of the Office of the United Nations High Commissioner for Refugees." Report 2017/122.

Vaca, Fermín. 2018. "'Correa ordenó no patrullar la frontera': René Yandún." *Plan V*, June 4. http://www.planv.com.ec/historias/entrevistas/correa-ordeno-no-patrullar-la-frontera-rene-yandun.

Valdivia, Gabriela. 2017. "Oil Citizens of the Revolution." *NACLA Report on the Americas* 49, no. 4: 429–35.

Van Cott, Donna Lee. 2006. "Dispensing Justice at the Margins of Formality: The Informal Rule of Law in Latin America." In Gretchen Helmke and Steven Levitsky, eds., *Informal Institutions and Democracy*. Baltimore, MD: Johns Hopkins University Press.

van Meeteren, Masja. 2010. *Life without Papers: Aspirations, Incorporation and Transnational Activities of Irregular Migrants in the Low Countries*. Rotterdam: Erasmus Universiteit.

Van Praag, Oriana, and Cynthia Arnson. 2020. "A Crisis within a Crisis: Venezuela and COVID-19." Wilson Center Report. https://www.wilsoncenter.org/publication/crisis-within-crisis-venezuela-and-covid-19.

Vaughn, Michael, Christopher P. Salas-Wright, Matt DeLisi, and Brandy R. Maynard. 2014. "The Immigrant Paradox: Immigrants Are Less Antisocial Than Native-Born Americans." *Social Psychiatry and Psychiatric Epidemiology* 49, no. 7: 1129–37.

Von Bülow, Marisa. 2010. *Building Transnational Networks: Civil Society and the Politics of Trade in the Americas*. New York: Cambridge University Press.

Wade, Peter. 1993. *Blackness and Race Mixture: The Dynamics of Racial Identity in Colombia*. Baltimore, MD: Johns Hopkins University Press.

Walzer, Michael. 1983. *Spheres of Justice: A Defense of Pluralism and Equality*. New York: Basic Books.

Weiner, Myron. 1995. *The Global Migration Crisis: Challenges to States and to Human Rights*. New York: HarperCollins.

Weiner, Myron. 1996. "Bad Neighbors, Bad Neighborhoods: An Inquiry into the Causes of Refugee Flows." *International Security* 21, no. 1 (Summer): 5–42.

Whitten, Norman. 1965. *Class, Kinship, and Power in an Ecuadorian Town: The Negroes of San Lorenzo*. Stanford, CA: Stanford University Press.

Wibben, Annick T. R. 2016. "The Promise and Dangers of Human Security." In Jonna Nyman, Anthony Burke, eds., *Ethical Security Studies: A New Research Agenda*, ch. 7. New York: Routledge.

Wilentz, Amy. 2008. "Who's Afraid of Jimmy Carter?" *New York Magazine*, July 20. http://nymag.com/news/politics/48675/.

Williamson, Vanessa, Theda Skocpol, and John Coggin. 2011. "The Tea Party and the Remaking of Republican Conservatism." *Perspectives on Politics* 9, no. 1: 25–43.

Wilson, Maya, David Davis, and Amanda Murdie. 2016. "The View from the Bottom: Networks of Conflict Resolution Organizations and International Peace." *Journal of Peace Research* 53, no. 3: 442–58.

Wong, Wendy. 2012. *Internal Affairs: How the Structure of NGOs Transforms Human Rights* Ithaca, NY: Cornell University Press.

Woolcock, Michael. 1998. "Social Capital and Economic Development: Toward a Theoretical Synthesis and Policy Framework." *Theory and Society* 27: 151–208.

World Food Programme (WFP). "Protracted Relief and Recovery Operations Approved by the Executive Director: Food Assistance for the Refugee Population Affected by the Internal Conflict in Colombia." Report to the Executive Board on Ecuador Project 10443.0, Document #WFP/EB.A/2008/11-C/1. Rome, May 2.

Xiang, Biao, and Johan Lindquist. 2014. "Migration Infrastructure." *International Migration Review* 48 (S1): S122–S148.

Yashar, Deborah J. 2005. *Contesting Citizenship in Latin America: The Rise of Indigenous Movements and the Postliberal Challenge*. Cambridge: Cambridge University Press.

Young, Elliott. 2014. *Alien Nation: Chinese Migration in the Americas from the Coolie Era through World War II*. Chapel Hill: University of North Carolina Press.

Zaragocin, Sofia. 2019. "Gendered Geographies of Elimination: Decolonial Feminist Geographies in Latin American Settler Contexts." *Antipode* 51, no. 1: 373–92.

Zepeda, Beatriz, and Francisco Carrión. 2015. *Las Américas y el mundo: Ecuador 2014*. Quito: FLACSO.

Zepeda-Millán, Chris. 2017. *Latino Mass Mobilization: Immigration, Racialization, and Activism*. New York: Cambridge University Press.

Zolberg, Aristide, and Long Litt Woon. 1999. "Why Islam Is Like Spanish: Cultural Incorporation in Europe and the United States." *Politics and Society* 27, no. 1: 5–38.

Zolberg, Aristide R., Astri Suhrke, and Sergio Aguayo. 1989. *Escape from Violence: Conflict and the Refugee Crisis in the Developing World*. New York: Oxford University Press.

Index